Language in Society

Language in Society

An Introduction to Sociolinguistics

Second edition

Suzanne Romaine

OXFORD
UNIVERSITY PRESS

Great Clarendon Street, Oxford OX2 6DP

Oxford University Press is a department of the University of Oxford.
It furthers the University's objective of excellence in research, scholarship, and education by publishing worldwide in

Oxford New York

Auckland Cape Town Dar es Salaam Hong Kong Karachi Kuala Lumpur Madrid Melbourne Mexico City Nairobi New Delhi Shanghai Taipei Toronto

With offices in

Argentina Austria Brazil Chile Czech Republic France Greece Guatemala Hungary Italy Japan South Korea Poland Portugal Singapore Switzerland Thailand Turkey Ukraine Vietnam

Published in the United States by Oxford University Press Inc., New York

First edition published by Oxford University Press 1994

British Library Cataloguing in Publication Data

Data available

Library of Congress Cataloging in Publication Data

Data available

ISBN 0-19-873192-2

7 9 10 8

Typeset by RefineCatch Limited, Bungay, Suffolk
Printed in Great Britain by Biddles Ltd., King's Lynn, Norfolk

Contents

List of Figures

List of Tables

Preface

MODERN linguistics has generally taken for granted that grammars are unrelated to the social lives of their speakers. Thus, linguists have usually treated language as an abstract object which can be accounted for without reference to social concerns of any kind. Sociologists, for their part, have tended to treat society as if it could be constituted without language. I have called this book *Language in Society*, which is what sociolinguistics is all about.

The term 'sociolinguistics' was coined in the 1950s to try to bring together the perspectives of linguists and sociologists to bear on issues concerning the place of language in society, and to address, in particular, the social context of linguistic diversity. Although it is still a young field of research, it gathered momentum in the 1960s and 1970s and continues to do so today. Educational and social policies played a role in the turning of linguists' attention to some of these questions, as did dissatisfaction with prevailing models of linguistics. Since the late 1950s mainstream linguistics has been conceived of as a largely formal enterprise increasingly divorced from the study of languages as they are actually used in everyday life.

Sociolinguistics has close connections with the social sciences, in particular, sociology, anthropology, social psychology, and education. It encompasses the study of multilingualism, social dialects, conversational interaction, attitudes to language, language change, and much more. It is impossible to put all the different approaches to the topic into neat pigeonholes, each of which is distinct in terms of methodology, goals, etc. There is considerable overlap, so that for instance, while dialectologists have studied speech varieties and language change, subjects of paramount interest to many sociolinguists, they have generally employed quite different methods of data collection and concentrated on rural rather than urban speech (see Chapter 5).

Different authors writing about what has now become a very broad field have divided it up in various ways. Some distinguish, for instance, between theoretical and applied sociolinguistics. The former is concerned with formal models and methods for analysing the structure of speech communities and speech varieties, and providing a general account of communicative competence. Applied sociolinguistics deals with the social and political implications of fundamental inequalities in language use in various areas of public life, e.g. schools or courts. A glance at the two-volume work *Sociolinguistics: An International Handbook of the Science of Language and Society* (1987–8, Mouton de Gruyter), which contains entries for nearly 200 topics, will give an indication of the multifaceted nature of the field.

More often, however, the field is subdivided into two broad headings: macro- and micro-sociolinguistics, with the macro domain sometimes also referred to as the 'sociology of language'. Macro-sociolinguistics takes society as its starting point and deals with language as a pivotal factor in the organization of communities. Micro-sociolinguistics begins with language and treats social forces as essential factors influencing the structure of languages. A recent example of this approach can be found in a two-volume work, one volume of which deals with what is referred to as the 'sociolinguistics of society' and the other with the 'sociolinguistics of language'. In his preface to the second volume, the author says he is not able to see much in common between issues about form and use of language on a small scale and large-scale socio-political issues. Thus, he presents sociolinguistics as a series of unconnected topics because he finds no common theoretical framework within which to link them.

I have always seen this division into two subfields as an artificial and arbitrary division of labor, which leads to a fruitless reductionism. It is no accident in my view that no convincing sociolinguistic theories exist. As long as scholars are prepared to ignore the forest for the trees, no theory is likely to be forthcoming.

Joshua Fishman, whose work is generally thought of as belonging to the sociology of language, said recently that the sociolinguistic enterprise is undergoing a mid-life crisis. Instead of progressing firmly on two legs (one propelled by linguistic matters and the other by sociological matters), it is trying to move ahead primarily on the linguistic front while merely shuffling on the social. He would like to see the 'socio' put into more prominence. One reason why I have called this book language *in* society rather than language *and* society is to emphasize the fact that the study of society must accord a place to language within it at the same time as the study of language must take account of society.

I cannot promise to produce a sociolinguistic theory in this book. Nevertheless, I hope that some of what I say might contribute to such a framework in the long term. What I offer in this short introductory text is an overview of the field by someone who has spent rather more time among the trees, while trying not to lose sight of the forest. The choice of which topics to include in a small survey of what is now a large and diverse field is to a great extent arbitrary. Every book inevitably reflects its author's assumptions about what is most interesting and important. I have made my choices based on those areas where there has been significant growth in terms of research findings, and also those areas where I have first-hand experience myself.

My research over the past fifteen years has involved me in trying to come to grips with problems of societal multilingualism, language change, and language contact in the broadest sense, initially with respect to the status of the languages spoken by ethnic minorities in the UK and elsewhere in Europe, and more recently, through my research on the pidgin and creole languages of the Pacific, particularly in Papua New Guinea and Hawai'i. My recent work in Papua New Guinea, in particular, has convinced me that there are crucial connections between the large-scale socio-political issues typically addressed by the sociology of language on the one hand, and the forms and uses of language on a small scale dealt with by sociolinguistics on the other. They are manifestations of similar principles, albeit operating at different levels. Variability is inherent in human behavior.

In preparing the second edition of this book, I have benefited from discussions, comments, and reviews, and have incorporated some of the ideas which have emerged. However, the old adage about not being able to please all of the people all of the time, let alone even some of the people some of the time, very much applies to authors and their audiences. What one reviewer or colleague loved about the book, another hated. Chapter 4 on language and gender proved, not surprisingly, to be one of the most controversial. Since then, I have given that topic a book-length treatment, which made it even more difficult for me to confine myself to a chapter. Although some readers would have liked to see additional chapters on discourse and pragmatics, I have kept the same choice of topics. My main aim in this edition is to update the material to take account of works published since I first wrote the book in the early 1990s. Although I had hoped to keep this edition about the same length, it has inevitably ended up slightly longer.

Likewise, some readers liked the system of referencing I adopted with no in-text citations; others abhorred it, with one even considering that it set a bad example for students. This edition, however, does incorporate a general bibliography in addition to the annotated bibliographies at the end of each chapter, which I have correspondingly shortened.

Oxford S. R.
2000

Acknowledgements

I WROTE the first edition of this book while I was a visiting professor in Sweden in 1991–2. My biggest debt is therefore to my colleagues at FUMS (Avdelningen för forskning och utbildning i modern svenska) in the Institute for Nordic Languages at the University of Uppsala and to the Swedish Research Council for the Humanities and Social Sciences for awarding me the Kerstin Hesselgren visiting professorship which made my stay possible and rewarding both intellectually and personally. My perception of fundamental sociolinguistic problems has been sharpened by my interaction with my colleagues at FUMS, whose interests and expertise span virtually the whole field of sociolinguistics.

I would also like to thank Isabel Forbes for sending me the article on French usage, and my colleague Olle Josephson at FUMS for bringing the case of *nörd* to my attention, both of which provide examples for my discussion of linguistic change in Chapter 6. Thanks also to Gunnel and André Melchers for discussion of the Swedish T/V system. I am also grateful to Nancy C. Dorian for helping me to locate various pieces of information I needed, and to Jim and Lesley Milroy, and John Rickford, for their helpful comments on a first draft of this book. Thanks also to the many readers who provided feedback.

Chapter 1

Language in Society/Society in Language

I NOTED in my Preface how prevailing trends in linguistics have marginalized the study of the social role of language. In discussing the differences between the concerns of sociolinguistics and mainstream linguistics, Noam Chomsky, who is the leading figure in theoretical linguistics, observed that sociolinguistics was not concerned with 'grammar' but with concepts of a different sort, among them perhaps 'language'. To this he added, 'if such an object can become an object of serious study'. Chomsky then goes on to say that questions of language are basically questions of power, but these are not the sorts of issues which linguists should address. He is certainly right about the former. The latter is a matter of opinion. The narrowing of modern linguistics to the study of grammar has ruled out investigation of many interesting questions about how language functions in society. This book is about some of these issues which form the subject matter of sociolinguistics, chief among them being the question of what we mean by a language.

I can't begin to estimate how many times people have asked me questions such as how many languages there are in the world, how many dialects of English there are, and whether American English is a language or a dialect of English. I am sure my answers are generally seen as unsatisfactory because I invariably reply that it depends on what we mean by terms such as 'language' and 'dialect' and that these are not linguistic but rather social matters. It may at first glance seem incredible to non-linguists that linguists cannot define such essential and basic concepts in purely linguistic terms. The purpose of this chapter is to explain why the notions of language and dialect are fundamentally social and not linguistic constructs. I will also introduce other concepts such as 'communicative competence' and say why these too are primary concerns of sociolinguistics because they depend on society in crucial ways.

Language v. dialect

The term 'dialect' has generally been used to refer to a subordinate variety of a language. For example, we are accustomed to saying that the English language has many dialects. These dialects may be of different kinds. A 'regional dialect' is a variety associated with a place, such as the Yorkshire dialect in England or the Bavarian dialect in Germany. Dialects of a language tend to differ more from one another the more remote they are from one another geographically. In this respect the study of dialects or dialectology has to do with boundaries, which often coincide with geographical features such as rivers and mountains (see Chapter 5 for further discussion). Boundaries are, however, often of a social nature, e.g. between different social class groups. In this case we may speak of 'social dialects' (see Chapter 3 for a discussion of these). Social dialects say who we are, and regional dialects where we come from.

The term 'dialect' also has historical connotations. Historical linguists, for instance, speak of the Germanic dialects, by which they mean the ancestors of language varieties now recognized as modern Germanic languages, such as English, Dutch, and German. The entities we label as the 'English language' or 'Flemish dialect' are not, however, discrete. Any variety is part of a continuum in social and geographical space and time. The discontinuities that do occur, however, often reflect geographical and social boundaries and weaknesses in communication networks.

Language and dialect in Papua New Guinea

A preliminary example from north-west New Britain in the Pacific region will illustrate the problems in applying purely linguistic criteria in deciding what counts as a language or dialect. The Pacific is a good place to begin because it is a vast area containing many indigenous languages, whose number must have been even greater before European contact. In many parts of the region there are extensive chains of interrelated varieties with no clear internal boundaries. The greatest concentration of diversity is found in Melanesia (an area comprising the south-west Pacific island nations of Papua New Guinea, the Solomon Islands, Vanuatu, New Caledonia, and Fiji), where up to 1,500 languages are spoken, with as many as half found in Papua New Guinea alone. Most of the languages in Papua New Guinea are spoken by small groups; probably 40 per cent have fewer than 500 speakers. There is a great diversity of language types and only a handful of these languages has been investigated in any detail. New

Britain is one of the larger islands in the Bismarck Archipelago off the north-eastern coast of the island of New Guinea, which lies just 100 miles north of the tip of Queensland, Australia. Politically, the islands are part of Papua New Guinea (independent since 1975), and the island of New Britain is divided into two provinces, East and West New Britain (see Fig. 1.1). In the part of north-west New Britain to be discussed here people live in small villages along the coast and in the interior. All are multilingual and it is not uncommon for people to be able to speak four or five languages.

The following ten examples illustrate how people in different villages would request someone to give them betelnut to chew. For the moment, let's use the term 'variety' as a neutral term which does not commit us to any decision about whether the varieties concerned have the status of language or dialect. The grammar is the same in all cases: first, the item desired is named (in this case, betelnut), then follows a third person singular form of the verb 'come', and finally, a first person verb phrase indicating what the person requesting the item is going to do with it. Literally, the request means 'betelnut, it comes, I chew', or loosely, 'give me some betelnut to chew'. Betelnut is the small green nut of the betel palm, which when chewed is a mild intoxicant (and also carcinogen). It is typically chewed with lime pepper and it turns the mouth a bright reddish-orange. Later, it is spat out. Sharing betelnut and other items such as tobacco or yams is culturally important in north-west New Britain and other parts of Papua New Guinea. Offering these items is a sign of friendliness on the part of those who give them, while accepting or requesting them indicates trust that a spell has not been cast over them.

1.	*ezim*	*o-mên*	*da-kîn*
2.	*eliep*	*max*	*nga-ngas*
3.	*bile*	*me*	*nge-nges*
4.	*bile*	*me*	*nga-nges*
5.	*bile*	*me*	*nga-nges*
6.	*vua*	*i-nama*	*nga-songo*
7.	*vua*	*i-nama*	*nga-songo*
8.	*bua*	*i-nam*	*nga-songo*
9.	*vua*	*i-mai*	*nga-songo*
10.	*eilep*	*i-me*	*a-ngas*
	betelnut	3 sing. *come*	1 sing. *chew*

Let's for the moment try to sort these ten utterances into groups based on how similar they are to one another in terms of the words they use and see if we can make a guess at how many languages and dialects there are here in purely linguistic terms. We would certainly want to recognize the first variety as a separate language since it seems to share none of its vocabulary with any of the

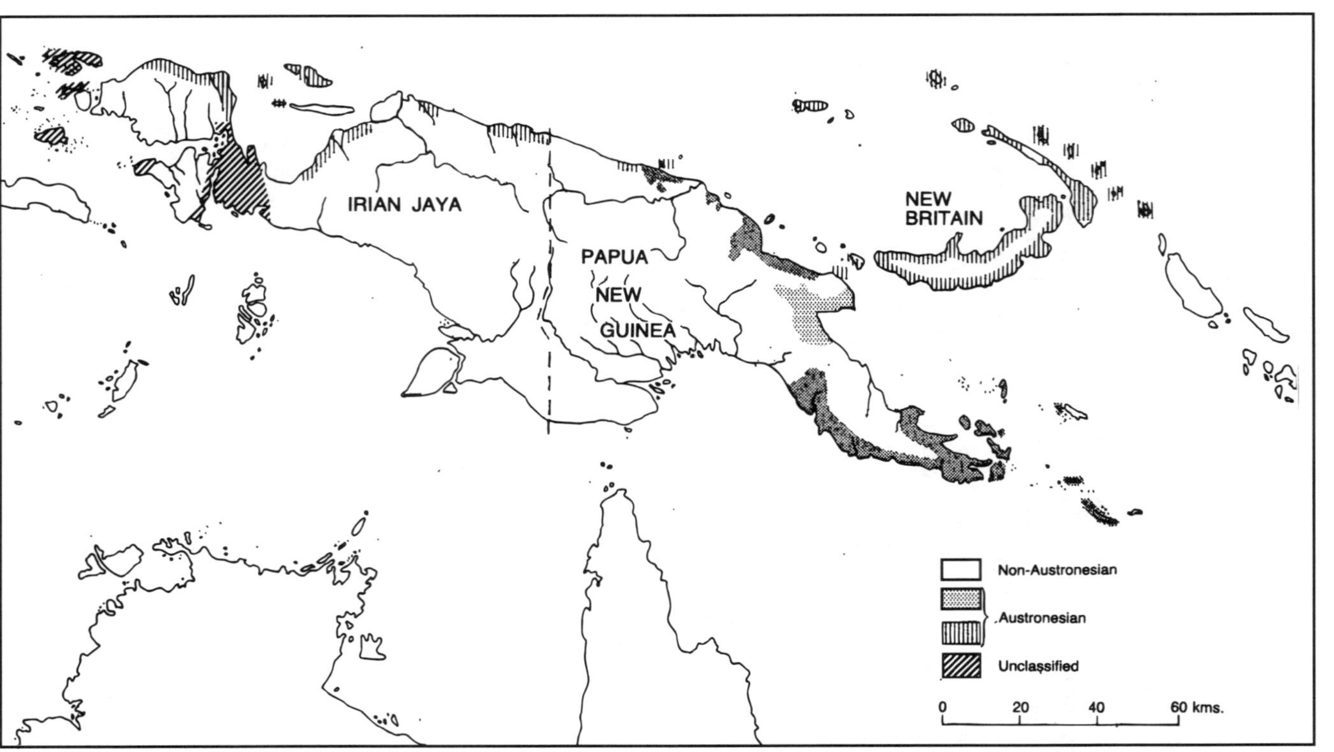

FIG 1.1 Map of Papua New Guinea showing New Britain and the distribution of Austronesian and non-Austronesian languages

other varieties, except possibly some remote similarity in the verb 'to come'. The other varieties, however, obviously have some lexical relationship to one another, though some more so than others. For instance, varieties (6) and (7) are identical, therefore it seems reasonable to suppose that the villages speaking these varieties do not have totally different languages, but rather dialects of the same language, or even the same language. Varieties (8) and (9) are also very similar to (6) and (7), differing only slightly in the pronunciations of the words for 'betelnut' and 'come'. So we might plausibly imagine that these four varieties constitute dialects of one language. Varieties (3), (4), and (5) also show a close relationship, differing only in terms of the vowels in the root and in the prefix for the verb 'chew', so we might consider them dialects of one language. Variety (10) is also not so very different, apart from its use of *eilep* instead of *bile* for 'betelnut' (which is similar to variety 2) and its lack of an initial consonant in the verb prefix for 'chew'.

There are some explicit linguistic procedures we could invoke to back up this impressionistic view. In fact, most of what is known about linguistic relationships in Papua New Guinea has relied on a measure called 'lexico-statistics', a method which still remains extremely popular because it provides a simple means of comparing the speech of different communities. The method relies on counting percentages of apparent cognates, i.e. related forms meaning the same thing, in a word list of 100 or 200 items. Those who use this method generally regard varieties sharing between 81 and 100 per cent cognates as dialects within a language. If there are between 28 and 81 per cent cognates, then the varieties count as languages within a family. Fewer cognates indicate a more distant relationship. These measures of course tell us nothing of what the speakers themselves consider the status of these language varieties to be.

When we ask what varieties the speakers themselves consider to be separate languages, we see that the linguistic evidence is interpreted in another way. We can get an answer to this question by looking at the names given to the ten varieties. In fact, all the varieties are recognized as separate languages each with its own name. They are shown in Fig. 1.2 in a grouping which is based on their linguistic similarities and their supposed historical relationship. The names used by the speakers are given here along with the numbers I used above.

Linguists generally recognize two major language families in Papua New Guinea comprising between 700 and 800 languages, Austronesian and non-Austronesian (or Papuan). We are still a long way from arriving at a generally accepted classification of these languages, particularly the non-Austronesian or Papuan group. It is, however, usually agreed that speakers of the latter group of languages arrived in Oceania long before the speakers of Austronesian languages. The coastal distribution of most of the Austronesian languages, which

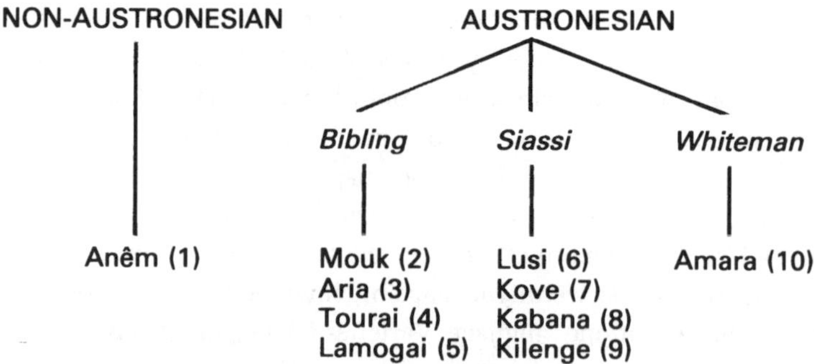

FIG 1.2 Languages of north-west New Britain

can also be seen in Fig. 1.1, is commonly taken to indicate the later arrival of their speakers.

The Anêm language spoken in north-west New Britain is a member of the non-Austronesian family and is not lexically related to any other language known in Papua New Guinea as far as we can tell at the moment. In fact, the Anêm-speaking people claim theirs is the original language of the area. This is probably correct. It is also likely that Anêm is the sole survivor of a group of non-Austronesian languages which were once spread over a wider area of New Britain. Thus, by anyone's criteria, Anêm has to be recognized as a separate language, at least at the level of vocabulary. It is at present the language of four villages, three of which are on the coast and the other in the interior, separated from the coastal speakers by Lusi territory. The interior Anêm speakers have intermarried with Mouk, Aria, and Lusi speakers. The latter speak languages which are all classified as Austronesian, although on the basis of a more precise linguistic analysis we can divide them into three subgroups: Bibling, Siassi, and Whiteman. However, these Austronesian languages are structurally unlike those spoken outside the Melanesian area. Languages which are geographically adjacent are the most similar and those languages that have been in close association the longest exhibit structural similarities which are due to contact rather than inheritance.

Mouk is most closely related to Aria and many Mouk, especially older men, know a fair amount of Anêm. Due to their interaction with Anêm speakers, Mouk and Anêm now share certain linguistic features to the exclusion of the neighboring languages. Within the Bibling group Aria, Lamogai, and Tourai are closely related and the people who call themselves Tourai consider their language to be intermediate between Aria and Lamogai but more closely related to Aria, an impression which is supported by linguistic evidence. Within the Siassi group Lusi and Kove are very similar and some linguists have taken Lusi and Kove to be dialects of one language, ignoring the claims of the speakers. Kilenge is less closely related to Lusi, Kove, and Kabana. Amara, the only representative of the Whiteman group in this area, is apparently near extinction. The Amara and Kabana interact so closely with each other that Kabana is quickly becoming the language of first choice among young Amara children.

It is obvious that the boundaries reflected by the names given to these varieties are socially rather than linguistically constructed. But how is it that all these varieties emerge as entities autonomous enough to be named separate languages by their speakers when some of them are virtually identical from a linguistic point of view? Not surprisingly, early investigators were puzzled by the complex nature of linguistic relationships in the New Guinea area. Historical connections are complicated by such extensive long-term contacts and movements between Austronesian and non-Austronesian-speaking peoples which has also brought about drastic grammatical convergence. There is still some dispute over the membership of many languages since linguists have been reluctant to accept that a language might be 20 per cent Austronesian and 80 per cent non-Austronesian. Lexical relationships have been taken as primary in historical classification. Moreover, we can see that it is largely on the basis of lexical forms that the people of north-west New Britain see their varieties as being separate languages.

The names given by the early European government patrol officers to villages and census divisions do not always correspond to linguistic differences, although some have made this assumption. Most of the names given on maps are administrative names of subdistricts and cannot be relied upon to yield the linguistic composition of an area. Europeans often arbitrarily chose the name of one of the constituent clans for a group of clusters they took as members of a village. The term 'village', however, suggests a degree of centralization not found in traditional societies, where residential units were not compact. Villages are simply points of contact between the administration and the local populace, who may not actually occupy that particular place. From the European perspective, it seemed natural to expect that a place name, the names of people occupying that place, and the name of a language spoken there should be the same. That is what typically happens in Europe, where there is a close association between the names of countries, peoples, and languages, as can be seen in sets of names such as England/English/English, Germany/German/German, France/ French/French.

However, in Papua New Guinea there is no one-to-one mapping between village names, groups, and language names. Sometimes up to four local names apply to what a district officer decided to call 'one' village, and some names are common to three or four sites. In addition, many groups have no special names for their languages. The Sare people of the Sepik, for example, call their language Sare, but this means simply 'to speak or talk'. There are probably many more languages than the actual names indicate and the boundaries between them are fuzzy. Much of the early information contained in explorers' accounts and the reports of patrol officers is anecdotal. What is now called Kabana by some linguists was earlier called Barriai by one observer, which is a name given by the Kabana and Amara people to their land. Lusi was called Kaliai-Kove in an earlier description in recognition of the near identity of grammar between Kove and Lusi and also because the people of this area are commonly called Kaliai by people outside the region. Kaliai is the name of one of the Lusi clans. The Mouk-speaking village of Salkei was counted as Aria-speaking because fieldworkers unwittingly collected their data from an Aria speaker who happened to be visiting the aid post there rather than from a local resident.

Even if we had descriptions of all the varieties spoken in each village, it would still pose considerable problems to say which constituted languages and which dialects since the point of view of the speakers themselves will differ from the linguistic evidence. Moreover, the views of speakers themselves may vary a great deal. For example, we saw how Tourai and Aria could on linguistic grounds be thought of as dialects of a single language, but Tourai speakers (as well as those of Lamogai and Aria) consider them separate languages. The language spoken in Bolo village is also from a linguist's point of view identical to Aria, but Aria speakers from other villages say it is not Aria. They say Bolo villagers really speak Mouk. However, the people of Salkei village, who speak Mouk, say that Bolo people speak Aria. As for the Bolo themselves, they claim to be Anêm speakers! While traditionally this was true, only a handful of older men now know the language and people generally recognize that Anêm is no longer spoken there. For their part, the Anêm people do not think the Bolo speak acceptable Anêm anymore. Thus, this one village of Bolo, which is said to be Anêm-, Aria-, and Mouk-speaking, speaks a variety which no one else accepts as a legitimate member of their own language group.

The counterpart to this at the level of linguistic form is that there are words widely used in the region for intergroup communication which no one accepts as part of the 'true' vocabulary of their language. Each group speaking what it regards as a separate language has what it considers its own true lexicon, but there are also synonyms, which are identical in form to the words used by others speaking different languages. Here, for example, is a list of words (not complete) meaning 'wallaby' in some of the languages:

Anêm: *apose, gauxu, kis, nautus, zei*
Amara: *natus, kope, *kio*
Mouk: *natus, apose, sokolo*
Aria: *apare,*apose*
Tourai: **apare, apose*
Lamogai: *airok, apare, keneng*

Those marked with an asterisk are words which the people of that particular language consider as their own true word for 'wallaby', while the others are seen as equivalents. The use of such synonyms aids intergroup communication at the same time as it allows each group to claim at least one word as its own. This permits each group to maintain its distinctiveness. There are, however, other words known among the groups which no one claims as a true word of their own language. The extensive overlap in vocabulary from one language to another facilitates what has been called 'dual-lingualism', where speakers communicate with one another while each speaking their own language. It also facilitates active learning of other languages.

The Siassi languages function widely as lingua francas (i.e. additional languages used across wide areas for intergroup communication) in this area and most people speak either Lusi, Kove, or Kabana well. The Bibling languages also function dual-lingually so that knowing one gives access to understanding the others. Anêm and Amara, however, have no value as lingua francas since neither can be used dual-lingually with any other language. Since European contact in the nineteenth century, another language has been added to the villagers' repertoire, an English-based pidgin called Tok Pisin ('talk pidgin'), a language which developed from a contact language which emerged on plantations in Queensland, where Pacific Islanders worked as contract laborers. Recruiting was particularly heavy in the Bismarck Archipelago; at one time, few men were left in the villages. When the laborers returned, they often taught Tok Pisin to the younger male generation (see Chapter 6 for further information about Tok Pisin and other pidgins and creoles). Tok Pisin eventually became such a useful additional language that it spread throughout mainland New Guinea and today it is the most widely spoken lingua franca in the country. It has been used in New Britain for at least eighty years and all the languages of north-west New Britain have now incorporated Tok Pisin words into their vocabulary.

A number of explanations have been proposed for the existence of such extreme linguistic fragmentation of New Guinea. First, a span of 40,000 years of human habitation affords sufficient time-depth for natural processes of change and diversification to produce a multitude of languages. Secondly, the rugged nature of the terrain poses physical barriers to human social interaction. Thirdly, cultural attitudes play an important role in fostering and maintaining diversity. Diversity is cultivated in Melanesia as a badge of identification and is largely a conscious reaction. However, even more important, in my view, is that none of the pressures towards convergence found for a long time in Europe and elsewhere, such as literacy, standardization, centralized administrative control, schooling, media, was present to any great degree in precolonial days. These factors have, however, become relevant since European contact and have favored the spread of lingua francas such as Tok Pisin and metropolitan languages such as English.

Traditional dialectologists believed that isolation led to linguistic diversity, while mixing of populations created uniformity. Yet it is clear that geography alone is not sufficient to explain diversity, nor is the concentration of people in one area or isolation a guarantee of uniformity or conservatism, as research on urban social dialects has shown (see Chapter 3). Compare, for instance, one of the areas of greatest diversity, the easily navigable Sepik River, with Enga in the interior Highlands, which has some of the most rugged terrain in the country and is an area with much less diversity. The north coastal areas, where there are more small, unrelated language groups, are more linguistically diverse than the more isolated areas of the interior.

The distribution of linguistic diversity implies demographic factors as additional contributory causes. It seems likely that the existence of endemic diseases such as malaria in the coastal lowlands restricted not only mobility, but also population growth. In the Highlands, which are largely malaria-free, language groups are larger than on the coast. Compare Enga which has over 150,000 speakers with Erima, a language spoken in only four villages, with only 400 speakers. The threat of disease therefore probably limited the possibility for groups to expand much beyond their immediate territory, and thus impeded the spread of any one language or group of languages.

Since the imposition of colonial administration in various Pacific islands such as Papua New Guinea, there has no doubt been a decline in the number of languages. Moreover, dramatic changes have taken place in those which survive, often through contact with major metropolitan languages. New lingua francas arose as a result of contact with Europeans; the most important of these were languages like Kâte and Yabem, spread by missionaries as church lingua francas, and Tok Pisin and Hiri Motu.

Any estimate of the number of languages spoken in an area like Papua New Guinea is fraught with difficulties due to the problems inherent in defining terms such as 'language' and 'dialect'. The very concept of discrete languages is probably a European cultural artefact fostered by processes such as literacy and standardization. Any attempt to count distinct languages will be an artefact of classificatory procedures rather than a reflection of communicative practices. Lexico-statistics will not yield any non-arbitrary technical definition of terms such as 'language', 'dialect', or 'family'.

Language and dialect in Europe

Other examples from Europe can be taken to illustrate the arbitrariness of linguistic criteria, and the importance of social factors in deciding what counts as a language or dialect. Some classic cases are the West Romance and Germanic dialect continua. The West Romance dialect continuum stretches through rural communities from the Atlantic coast of France through Italy, Spain, and Portugal. Mutual intelligibility exists between adjacent villages, although speakers of the standard varieties of French, Italian, Spanish, and Portuguese find one another mutually unintelligible to varying degrees. Similarly, the Germanic dialect continuum connects a series of historically related varieties that differ from one another with respect to one or more features.

Degree of mutual intelligibility is greatly affected by the extent of social and other contact between the groups concerned as well as their attitudes to one another and does not necessarily have much to do with lexico-statistical relationships. In Scandinavia, for instance, if a traveller knows Danish, Swedish, or Norwegian, it is possible to communicate across language boundaries. Certainly, linguistically the languages are very close, in fact close enough from a linguistic point of view to be considered dialects of one language. Indeed, structurally they form a nice parallel to the linguistic situation in parts of north-west New Britain because their grammar is very similar and most of the distinctive differences lie in vocabulary, and pronunciation, although the differences here are also not very great in many cases. Danish and Norwegian have a great deal of vocabulary in common, but differ in pronunciation, while Swedish and Norwegian differ more in vocabulary, but have a more similar pronunciation. In a sample of 1,000 words from Norwegian, as many as 50 per cent of the words are identical and another 25 per cent are variants of the same form. A further 15 per cent have the same pronunciation but are spelled differently, while only 10 per cent are essentially different. Some of the superficial similarities can be seen in these examples.

Danish: *Hun sidder i vinduet og ser ud over gaden.*
Norwegian: *Hun sitter i vinduet og ser ut over gatan.*
Swedish: *Hon sitter i fönstret och ser ut över gatan.*

The modern languages are derived historically from a common Nordic ancestor and their increasing fragmentation reflects political history. It is largely for political reasons that they are regarded as separate languages. By 1700 Swedish and Danish standards were firmly established, but Norway was still under Danish rule. When these languages were standardized, differences between

FIG 1.3 Dialect continua in Europe

them were consciously exaggerated. For instance, before 1906 all three languages wrote the word meaning 'what' unphonetically as *hvad*. Now only Danish does. Swedish spells it as *vad* and Norwegian as *hva*. Thus, orthographic differences now disguise what is a similar pronunciation and make the languages look more different in their written form than they are when spoken.

In studies of mutual intelligibility some interesting asymmetries emerge. Danes claim to understand Norwegians much better than Norwegians claim to understand Danes. The poorest understanding is between Danes and Swedes and the best between Norwegians and Swedes. However, Norwegians and

Danes claim to understand Swedes better than Swedes claim to understand either Norwegians or Danes. How can this be? Studies of mutual intelligibility are not really about linguistic relationships between varieties, but about social relationships since it is people and not the varieties who understand or do not understand one another. More Norwegians and Danes have been in Sweden than Swedes have been in the other two countries. Only one-quarter of Swedes claim to read anything in the other two languages. While 41 per cent of Danes and 52 per cent of Norwegians listen to Swedish radio, only 9 per cent of Swedes listen to Norwegian or Danish radio. It is obvious that more accommodation is made towards Sweden and Swedish by Danes and Norwegians because Sweden is a larger and wealthier country. It is much more self-contained both economically and intellectually. Not surprisingly, Swedes show the least interest in Nordic cooperation, while the Danes favor it most, no doubt because they stand to gain the most from it. They are generally less well understood than Norwegians or Swedes.

A Danish school principal told the story of how she gave a lecture to an audience in Stockholm from a manuscript which had been translated into Swedish. She said, 'They understood me very well. Then I fumbled for an expression, and the audience cried out, "just talk Danish, you are so easy to understand". I switched to Danish, to the great surprise of the Swedes, who understood nothing! They had thought I was talking Danish all along.' Under the present political circumstances, convergence towards a common inter-Scandinavian speech form could be brought about only by conscious language planning and increased social contact.

The dividing line between the languages we call Swedish, Norwegian, and Danish is linguistically arbitrary but politically and culturally relevant. Max Weinreich's often quoted dictum, 'a language is a dialect with an army and a navy', attests the importance of political power and the sovereignty of a nation-state in the recognition of a variety as a language rather than a dialect. Situations in which there is widespread agreement as to what constitutes a language arise through the interaction of social, political, psychological, and historical factors, and are not due to any inherent properties of the varieties concerned. In China, a range of mutually unintelligible varieties which a linguist would certainly call separate languages are nevertheless considered dialects of Chinese because they are linked by a common writing system. While speakers of varieties such as Cantonese and Mandarin would not be able to communicate in the spoken language, they would share the same writing system. Each would write the same symbol for the 'same' words, even though their spoken forms would be completely different. This is really in a sense the opposite of what exists in Scandinavia, where differences in writing obscure basic similarities in pronunciation. Many speakers of what is sometimes called

Serbo-Croatian, the standard language of the former Yugoslavia, and current standard of the Federal Republic of Yugoslavia, say it is really two languages rather than one because Croats write their variety in Roman script, while Serbs write theirs in Cyrillic.

Certain varieties of the West Germanic dialect continuum are considered to be dialects of Dutch and others dialects of German because of the relationship these varieties have to their respective standard languages. The process of standardization is connected with a number of socio-historical factors such as literacy, nationalism, and cultural and ethnic identity. It results in the selection and fixing of a uniform norm of usage, which is promoted in dictionaries, grammars, and teaching. A standard language is a variety that has been deliberately codified so that it varies minimally in linguistic form but is maximally elaborated in function. Most of the European languages became standardized under periods of intense nationalism. The standardization and promotion of a common language was seen as an important symbol of the process of political unification. Some of the consequences of this will be discussed in Chapters 3 and 7.

Some linguists have found the terms 'autonomous' and 'heteronymous' speech varieties useful as alternative labels to language and dialect. Thus, we can say, for instance, that the Dutch dialects are dependent on or 'heteronymous' with respect to standard Dutch, German dialects to standard German, etc. This means that because speakers of German watch German TV, are taught standard German in school, read in standard German etc., they look to standard German as a reference point. There will be more linguistic similarities between the varieties of German and Dutch spoken close to the border between those two countries than there will be between standard German and standard Dutch. Nevertheless, a standard language serves to create a feeling of unity among the speakers who take it as a reference point, particularly those who speak varieties far removed from one another geographically. Thus, for speakers of Cockney English in London and speakers of local dialects in Tyneside, in the north-east of England, the linguistic differences may be so substantial as to prevent easy spoken communication, but both groups would say in a larger sense they 'speak the same language' since both have standard English as a superordinate variety.

The term 'language' is employed for a variety that is autonomous, together with all those varieties that are heteronymous upon it. Because heteronomy and autonomy reflect political and cultural rather than purely linguistic factors, they can change. Often due to political developments formerly heteronymous varieties can achieve autonomy, as is the case with Afrikaans in South Africa, which was standardized in the 1920s and recognized as a language and not a dialect of Dutch. Conversely, autonomous varieties may lose their autonomy, as Scots English did when it ceased to function as the language of the Scottish court after the Union of Crowns in 1603. There is nothing inherently better about a variety which achieves autonomy, and autonomy can always be challenged. Political and social factors are responsible for the selection of one out of many varieties which could have been candidates for standardization (see further in Chapter 3).

Disputes about the status of a variety are often used to bolster claims about the ethnic membership of the speakers or political status of territory with which it is associated. The present-day nation calling itself Macedonia was once the heart of an empire that stretched from Gibraltar to the Panjab, and its 2 million people live on land that until 1991 was part of Greece, Yugoslavia, Bulgaria, and Serbia, all of whom have taken chunks of its territory. When Macedonia was one of five constituent republics of Yugoslavia (along with Serbia, Montenegro, Croatia, Bosnia-Herzogovina, Slovenia) from 1944 to 1991, Macedonian was subordinate to Serbo-Croatian. Extremist Serbian politicians in now independent Serbia have publicly denied the legitimacy of Macedonian language and nationality and called for the reabsorption of Macedonia into Serbia. Although Bulgaria recognized the independent republic of Macedonia in 1992 after the break-up of the Socialist state of Yugoslavia, it still insists that Macedonian is a dialect of Bulgarian.

Meanwhile, neighboring Greece, which claims Alexander the Great (b. 356 BC), probably the most famous Macedonian, as the founding father of Greek nationhood, has always officially denied both Macedonian nationality and language, insisting instead that Ancient Macedonian was a dialect of Greek. It regards the existence of an independent Macedonia as an assault on Greek sovereignty. When Macedonia became independent in 1991, Greece blocked its entrance to the United Nations under its own name because Greece uses the same name to refer to a province of its own territory and claims exclusive right to the name *Makedonia*. The extension of Greek national sovereignty over parts of the territory of Makedonia was accompanied by particularly aggressive measures aimed at Hellenization of the Slavic-speaking population, among them the prohibition of the use of any language but Greek in public. People were fined, sent to prison, or forced to drink castor oil, and children thrashed at school, if they were caught speaking their own language.

In 1993 newly independent Macedonia joined the UN under the rather unwieldy euphemism 'Former Yugoslav Republic of Macedonia'. Greece imposed an economic blockade that was not lifted until Macedonia agreed to alter a disputed symbol in its flag. Greek authorities also grounded a Macedonian passenger aircraft until the word Makedonia on its fuselage was painted over.

What light can historical and linguistic evidence shed on these competing claims from Greece, Serbia, and Bulgaria? The Macedonians are descended from

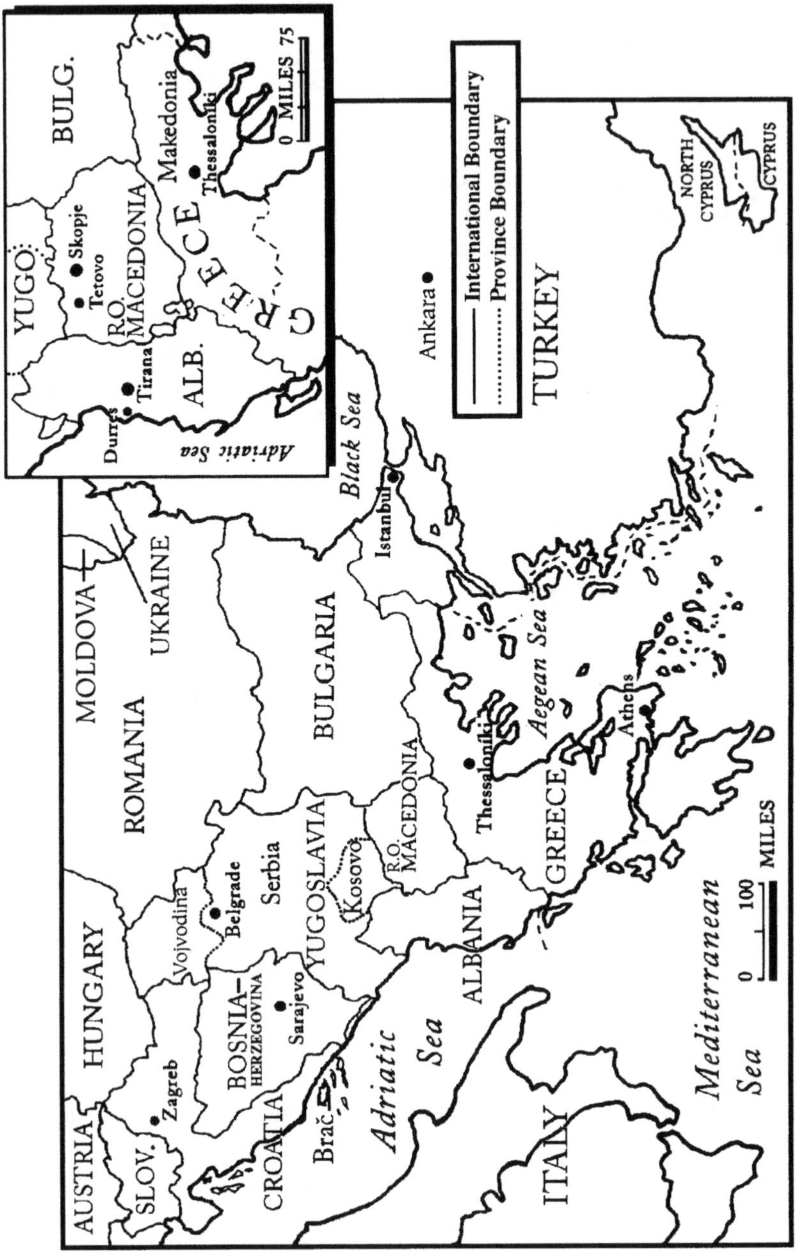

FIG 1.4 Map of the south Balkan region

Slavs who settled in the Balkan Peninsula from north of the Carpathian range around AD 550 to 630 and linguistic evidence indicates that Ancient Macedonian was in fact separate from what later became Greek. At the time of the Slavic invasions, the territory of Macedonia was part of the Byzantine Empire. Thereafter, it shifted between Greek and Slavic domination until the end of the fifteenth century when it became part of the Ottoman Empire. It then passed from Ottoman to Serbian control as a result of the Balkan wars of 1912 and 1913 until it became a republic of Yugoslavia in 1944 under the Communist regime.

Macedonian is part of the South Slavic dialect continuum at the ends of which are Serbian and Bulgarian, both of which served at one time as languages of education for many Macedonians. Longstanding contact and multilingualism in the Balkan region between Slavic languages such as Bulgarian, Macedonian, and Serbian and non-Slavic languages such as Greek, Turkish, and Albanian have led to linguistic convergence of the type found in north-west New Britain. Turkish, for instance, contributed a significant amount of vocabulary to Macedonian, because it was the language of administration in Macedonia from the fourteenth century to the beginning of the twentieth, as well as a language of considerable economic and cultural prestige. Macedonian shares some similarities with Serbian and some with Bulgarian. The variety of Macedonian spoken in the capital, Skopje, for example, shares some of its most salient features with Serbian. This allows some Serbian authors to cite certain linguistic similarities between Serbian and Macedonian to bolster their territorial claims, at the same time as Bulgarians can use other linguistic features shared between Bulgarian and Macedonian to support their view that Macedonian is a dialect of Bulgarian. Not surprisingly, given the territorial ambitions of their Greek, Bulgarian, and Serbian neighbors, many Macedonians perceive themselves as linguistically and culturally threatened even in their own country.

English: language and dialect

So the answer to one of the questions I am often asked about whether American English is a dialect of English or a separate language depends on your point of view. George Bernard Shaw characterized England and America as two nations divided by a common language. When H. L. Mencken decided to call his book *The American Language* rather than *The English Language in America*, he was making a political statement. Similar sentiments had been expressed earlier by Noah Webster when he authored his dictionary of American

English and consciously employed spellings for certain words which were different from British English norms, e.g. *color*, *criticize*. In fact, Webster noted over a century ago that 'the taste of her [i.e. Britain's SR] authors is already corrupted, and her language on the decline'. Webster's remarks about British English being eclipsed by American English seem now to give at least some Britons and the British Council pause as they seek to guarantee the supremacy of the British variety of the language, particularly in the lucrative export market for English as a second language. But all this talk about language is really about politics, and Britain no longer exerts as much influence as a superpower as does its former colony. In an interview the former British Prime Minister Margaret Thatcher (*Newsweek*, 8 October 1990), who stood much to gain from aligning her own political views with those of former President Reagan, very generously conceded that Shakespeare belonged as much to Americans as to the British in characterizing the 'special relationship' that exists between the United States and Britain. Speaking to an American interviewer, she observed:

> The Magna Carta belongs as much to you as it does to us; the writ of habeas corpus belongs as much to you as it does to us.... There is such a common heritage as well as the language. Shakespeare belongs as much to you as he does to us ... That is what unites us and has united us—rather more than a philosophy, but history as well, and language and mode of thought.

America's linguistic declaration of independence was unparalleled in Australia until the appearance of Sidney Baker's book *The Australian Language* (1945), whose title confidently asserted the autonomy of Australian English in the same way that Mencken's had attempted to do for American English. Baker noted that Australians 'have to work out the problem from the point of view of Australia, not from the viewpoint of England and of the judgements she passed upon our language because she did not know it as well as we do'. Still, it was a long time before many Australians were to feel confident about sounding Australian, and many still do not today. While some linguists declared there was nothing wrong with Australian speech, they still compared Australian accents with educated southern British English ones. For some, this was an unpleasant reminder of the extent to which Australian English deviated from what was seen as a prestige standard. The Australian Broadcasting Corporation, created in 1932, endorsed the British norm as the one to be used on the radio and most of those recognized as suitable announcers were Englishmen. Today a British accent is no longer needed for the ABC. Since 1983 Australians who sound distinctly Australian can be heard on radio and television and all questions concerning pronunciation, style, and usage are referred to an Australian dictionary, not a British one. The upsurge of interest and even pride in rather than embarrassment at Australian English represents a decided move away from what has been called the 'cultural cringe'.

A dialect continuum can also be primarily social rather than geographical in nature. A good example is found in Jamaica, where at one time those at the top of the social scale—the British—spoke English, while those at the bottom spoke Jamaican Creole. Over time the gap between the two has been filled by a range of varieties that are either more like the creole or more like English (see further in Chapter 6). Most speakers use several varieties that span a range on this post-creole continuum and shift among them according to context or addressee. Any division of the Jamaican social dialect continuum into English versus Jamaican Creole would be linguistically as arbitrary as dividing the Germanic dialect continuum into Dutch and German. There is no social, political, or geographical reason for saying that English begins at one particular point and Jamaican Creole at another.

Accent v. dialect

Some linguists make a further distinction between 'accent' and 'dialect'. An accent consists of a way of pronouncing a variety. A dialect, however, varies from other dialects of the same language simultaneously on at least three levels of organization: pronunciation, grammar or syntax, and vocabulary. Thus, educated speakers of American English and British English can be regarded as using dialects of the same language because differences of these three kinds exist between them. In practice, however, speakers of the two varieties share a common grammar and differ from each other more in terms of vocabulary and pronunciation. Some examples of these differences are illustrated in Table 1.1.

Table 1.1 Some differences between American and British English

	American	British
Pronunciation: *ate*	/eit/ (rhymes with *mate*)	/ɛt/ (rhymes with *Met*)
Grammar/syntax	Jane had *gotten* used to it.	Jane had *got* used to it. (Past participle of *get*)
Vocabulary	Sam took the *elevator* rather than the stairs.	Sam took the *lift* rather than the stairs.

People have strong views on accents, including the idea that it is always others who have accents and never themselves! Strictly speaking, however, it is impossible to speak any variety without some accent. Evaluational studies of accents have found that in Britain people rate the speech of urban areas such as Birmingham, Liverpool, and Glasgow much less favorably than accents of rural areas such as Devon and Cornwall. These differences in judgement reflect views about the nature of urban v. rural life rather than anything inherent in the accents themselves. Outsiders who do not know where the accents are used do not uniformly rate them unfavorably. In Britain the prestige of one variety called RP (received pronunciation) is so high that people often imagine themselves to use RP forms when they don't. RP is the speech variety used by those educated at public (i.e. private) schools and is not tied to any particular locality. RP is sometimes considered the equivalent of a standard English pronunciation, particularly in England. It is sometimes also referred to as BBC English, Oxford English, and the King's English, and is the accent taught to foreigners who are learning British rather than American English. While it is spoken by only about 5 per cent or less of the population (and therefore hardly has wide currency), it is nevertheless considered a prestigious accent throughout the UK and the British Commonwealth. As seen in my comments about Australia, RP has long served overseas as an important prestige norm.

There is a story (possibly apocryphal) about Daniel Jones, a phonetician largely responsible for establishing the use of the term RP in its present sense and who based his description on his own speech. Upon being asked how many RP speakers there were in his department at London, he replied after a pause 'two'. He did not, however, reveal the identity of the second person.

The relatively arbitrary nature of the features which come to have prestige (and by contrast those which do not) and the role of the socially and politically powerful in defining them is well illustrated in the following incident. During the administration of President Jimmy Carter, a Georgian with a local Georgian accent, a popular American television program had a character representing a state department official, who spoke conspicuously like a Georgian. When a New Yorker next to him called attention to his Georgian accent, he replied, 'We don't have an accent anymore. You do.' What causes a particular way of speaking to be perceived as superior is the fact that it is used by the powerful. I will say more about accent prejudice in Chapters 3 and 4, and examine how some varieties get to be regarded as more prestigious than others simply because the people who speak them are thought to have higher status. Some practical consequences of this are discussed in Chapter 7.

Register and style

We have seen that we can regard varieties as a clustering of features. In addition to regional and social dialects, two other varieties often discussed by sociolinguists are register and style. While regional dialect reveals where we come from and social dialect what our status is, register gives a clue about what we are doing. The concept of register is typically concerned with variation in language conditioned by uses rather than users and involves consideration of the situation or context of use, the purpose, subject matter, and content of the message, and the relationship between participants. For example, two lawyers discussing a legal matter use the register of law; the language of police detectives reviewing a case reflects a register particular to their profession and the topic under discussion. If we hear words such as 'Our merciful Father in heaven, grant us the strength to do Thy will', we know instantly that we are dealing with the register of religion. Similarly, if we read something such as '"The Colts have reached an agreement with veteran quarterback Joe Ferguson as a backup to current starter Jack Trudeau", said coach Ron Meyer. The quarterback move was prompted by injuries to rookie Jeff George and veteran Mark Herrmann,' we recognize the register of sports reporting. Vocabulary differences—either a special vocabulary or special meanings for ordinary words—are most important in distinguishing different registers.

Other good examples of register variation can be found in other languages such as Javanese spoken in Indonesia, where there are a number of distinct levels of speech or varieties whose use is determined by the social status of the addressee. There are at least three levels of speech which can be distinguished in terms of selections of near synonyms for certain words: a 'high' (*krama*), 'middle' (*madya*), or 'low' (*ngoko*) variety. This sentence illustrates the three levels, with the highest first:

menapa	*pandjenengan*	*badé dahar*	*sekul*	*kalijan*	*kaspé*	*samenika?*
napa	*sampéjan*	*adjeng neda*	*sekul*	*lan*	*kaspé*	*saniki?*
apa	*kowé*	*arep mangan*	*sega*	*lan*	*kaspé*	*saiki?*
'Are	you	going to eat	rice	and	cassava	now?'

The speech register used for the highest-status persons is more elaborate than that used for lower-status persons. Note too that there are greater linguistic differences between the speech levels within Javanese than there are between the varieties labelled as separate languages by speakers in north-west New Britain, illustrating again the relative nature of the terms 'language' and 'dialect'.

The so-called 'mother-in-law' language found in most of the Aboriginal languages of Australia is another example of register variation. The mother-in-law register consists of a special way of speaking which men must use when addressing their mothers-in-law and certain other female relatives regarded as taboo. It has the same grammar and sounds as everyday speech, but a totally different vocabulary. Here are the words for 'sun' in some of the dialects of Dyirbal, a language spoken in north Queensland, compared with everyday (Guwal) and mother-in-law language (Dyalnguy). The varieties used by the different tribes are similar enough from a linguist's point of view to be varieties of the same language but each tribe considers its own speech to be a different language from that of its neighbors. These 'languages' of the different tribes (Yidin, Ngadyan, and Mamu) have almost identical grammars and sound systems. They also share between 80 and 90 per cent of their vocabulary. We can note again that the difference between registers is greater than that between varieties considered to be regional dialects. Each tribe, however, has its own Guwal and Dyalnguy varieties. Nevertheless, what is a Guwal form for one tribe may turn up as the Dyalnguy word of a neighboring group. For example, the Yidin everyday word for 'sun' is *bungan*, but in the Ngadyan tribe's language, that is the 'mother-in-law' word.

	Guwal (everyday)	Dyalnguy (mother-in-law)
Yidin	*bungan*	*gari:man*
Ngadyan	*gari*	*bungan*
Mamu	*gari*	*gambulu*

A notion related to register is that of 'style', which can range from formal to informal depending on social context, relationship of the participants, social class, sex, age, physical environment, and topic. Stylistic differences can also be reflected in vocabulary, as in 'The teacher distributed the new books' versus 'The teacher gave out the new books'; syntax, as in an increased use of the passive voice (in English) in formal speech ('The meeting was canceled by the president' versus 'The president called off the meeting'); and pronunciation (compare, for example, colloquial pronunciations such as 'readin', 'singin' with more formal ones such as 'reading', 'singing'). I will say more about such stylistic differences in Chapter 3.

Speech communities and communicative competence

What general lessons can be drawn from the examples given in this chapter for the study of language in society? I have shown how society impinges on language in various ways; in fact, the very existence of languages critically depends on the availability of a social group who claims a variety as their own and maintains its distinctiveness from the varieties spoken by its neighbors. Such a group can be called a 'speech community' and the conventions they share about their speech variety can be called 'communicative competence'. Distinctiveness can be either wholly or partly imagined, as our examples from northwest New Britain show. Languages and nations are continually used to validate one another in acts of identity.

The notions of 'speech community' and 'communicative competence' are fundamental to understanding the ways in which social groups organize their linguistic repertoires. A speech community is not necessarily coextensive with a language community. A speech community is a group of people who do not necessarily share the same language, but share a set of norms and rules for the use of language. The boundaries between speech communities are essentially social rather than linguistic. This means that terms such as 'language' and 'dialect' are, from a linguistic point of view, non-technical notions because there is no objective way to determine when two varieties will be seen by their speakers as sufficiently similar to warrant calling them the 'same' language. Any attempt to count distinct languages will be an artefact of classificatory procedures rather than a reflection of communicative practices. In Papua New Guinea people pay very great attention to small linguistic differences in differentiating themselves from their neighbors. People in one village or clan insist they speak a different language from the next village, although there is often a high degree of mutual intelligibility between them. Degree of mutual intelligibility is itself a function of the extent of social and other contact between the groups concerned and does not necessarily have much to do with actual linguistic differences.

Patterns of social interaction often transcend language boundaries. The so-called Prague School linguists introduced the notions of 'Sprechbund' (speech bond) and 'Sprachbund' (language bond), with a Sprechbund involving shared ways of speaking which go beyond language boundaries; and Sprachbund, relatedness at the level of linguistic form. A Sprachbund and a Sprechbund may not necessarily coincide. Membership in a community may be established and maintained primarily in terms of interactional rather than language norms. In some bilingual Gaelic/English communities along the east coast of Sutherland in Scotland, speakers who have only a receptive competence in Scottish Gaelic nevertheless are able to share in conversations and interactions with more fluent speakers. Even though they do not control the language well enough to use it, they understand what goes on and what behavior norms are appropriate. They have what we can call 'communicative competence' even though their grammatical competence in Gaelic is weak. The community as a whole shares certain norms for interacting, whether in fluent Gaelic, non-fluent Gaelic, or English. Conversely, sharing a grammar does not necessarily entail that communication will be successful. Speakers who speak the same language do not always understand each other because they do not necessarily share the same conventions for interpreting each other's speech or use speech in the same way.

Successful conversation for many English speakers involves filling any gaps with talk. Silence, in other words, is regarded as awkward. This is not true in all English-speaking communities, however. In Belfast, for instance, a neighbor may visit another and sit in her kitchen silently for an hour or more. Likewise, in some Aboriginal communities, people may sit silently for hours, with only an occasional obvious comment. Although most Aboriginal people in Australia have shifted from their ancestral languages to English, some of them carry over in the varieties of English they speak rules of communicative competence inherited from Aboriginal languages. The mistake other English speakers make in such situations is to feel they have to make remarks to keep the conversation going.

Talking about the weather is a stereotype often associated with speakers of British rather than American English. There are obvious reasons why the weather proves to be such a common topic in Britain. One is certainly the changeability and often unpleasant nature of the climate. Most important, however, is that the weather is a safe, impersonal topic that can be discussed between two strangers who want to be friendly but not too friendly. A common British stereotype about Americans is that they show too much familiarity with strangers and ask personal questions which are perceived as unwelcome intrusions. Americans, however, say they are simply showing interest by asking questions.

Yet Americans too consider the weather a safe topic for public discussion. This was evident in First Lady Hilary Rodham Clinton's 1999 visit to Egypt in the wake of her husband's infidelity which had led to his impeachment trial. At the same time, there was much speculation that she would run for election as senator in New York. Noting that she had just spoken on the telephone to her husband, the press was naturally eager to know what they had talked about. Clinton admitted only to having discussed the weather with the President.

Speakers of American English also offer each other more compliments than do English speakers in South Africa. Interestingly, Americans also accept more of the compliments they are given than do South Africans. Children in many communities are taught simply to accept a compliment such as 'That's a nice sweater' by saying 'Thank you'. However, studies of compliments have shown that two out of three responses to compliments are not of this type. More often, speakers are likely to avoid outright agreement and acceptance of the compliment by saying something like, 'It's really quite old', 'My mother made it for me', 'I bought it for wearing around the house', or even questioning the compliment, 'Do you really think so?', or returning it, 'So's yours'. There are also gender differences, some of which we will look at more carefully in Chapter 4. Compliments from women have the least likelihood of being accepted with simple thanks by both men and women. Compliments given by men, especially to women, are more likely to be accepted. While it appears to be important in American society to show solidarity by offering compliments, there is also an opposing but unstated principle, which seems to be that the receivers should avoid self-praise.

The term 'communicative competence' is used by sociolinguists to refer to a speaker's underlying knowledge of the rules of grammar (understood in the widest sense to include phonology, grammar, lexicon, and semantics) and rules for their use in socially appropriate circumstances. Native speakers of English know, for instance, that an utterance like *I now pronounce you man and wife* is something which can be said by someone with the authority to perform a marriage ceremony. They also know that an utterance such as *Would you mind setting the table?* is not usually a question requiring a yes or no answer, but instead is a polite request to set the table. Young children and foreigners may not at first understand these non-literal meanings since they are conventions which are learned through socialization in a community of native English speakers, just as Javanese children are taught how to use the various speech levels. Javanese children who are barely able to speak are held up by their caregivers facing an addressee while the caregiver speaks for the child to model the correct level of politeness, just as English-speaking children are prompted by adults into saying *thank you*, *goodbye*, etc. at the right time. Thus, social knowledge is essential for membership in a speech community.

Language, society, and reality: different words, different worlds?

There is no necessary one-to-one relationship between language and society. As a working premise, however, we can assume there probably aren't any speech communities in which aspects of society have no impact on language whatsoever. It is part of the task of sociolinguistics to examine the various possible connections between the two which may obtain. Some time ago, one linguist commented that no two languages are sufficiently similar to be considered as representing the same social reality. This is an acknowledgement of the crucial role language plays as an agent for the transmission of culture. It is often said that the vocabulary of a language is an inventory of the items a culture talks about and has categorized in order to make sense of the world. However, language is not simply a reflection of some external 'objective' reality which gets carved up in different ways in different languages. Language helps us to make sense of the world. By classifying things, we impose a structure on the social world, and language helps us to construct a model of it. A good example is our western notion of a seven-day week containing five work days and a weekend. Time does not naturally divide itself up into such units. These concepts reflect the interaction of humans with the environment and a conscious agreement on the part of particular societies that time will be regarded as divided into chunks of this size. Different cultures have different concepts of time.

All languages give names to concepts of cultural importance and mark certain conceptual categories in their grammars, e.g. differences between male and female, differences between one and more than one, etc. The many languages of the world are therefore a rich source of data concerning the structure of conceptual categories. An ancient Chinese encyclopedia supposedly divided up the animal world into the following categories: (*a*) those that belong to the emperor; (*b*) embalmed ones; (*c*) those that are trained; (*d*) suckling pigs; (*e*) mermaids; (*f*) fabulous ones; (*g*) stray dogs; (*h*) those that are included in this classification; (*i*) those that tremble as if they were mad; (*j*) innumerable ones; (*k*) those drawn with a very fine camel's hair brush; (*l*) others; (*m*) those that have just broken a flower vase; (*n*) those that resemble flies from a distance.

Much has been made of linguistic facts such as that English has no word corresponding to German *Schadenfreude* 'happiness about someone else's misfortune', or that in many languages spoken in Papua New Guinea the same word is used for 'hair', 'feather', and 'fur' (see further in Chapter 6), or that in Russian *mir* can mean both 'peace' and 'world', etc. To take what is the most often mentioned case, we can note the existence of several words in Eskimo to refer to 'snow' compared to only one in English. Of course, we can easily see why some of these differences occur. Snow is important to the Eskimo, while to most English speakers the precise state of snow is not very important, unless they are planning a skiing expedition. But we need to be careful in making generalizations such as this. English speakers are perfectly capable of talking about different kinds of snow such as *powdery snow*, *packed snow*, although they have to use phrases instead of a single word to talk about them. There are probably no important conceptual differences which result from lexical variation of this type between languages.

An examination of kinship terminology in different languages will reveal how the categories of relatives which are distinguished reflect the social construction of reality for a particular culture speaking a particular language. Even closely related languages such as English and Swedish differ. English has terms such as *aunt*, *grandfather*, and *grandmother* which distinguish the gender of certain relations, while Swedish must distinguish not just gender, but also whether an aunt is a father's sister (*faster*, literally a combination of the words for 'father' and 'sister') or mother's sister (*moster*, a combination of the words for 'mother' and 'sister'), and a grandfather is a father's father (*farfar*, a repetition of the word for 'father') or mother's father (*morfar*, a combination of the words for 'mother' and 'father'). In the Native American language Fox, uncles, great-uncles, and nephews are all called by the same term.

Categorization of the world by language is an ongoing social activity since new things have to be named. Conversely, in some cultures, when a person dies, his or her name and similar sounding words may be tabooed, so new words have to be coined or borrowed. We put things and concepts into categories only partly on the basis of perceived similarities. Categorization also has a cultural basis, and items which are characterized as similar in one culture may not be seen as such in another. There is, of course, a substantial overlap among the categories selected for encoding by human languages. It would be most unusual, for instance, to find that any language marked in some way as members of the same category 'things to take home from the office on a weekend', although it is one of some importance to academics and others who regularly take home work from the office.

A look at a non-western language such as Dyirbal reveals a four-way classification, so that each noun must be preceded by a classifier telling what category it belongs to. The *bayi* class includes men, kangaroos, possums, bats, most snakes, the moon, etc. The *balan* class includes women, bandicoots, dogs, anything connected with fire or water, sun, stars, etc. The *balam* class includes all edible fruits and the plants that bear them, ferns, honey, cigarettes, etc. The *bala* class includes body parts, meat, bees, most trees, mud, stones, etc. What organizing principles lie behind this system? The first class obviously includes human males and animals, while the second contains human females, birds, water and fire. The third has non-flesh food; and the last, everything not in the other classes. There is also a general rule at work that puts everything associated with the entities in a category in that particular class. Fish are in the *bayi* class with men because they are seen as animals, and so are fishing lines, spears, etc. because they are associated with fish. This shows that sharing similarities is not the only basis for categorization.

Cultural beliefs too affect classification. In order to understand why birds are not in the first category one has to understand that to the Dyirbal birds are the spirits of dead human females. Therefore, they belong in the second class with other female beings. The affinity between birds and female spirits is more obvious in mother-in-law language, where both are referred to by the same word. Similarly, according to Dyirbal myth, the moon and sun are husband and wife, so the moon goes in the class with men and husbands, while the sun belongs with females and wives.

There is one further principle at work. If some members of a set differ in some important way from the others, usually in terms of their danger or harmfulness, they are put into another group. Thus, while fish are in class one with other animate beings, the stone fish and gar fish, which are harmful and therefore potentially dangerous, are in class two. There is nothing in objective reality corresponding to the Dyirbal noun categories in the sense that the classes do not correspond to groups of entities which share similar properties, but the rationale for the categorization tells us something about how Dyirbal people conceive of their social world and interact with it.

A useful way of conceptualizing differences between languages is to think of them as varying not so much in what it is possible to say, as in what is unavoidable to say. Although English is a relatively impoverished language by comparison with others such as Javanese in terms of the social distinctions that have to be expressed in its grammar, the grammars of other languages are much more permeable to society, as can be seen by looking at Japanese, where the concept of self depends on social relations. While in English speakers can usually refer to themselves as 'I', in Japanese there are four pronouns, depending on the formality of the occasion and the status of one's interlocutor. In some Aboriginal languages of Australia pronominal forms are used to mark kinship relations, so that in Adnyamadhanha there are ten different pronouns which are the English equivalents to 'you and I' (we), which depend on clan membership, kin relation, and generation level. Thus, we can conclude that there are cultural prerequisites to formal grammatical analysis of Adnyamadhanha. In Chinese, the forms which are equivalent to the English first person pronoun are actually more like titles since they mean 'younger brother', 'less worthy one', 'the fool', while the forms for 'you' mean 'big brother', 'wise one', etc.

In such languages speakers cannot even refer to themselves without taking into account how they fit into society. A Korean/English bilingual student of mine told me that when he met Korean/English bilinguals in the USA, he preferred to speak English with them since he could then avoid any possible embarrassment that might arise if he incorrectly assessed his addressee's age and status. In English he could simply say 'you' and 'I'. Thus, in Japanese it is not possible to refer to oneself without making certain social distinctions, just as it is not possible to say 'you are tired' in Spanish and many other European languages without indicating the sex of the person spoken to and the relationship the speaker has to the addressee. To say, *estás cansada* means not simply 'you are tired', but that the speaker is female (cf. masculine *cansado*) and the speaker knows her well enough to address her in the intimate second person singular form (compare the polite form *está*).

Most of the languages of Europe except English require speakers to choose between pronouns meaning 'you' according to the location of the speaker and hearer in a multidimensional social space, where considerations of solidarity, status, age, etc. are taken into account. Comparing English and Spanish in this regard, we can say that Spanish speakers are obliged by virtue of the fact that they speak Spanish to make such distinctions of status and gender. These distinctions have been 'grammaticalized', or made obligatory, in Spanish, whereas they have not in English. It is not the case that English cannot make such distinctions. It can, but they have to be encoded in other ways such as through the use of titles, and such distinctions are not obligatorily encoded for pronouns. Pronoun systems are one important part of the grammar of languages where these kinds of distinctions are often grammaticalized and can be used to maintain, create, or transform social relations.

English does, in fact, encode other social distinctions such as gender in its third person pronouns, i.e. *she/he*, *her/him*, *hers/his*, while Finnish does not. In Chapter 4 I will examine some of the claims made by women that English and other languages encode a sexist view of society, and consider what can be done about it. In Chapter 5 I will look at how changes in the grammatical encoding of social distinctions such as these reflect changing concepts of self in society.

We can conclude from these examples that no particular language has a privileged view of the world as it 'really' is. The world is not simply the way it is, but what we make of it through language. The domains of experience which are important to cultures get grammaticalized into languages. Grammaticalized concepts are more fundamental than concepts associated with lexical items. Our understanding of these concepts contributes to our view of cognitive categories. These multiple points of view are not just simply products of speaking different languages with different categories, but are constantly available to all of us. There is then a sense in which all communication is cross-cultural. For instance, if different people see a man out mowing his lawn early Saturday morning and are asked what he is doing, one may see him as a good citizen keeping up appearances and property values in the neighborhood, while a next-door neighbor who likes to sleep late on Saturdays may see him as engaging in an antisocial activity. We might also ask ourselves whether the man mowing his lawn is 'working'.

As English speakers, we are accustomed to going to the dictionary to find out what a word 'really' means. I consulted one dictionary and found several entries for 'work'. Among them were the following: physical or mental effort or activity directed toward the production or accomplishment of something, employment, a job; the means by which one earn's one's living. How does mowing the lawn fit into these definitions? I am generally amused by the fact that when my neighbors see me at home on a weekday during the daytime, they assume I am not 'working'. For them, the home is not a workplace and things done outside normal working hours do not count as work. Even my parents, who have a better idea of what my 'work' involves than most of my neighbors, expressed puzzlement at what I was going to be doing on my sabbatical if I was not teaching. Academics often complain that much of the time spent on research is 'unseen' and therefore unvalued, even though most of us are expected to spend a significant amount of time engaged in it. I and other academics I have talked to are accustomed to making a distinction between 'job' and 'my work'. If I talk about 'my work' to another academic, I am talking about my research and not about the teaching I am doing. The contrast was recently made clear to me by a colleague who wrote to say that her work (i.e. 'paid work', she added) was not going all that well. By further qualifying the notion of work with the word 'paid' she wanted me to know that she was complaining about her teaching and administrative duties as a professor rather than her own research.

This example shows the context relativity of all observation at the same time as it demonstrates that social context and intention play a role in our judgements of what it means to 'work'. Meaning is affected by our understanding of a situation. It is not the case that any one particular interpretation is the 'correct' one or corresponds to the 'truth', but rather that individuals bring different conceptual frames, background knowledge, and assumptions to an event or situation and arrive at an interpretation which is consistent with the alternatives available to them. We all have multiple conceptualizations of the 'same' events even when we are speaking the 'same' language. This is all part of our communicative competence.

The notion of communicative competence in sociolinguistics is intended to replace the dichotomy between competence and performance central to mainstream linguistics. The knowledge of rules of grammar is called 'competence' (as distinct from 'performance', which refers to how the rules of grammar are used). Speakers draw on their competence in putting together grammatical sentences, i.e. those which can be derived by the rules of grammar. Even though English has no grammaticalized distinctions in its pronominal system, not all grammatical sentences can be used in the same circumstances. Thus, *close the window, would you mind closing the window please?*, and *Do you think it is cold in here?* are all grammatical sentences of English, but they differ in terms of their appropriateness for use in particular situations. Speakers rely on their communicative competence in choosing what to say, as well as how and when to say it. In the next chapter I will examine some of the motivations behind speakers' choices.

Annotated bibliography

An overview of the intellectual concerns of Chomskyan linguistics can be found in Neil Smith and Deidre Wilson's book (1979). The example from north-west New Britain comes from William Thurston (1987). Further information about the linguistic situation in Papua New Guinea can be found in Stephen Wurm's book (1982) and his edited collection (1975, 1976, 1977), William Foley (1986), and many of the papers in Gillian Sankoff (1980). Jack Chambers and Peter Trudgill (1980) proposed the terms *heteronomy* and *autonomy* in their book, which is an excellent introduction to the study of dialects in the widest sense.

Anastasia N. Karakasidou's book (1997) relates the struggle between Greece and Bulgaria for the territory of Macedonia and Victor Friedman (1997, 1998) provides a fascinating analysis of the sociolinguistic situation in Macedonia.

The Javanese example is from Clifford Geertz (1972). Examples of mother-in-law language can be found in R. M. W. Dixon (1972). Benedict Anderson's (1991) book describes how nations may be brought into being through print literacy and standardization of national languages. The study of east Sutherland Gaelic is found in Nancy C. Dorian (1982). The notion of 'communicative competence' is discussed in Dell Hymes's article (1972). The study of mutual intelligibility in Scandinavia can be found in Einar Haugen's article (1972). The anecdote about accent was taken from Dwight Bolinger's book (1980). Research on compliments has been done by R. K. Herbert (1986). George Lakoff's book (1987) is a study of the relationship between cognitive and linguistic categories. For a discussion of the implications of the Eskimo example, see John B. Carroll (1956) and Geoffrey Pullum (1991). The example of the man mowing his lawn is taken from Ragnar Rommetveit (1980).

Chapter 2

Language Choice

> And the whole earth was of one language, and of one speech . . . And they said to one another, 'Go to, let us build us a city and a tower, whose top may reach unto heaven; and let us make a name, lest we be scattered abroad on the face of the whole earth'. And the Lord came down to see the city and the tower, which the children of men builded. And the Lord said, 'Behold, the people is one, and they have all one language, . . . let us go down, and there confound their language, that they may not understand one another's speech'. So the Lord scattered them abroad from thence upon the face of all the earth; and they left off to build the city. Therefore is the name of it called Babel: because the Lord did there confound the language of all the earth.
>
> (Genesis 11: 1–9)

MOST cultures have stories which seek to explain the origin of life and to explain why things are as they are in the world today. The story from Genesis would have us believe that linguistic diversity is the curse of Babel. In a primordial time, people spoke the same language. God, however, decided to punish them for their presumptuousness in erecting the tower by making them speak different languages. Thus, multilingualism became an obstacle to further cooperation and placed limits on human worldly achievements.

The idea that multilingualism is divisive, while monolingualism is a normal and desirable state of affairs, is still with us today. In a speech made on Australian radio in 1994 Rupert Murdoch claimed that multilingualism was the cause of Indian disunity, and monolingualism the reason for the unity of the English-speaking world. He rejoiced in the fact, however, that Hindi was finally spreading as a major lingua franca, due to the availability of Hindi TV programming being spread by his Asian television company, Star.

It takes but little reflection to find the many obvious flaws in Murdoch's reasoning and to come up with cases where the sharing of a common language has not gone hand in hand with political or indeed any other kind of unity. Northern Ireland is one such example from the English-speaking world that comes readily to mind. But there are many others from other parts of the globe. A very high degree of linguistic and religious uniformity in Somalia did not prevent a brutal civil war from breaking out there. Certainly, the attempt at Russification of the former republics of the Soviet Union did not ensure unity in that part of the world either. Indeed, one of the first political acts undertaken by the newly independent Baltic states was to reassert their linguistic and cultural autonomy by reinstating their own national languages as official in place of Russian. After the demotion in status of Russian, Russia was not slow to accuse these countries of depriving Russian speakers of their linguistic human rights.

Despite the emphasis of mainstream linguistics on monolingualism and homogeneous speech communities, widespread bilingualism and multilingualism of the type found in north-west New Britain discussed in Chapter 1 are actually more common. It has been estimated that there are some 5,000 languages in the world but only about 185 nation-states recognized by the United Nations. Probably about half the world's population is bilingual and bilingualism is present in practically every country in the world. I will use the terms 'bilingualism' and 'multilingualism' interchangeably. With the formation of new nation-states, the question of which language (or which version of a particular one) will become the official national language arises and has often led to bitter controversy. Even countries with more than one official language, such as Canada (where French and English share co-official status), have not escaped attempts by various factions to gain political advantage by exploiting issues of language loyalty.

A distinction is usually drawn between individual and societal multilingualism, although it is not always possible to maintain. Some countries, such as Canada, are officially bilingual in English and French, although not all Canadians are bilingual. There are many more French Canadians who learn English as a second language than English Canadians who learn French. In other countries such as India and Papua New Guinea there is a high degree of individual bilingualism with the average person knowing at least two languages. The connection between individual and societal bilingualism also becomes evident when we consider some of the reasons why certain individuals are or become bilingual. Usually the more powerful groups in any society are able to force their language upon the less powerful. If we take Finland as an example, we find that the Saami (Lapps), Romanies, and Swedes have to learn Finnish, but Finns do not have to learn any of these languages. Or similarly in Britain, the British child does not have to learn Panjabi or Welsh, but both these groups are expected to learn English.

The identification of schooling with the learning of a second language is a common situation in many parts of the world. In Papua New Guinea, for instance, almost all children will be educated in English, despite the fact that it is not widely known, because this language policy is a legacy of the country's colonial heritage. The middle-class anglophone parents in Canada who send their child to a French immersion school are, however, by contrast, under no obligation to do so. Many do so as a means of enriching their children's development and because they believe knowledge of another language is an advantage.

In Europe, it has generally been the case that language differences have been associated with distinguishable territories, and later, the nation-states occupying those territories. Language and nation coincide. Because of the identification of national entities with linguistic integrity, heterogeneity has tended to be limited to the frontiers and was for that reason local and peripheral, e.g. the Basques in Spain and France, and the 'Celtic fringe' in the British Isles and France. Thus, twenty-five out of thirty-six of the European countries are officially unilingual. In most of them, however, there are minorities (both indigenous and non-indigenous), whose languages do not have the same rights as those granted to the official languages. The marginalization of the languages and cultures of minority peoples in the European states can be seen as a form of 'internal colonialism'.

Some political scientists and linguists have used the term 'Fourth World' to label indigenous dispossessed minority peoples who have been encapsulated, within, and in some cases divided across, modern nation-states, e.g. the Saami and Inuit peoples of the Arctic region. They are people who do not have their own nation-state, but nevertheless regard themselves as ethnically and linguistically distinct from the majority population in the countries where they reside.

Because the boundaries of modern nation-states have been arbitrarily drawn in line with the political and economic interests of powerful elites, many indigenous people today like the Welsh, Hawaiians, and Basques find themselves living in nations they had no say in creating and are controlled by groups who do not represent their interests and, in some cases, actively seek to exterminate them, as is the case with the Kurds in Iraq and Turkey. More than 80 per cent of the conflicts in the world today are between nation-states and minority peoples.

All nation-states, whatever their political ideology, have persecuted minorities in the past and many continue to do so today. While not all states are actively seeking the eradication of minorities within their borders, they pursue policies designed to assimilate indigenous people into the mainstream or dominant culture. Many immigrants to the United States, for instance, were brainwashed into thinking that their languages and cultures were inferior and therefore had to be abandoned for the sake of being American. As recently as

1971 it was illegal to speak Spanish in a public school building in Texas. As we will see in Chapter 7, the widespread assimilation of minorities in this way in democratic countries such as the USA is generally ignored since it is assumed that assimilation is voluntary and not coerced. Consideration of the larger picture, however, reveals a fuzzy boundary between forced and voluntary assimilation.

Even in countries where minority languages are recognized for some purposes, what this means varies in practice. By minority language I mean one with a relatively small number of speakers living within the domain of a more widely spoken language, whose knowledge is usually necessary for full participation in society. Swedes in Finland probably have the best legal protection of any minority group in the world. The next strongest position is held by minority languages which have limited (often territorial) rights. This is the case in Canada, where certain provinces are officially declared bilingual, and others, like Ontario (where the national capital lies), are not. It would be naive, however, to assume that bilingual countries were created to promote bilingualism, rather than to guarantee the legal right to more than one language in a society. We can distinguish between de facto and de jure bilingualism. There are often fewer bilingual individuals in de jure bilingual states than in those where de facto bilingualism occurs. A good example is Switzerland, where territorial unilingualism exists under federal multilingualism. Of the twenty-six cantons, twenty-two are officially monolingual. Economic and political power is more greatly concentrated among German speakers. In a study done to investigate problems faced by non-German-speaking groups at the federal level, only German speakers considered having German as a mother tongue irrelevant for career purposes; all the other language groups saw it as more advantageous.

In all multilingual communities speakers switch among languages or varieties as monolinguals switch among styles. Language choice is not arbitrary and not all speech communities are organized in the same way. Through the selection of one language over another or one variety of the same language over another speakers display what may be called 'acts of identity', choosing the groups with whom they wish to identify. The aim of this chapter is to examine the motivations for such choices in different societies.

Societal multilingualism

The first step in understanding what choices are available to speakers is to gain some idea of what languages and varieties are available to them in a particular social context. Context in this case may be thought of in its widest sense as the varieties made available either officially or unofficially within boundaries of a nation-state such as Canada, or in a very narrow sense, as the varieties available on a particular occasion, e.g. shopping in an urban market in Ethiopia. Knowledge about the distribution of varieties in society has been obtained in a number of ways which reflect these differing perspectives.

Most of the studies of societal bilingualism have taken the nation-state as their reference point, and have relied on census data to determine the linguistic composition of these units. However, it must be remembered that large-scale surveys and census statistics will yield quite a different perspective on questions of language use from detailed case studies. Whether a variety constitutes a minority language varies according to the scale at which the observation is made, and is relative to the social context in which a language is used.

There are many problems in doing research on multilingualism using census statistics. The kinds of questions that can be asked about bilingualism are usually restricted by a variety of constraints. A census operates under limitations of time and money, and thus many facets of bilingualism, such as extent of interference between languages, or switching, cannot be investigated in any detail. On the other hand, large surveys can yield data on bilingualism for a population of much greater size than any individual linguist or team could hope to survey in a lifetime. In cases of de jure bilingualism, knowledge about the demographic concentration of particular ethnic minorities is necessary for the implementation of language legislation. In Canada, for instance, it is required in order that so-called bilingual districts are provided with services of the federal government in both French and English, which they are entitled to by law.

One major problem in such surveys has been touched on in Chapter 1 in my observation that it may not be easy to decide who speaks a particular language in north-west New Britain or elsewhere for that matter. Self-reports of language usage are subject to variance in relation to factors such as prestige, ethnicity, political affiliation. Even where these factors are not present to a great degree, a respondent and census taker may not share the same ideas about what terms like 'mother tongue', 'home language', etc. mean, especially since linguists themselves are not agreed on how bilingualism should be defined. Usually censuses do not recognize that an individual might have more than one 'mother tongue', or that the language learned first might not be the language best mastered. For example, until 1941 the Canadian censuses defined 'mother tongue' as the language first learned by the respondent and still spoken. From 1941 to 1976, however, it was taken to mean the language first learned and still understood, following the definition of mother tongue given in the Official Language Act of 1969. This change in the definition of 'mother tongue' makes longitudinal comparison of statistics difficult.

A more serious shift in the definition of mother tongue occurred in the case of second-generation immigrants in the United States. In 1910 and 1920 the second generation was classified by the mother tongue of the foreign-born parent. In 1940, however, the mother tongue was taken to be the language spoken at home from earliest childhood. Consequently, in the earlier censuses none of the second generation could be counted as English mother tongue speakers, unless their foreign-born parents used English at home before coming to the United States.

Like 'language' and 'dialect', 'mother tongue' is not a technical term and there are many problems with its use. In one of its popular senses, the term 'mother tongue' evokes the notion of mothers as the passive repositories of languages, which they pass on to their children. In some communities, however, it is fathers who transmit their language to their children. Such a case obtains, for example, in the Vaupes area of Columbia and Brazil. There groups are patrilineal and one's primary language is the language of the father. Because marriage is exogamous, one may not marry a person from one's own or a 'brother' language group. Husbands and wives communicate dual-lingually as in north-west New Britain. The children may become fluent in the language of both parents, but consider the father's language to be their own.

A widely cited and influential document arguing the advantages of vernacular education used the term 'mother tongue' (UNESCO 1953). It states: 'On educational grounds we recommend that the use of the mother tongue be extended to as late a stage in education as possible. In particular, pupils should begin their schooling through the medium of the mother tongue, because they understand it best and because to begin their school life in the mother tongue will make the break between home and school as small as possible.' Other influential pieces of legislation use the term 'mother tongue' too, such as the 1977 Directive of the Council of the European Community on the education of the children of migrant workers (Brussels 77/486/EEC). It instructs member states of the European Community to 'take appropriate measures to promote the teaching of the mother tongue and of the culture of the country of origin of the children of migrant workers, and also as part of compulsory free education to teach one or more of the official languages of the host state'.

When various minority groups campaign for provision of so-called 'mother tongue teaching', the question of what one's mother tongue is designated to be can be crucial because it determines who has a right to education in a particular language. In Britain, for example, Pakistani speakers of Panjabi will claim Urdu, the national language of Pakistan, as their mother tongue, and not Panjabi, which is a spoken language used in the home. For religious reasons Urdu provides a rallying point too for many Pakistanis, whereas Panjabi does not. Sikhs in Britain, however, will claim Panjabi as their mother tongue, for similar reasons. For them, it is both a home language and a public language. As the language of the Panjab state, it is an important regional language in India, and for Sikhs it has special significance as a religious language. Ethnic groups are often defined as belonging to a linguistic minority on the basis of their mother tongue. Some members of some minority groups such as West Indians in Britain would like to claim that varieties of West Indian creole constitute a language and therefore deserve recognition as their mother tongue. The belief that having one's own language is criterial for ethnicity may be used by a state and its mainstream population to deny the legitimacy of claims to special status and land rights made by a group who have shifted from their indigenous languages to the language of the majority. I will consider some of these practical implications in Chapters 6 and 7.

Returning to the case of Macedonia considered in Chapter 1, we can see that census data rarely capture the complex relationships among religion, language, ethnicity, and politics that define individual choices about national identity and designation of mother tongue. Looking at some census data from Macedonia around the turn of the century in Table 2.1, we can see how conflicting census statistics were used to bolster competing claims on the territory of Macedonia.

Each census reports a majority for its own group. Thus, the Bulgarian census from 1900 claims a majority of 52.31 per cent Bulgarians, the Serbian census of 1889 claims a majority of 71.35 per cent Serbs, and the Greek census of 1904 claims a majority of 37.85 per cent Greeks. These are the three states who fought one another over the territory of Macedonia in the second Balkan war in 1913. The Turkish figures from the 1905 Ottoman census likewise claim a majority of 51.80 per cent Turks.

In the case of the Greek and Turkish censuses, people were grouped according to religion or schooling or both. Thus, in privileging religion over language as the basis of identity, Greeks counted as Greek any persons who were members of the Greek Orthodox Church as well as anyone who went to a Greek

Table 2.1 Conflicting census figures for Macedonia 1889–1905 (%)

Ethnic group	Bulgarian	Serbian	Greek	Turkish
Bulgarians	52.31	2.01	19.26	30.8
Serbians	0.03	71.35	0.00	3.4
Greeks	10.13	7.01	37.85	10.6
Albanians	5.70	5.77	0.00	0.0
Turks	22.11	8.06	36.76	51.8
Others	9.72	13.86	6.13	3.4

Source: Adapted from Friedman 1996: Table A.1, p. 85.

school. Because schooling was controlled by religion, there was little choice for Macedonian Christians. Albanians do not appear as a separate group because they were counted as Turks, Greeks, or others on the basis of religion (Muslim, Greek Orthodox, Catholic). The Bulgarian figures assumed that any Slav was Bulgarian. Most importantly, however, what we do not see in these figures is how Macedonians identified themselves. Macedonian ethnic identity is totally suppressed.

The concepts of ethnicity, nationality, language, and religion have long been interrelated in complex ways in this region, leading to discrepancies between declared nationality and declared mother tongue. Some Macedonian-speaking Muslims, for instance, who have been manipulated by both Albanian and Turkish politicians into believing that they are Slavicized Albanians or Turks rather than Islamicized Slavs, will declare their nationality as Albanian or Turkish on the basis of religious affiliation. One result of this is that some census takers in Macedonian-speaking Muslim villages encountered monolingual families who demanded a bilingual Turkish or Albanian form with an interpreter but needed to have the form translated into Macedonian! In one monolingual Macedonian village parents even demanded an Albanian-language school for their children; other Macedonian-speaking Muslim families have been demanding Turkish-language schools. Meanwhile, some Albanian-speaking Christians declare their nationality as Macedonian because they equate Macedonian Orthodox Christianity with Macedonian ethnicity. Albanian politicians, however, declare such self-identified Macedonians to be Albanians.

Albanians, who make up the largest minority group in Macedonia, are demanding constitutional recognition as a nation and a redefinition of Macedonia as a bi-national state of Macedonians and Albanians. During the air strikes launched against Serbian military forces in 1999 which triggered a huge influx of Albanians from Kosovo into neighboring Macedonia, NATO was greatly concerned about destabilizing the situation in Macedonia and igniting ethnic conflicts. Even the most basic question such as how many ethnic Albanians there are in Macedonia is fraught with difficulty because both the Macedonian and Albanian language communities in Macedonia are divided by religious and ethnic cleavages.

As the Socialist Republic of Yugoslavia was collapsing, the 1991 census was conducted, although it was boycotted by ethnic Albanians, whose leaders insisted they would be purposely undercounted. Consequently, the Macedonian authorities determined the number of Albanians by statistical estimation. Albanian leaders refused to accept their estimate of 21.7 per cent of the population (against 65.3 per cent Macedonians), insisting instead that Albanians constituted as much as 40 per cent, or about 800,000 out of a population of just over 2 million. Several other minorities also claimed to have been undercounted.

Serbs, for instance, claimed up to 300,000 (instead of the Macedonian count of 42,775 or 2.1 per cent), Greeks up to 250,000 (instead of 474, less than 1 per cent), and Roms and Turks up to 200,000 each (instead of 52,103 or 2.6 per cent, and 77,080 or 3.8 per cent), etc. When added together, the population claims of all minorities far exceeded the republic's total population, even without counting Macedonians.

Under intense internal and external pressure an extraordinary census was conducted in 1994 by international organizations, who thought they were carrying out a purely mechanical exercise with no political dimensions, but soon discovered otherwise. Expecting to find a typical western European situation in which nationality is defined by equating language with state, they instead forced on people the kinds of choices that have long fuelled conflict in the Balkans. For one, the census form required people to choose a single mother tongue, which ignored long-standing multilingualism in the area. Intermarriage along religious lines but across linguistic ones produced bilingual children. When forced to declared their nationality, the children of a Turkish man and an Albanian woman might split along gender lines, with the daughters declaring themselves Albanians, and the sons Turks. Other such families might declare one son a Turk and another an Albanian.

In interpreting census statistics, we also run up against the language/dialect problem. As a rule, censuses are interested in languages, not dialects, even though, as we have seen in Chapter 1, from a linguistic point of view neither is a technical term. In India, for instance, Maithili was claimed as a mother tongue by over 6 million people in the 1971 census. It has its own script and literary tradition, but because it has borrowed much of its vocabulary from Hindi, it is considered a dialect of that language. In the state of Madras, speakers of Sourashtra petitioned the government for primary schools conducted in the medium of their own language. They were, however, refused on the grounds that Sourashtra was only a dialect. Interestingly, Sourashtra is listed among the languages of India in the 1950 census, but in 1960 it is classified as a dialect of Gujarati.

Such linguistic disputes are common in India. Rivalry between Hindi speakers, whose language has official status as a national language (replacing English), and speakers of other regional languages, like Panjabi and Urdu, is intense. Hindi, Panjabi, and Urdu are very closely related and, in most varieties, mutually intelligible, although they use different writing systems. After independence, Hindi leaders claimed that Urdu and Panjabi were dialects of Hindi, while some Sikh groups demanded a linguistically homogeneous Panjabi state. As a result of this antagonism, census authorities abandoned the separate tabulation of Hindi and Panjabi speakers in 1951. Thus, in the all-India census return, Hindi, Urdu, Panjabi, and Hindustani speakers were grouped together.

This fact was then taken up by Hindi leaders, who claimed that the combined total of all these languages was a legitimate reflection of the number of 'Hindi' speakers. A census interview is thus not a very good setting for obtaining a sociolinguistic profile of a country like India, as there is likely to be much over- and under-reporting of languages for reasons of nationalism, group solidarity, and prestige.

Even in nations with a lesser incidence of multilingualism there can be problems of definition in deciding what counts as a 'language' or 'dialect'. Within France the term 'bilingual' is usually applied only to persons who are able to handle two national languages. Thus, a Frenchman who spoke Breton and French would not be considered bilingual because Breton is of low status and considered a patois rather than a language.

In many parts of the world, there is often little language consciousness. In such cases, groups may have no special label for their language other than 'our language', but nevertheless regard it as distinct from the varieties spoken by their neighbors. The Gitksan people of British Columbia have no conventional native name for their language which sets it apart from other varieties such as Nisgha and Tsimshian. The Gitksan generally refer to their own language as *Sim'algax* [the real or true language], but the Nisgha and Tsimshian people do the same. Although linguistically these three could count as varieties of one language, the speakers comprise separate social and ethnic units within which there are distinct norms and standards relating to language. Some seemingly strange answers were recorded by immigration officers and in the 1910 census data for the United States by some of the peasantry of south-eastern Europe when asked what language they spoke. There are thousands of claimants of 'Slavish' and other varieties, which, from the linguist's point of view, are non-existent or inappropriately labelled languages.

Given all these problems, it is difficult to know what to ask. For example, some censuses have asked: what language is used in the home most frequently? The 1961 census in Scotland required the enumerator to check off those who spoke Gaelic only or both Gaelic and English. The interpretation given to 'speaking Gaelic' was left to the respondent. As we have seen in Chapter 1, in many parts of Scotland where Scottish Gaelic is dying out, it may not be clear to community members themselves who is or is not a proficient speaker of the language since speakers who have a very limited productive control of the language still participate in the speech community of Gaelic speakers by virtue of their communicative competence.

Neither is it clear what the status is of speakers who are represented in census statistics. If we look, for instance, at some of the results of the Irish census returns over the past century and a half summarized in Table 2.2, we can see that while Irish retreated dramatically from the mid-nineteenth century

Table 2.2 Speakers of Irish according to census returns

Census date	Speakers of Irish only	Total Irish speakers
1851	4.9	23.3
1901	0.5	14.4
1971		28.3
1981		31.6

Source: From Hindley 1990: 19, 23.

onwards, in 1971 it seems to have a great upsurge, with 28.3 per cent of the population claiming to speak it. This indicates a gain of nearly a quarter of a million speakers in a decade. The figures represent the number of children and adults who are recorded by heads of households as being able to speak Irish. In 1981 we might be tempted to conclude that the attempt to revive Irish appears to have reversed the enormous decline over the previous hundred years since, despite massive emigration in the intervening years, those able to speak Irish constitute almost a third of the total, or more than those reported for 1851.

However, on closer examination, the statistics represent the replacement of ever-decreasing numbers of native speakers by those whose first language is English, who for the most part are not fluent Irish speakers and hardly ever have occasion to use it. The 1926 census attempted to distinguish native from second language speakers, but ended up counting both simply as speakers of Irish. Over the years the census figures have become increasingly misleading. In one sense this does not matter. No state agency for language planning awaits the figures as a guide to policy, as would be the case in Canada, for instance, but it does mean that they are not a reliable diagnostic for determining the likelihood of the continued survival of the language among those who use it natively.

Since the foundation of the Gaelic League in 1893, which demanded recognition of Irish, the position of the language has been transformed although not always wholly to the advantage of Irish or its native speakers. Irish has continued to die as the language of a rural peasantry located in geographically well-defined areas, largely on the west coast. Respect for Irish, however, became an important part of the ideology of the Irish Free State established in 1922, when Irish was proudly proclaimed the national language in the new constitution and after which time all children began to study the language at school (at times compulsorily) either as a subject or through the medium of Irish. Once children had been taught Irish at school, there was a tendency to claim they were able to speak it.

At the time of the 1971 census a research team was investigating attitudes to Irish and they decided to look into the census returns since it was a matter of common knowledge that there were not 700,000-odd speakers of Irish. They found that the 28 per cent represented those who were strongly supportive of the language. In fact, only a very small number of Irish people are willing to express negative attitudes to Irish. The 'real' figure for first language speakers of Irish as a proportion of the total population was estimated to be around 2 per cent on the basis of the 1971 census data. The others are second language speakers. The latter, however, are an unrepresentative, though influential, sector of educated Irish society. Outside native Irish-speaking districts, fluent Irish is a fairly reliable indicator of middle-class status, while the working class remain ignorant of the language. The new bilinguals constitute a network, largely urban and middle class, not a community, and only a small number of them might be expected to pass the language on to the next generation. As one Irish person said, 'although we are all *for* Irish as we are for cheaper bus fares, heaven and the good life, nobody of the masses is willing to make the effort'. The urban middle class can in a sense afford the luxury of using Irish since they are comfortable in their status as English speakers, but it was this very group who jettisoned the language in their effort to obtain socio-economic security at a time when everyone spoke Irish.

A more recent estimate based on surveys of numbers of schoolchildren awarded grants as native speakers reached the conclusion that there were actually as few as 8,751 Irish speakers living in communities with sufficient attachment to the language to transmit it to the next generation as the language of the home. Even then, however, it proved difficult for an outsider to obtain reliable evidence since school officials were suspicious of questions about the extent of Irish spoken in their schools for fear of losing grants and subsidies. In former years, some inspectors had given grants to some families once they saw what poverty they lived in. While Ireland is unique among European nations by virtue of its declaration of what is in essence a minority language as its primary language, the fact that it is the only EEC member which did not require translation of all Community documents into what is constitutionally its first official language is indicative of the largely ceremonial and symbolic status of Irish. The native language of most Irish people is English.

We can see the problems posed by the fact that degree of bilingualism is usually left unspecified in most census questions. The question used in Canada for years was simply: can you speak French/English? In the Philippines census of 1960, a conversational criterion was stipulated: any person who can carry on a simple conversation in Tagalog, English, or Spanish on ordinary topics is considered 'able' (to speak) for the purpose of this census. In other cases, such as the Israeli census of 1948, respondents were asked to say only which languages they used rather than which ones they knew. The frequency with which respondents claimed to use Hebrew was probably exaggerated here too as it was in Ireland due to national pride during the early years of new nationhood. The question of whether a person uses a language also has to be viewed in context, since different languages and varieties are used for different things. Detailed information of this kind usually emerges from a different kind of study.

Domains

In research on the Puerto Rican community in New York City, a team of sociolinguists arrived at a list of five 'domains' in which either Spanish or English was used consistently. These were established on the basis of observation and interviews and comprised: family, friendship, religion, employment, and education. These domains served as anchor points for distinct value systems embodied in the use of Spanish as opposed to English. A domain is an abstraction which refers to a sphere of activity representing a combination of specific times, settings, and role relationships. They conducted further studies to support their claim that each of these domains carried different expectations for using Spanish or English.

The researchers constructed hypothetical conversations that differed in terms of their interlocutors, place, and topic. The way in which these variables were manipulated determined the extent to which the domain configuration was likely to be perceived as congruent or incongruent. For example, a highly congruent configuration would be a conversation with a priest, in church, about how to be a good Christian. A highly incongruent one would be a discussion with one's employer at the beach about how to be a good son or daughter.

People were asked to imagine themselves in hypothetical situations where two of the three components of the conversational context were given. For example, they might be asked to imagine they were talking to someone at their place of work about how to do a job most efficiently. They were then asked to whom they would most likely be talking and in what language. The respondents tended to provide congruent answers for any given domain, and their choice of language was consistent. The most likely place for Spanish was the family domain, followed by friendship, religion, employment, and education.

An earlier study of Japanese/English bilinguals in the United States highlighted a similar phenomenon, although it did not specifically invoke the concepts of domain or congruence. Three variables were involved: topic, listener, and language. Speech was disrupted when the bilinguals were asked to speak in English about Japanese topics to Japanese interlocutors. There were more instances of hesitation pauses, deviant syntax, and borrowing of Japanese words into English, which resulted from a violation of the usual co-occurrence constraint that Japanese should be used to speak about Japanese topics to Japanese interlocutors. The findings have important implications for the measurement of bilingual proficiency. Where testing contexts violate expectations about domain congruence, the bilingual's performance may be impaired (see Chapter 7).

In each domain there may be pressures of various kinds, e.g. economic, administrative, cultural, political, religious, which influence the bilingual towards use of one language rather than the other. Often knowledge and use of one language is an economic necessity. Such is the case for many speakers of a minority language, like Gujarati in Britain, or French in provinces of Canada where francophones are in a minority. The administrative policies of some countries may require civil servants to have knowledge of a second language. For example, in Ireland, knowledge of Irish is required. In some countries it is expected that educated persons will have knowledge of another language. This is probably true for most of the European countries, and was even more dramatically so earlier in countries like pre-revolutionary Russia, where French was the language of polite, cultured individuals. Languages like Greek and Latin have also had great prestige as second languages of the educated. As is the case with accent, the prestige of one language over another is a function of the perceived power of those who speak it. A bilingual may also learn one of the languages for religious reasons. Many minority Muslim children in Britain receive religious training in Arabic.

Due to competing pressures, it is not possible to predict with absolute certainty which language an individual will use in a particular situation. Variable language use can arise when domains become unclear and setting and role relationships do not combine in the expected way. In cases such as these, either the setting takes precedence over role relationship and the speaker chooses the language associated with that setting, or the role relationship takes precedence and the speaker uses the language associated with it. In Quechua-speaking parts of Peru, for instance, the indigenous language, Quechua, is identified with the physical territory of rural communities, while the colonial language, Spanish, is linked with the cities, mines, and coastal areas. Quechua speakers perceive Quechua to be the language for community/family/home (*ayllu*), and Spanish the language for everything outside those domains. Although in the past probably most, if not all, language interactions in the *ayllu* domains were in Quechua, and all interactions outside it were in Spanish, that is not true today. Spanish has gradually encroached on traditionally monolingual

Quechua-speaking communities so that some Spanish is used within the confines of the communities.

Not surprisingly, the school is the setting where mismatches often occur and speakers are presented with a choice. This is because the school, although physically located within the community, is not considered part of it. For instance, school pupils who would ordinarily address one another in Quechua as peers outside schools often do so inside the school, although they continue to address the teachers in Spanish. Here the role relationship takes precedence over the setting. In other cases the setting takes precedence over role relationship, e.g. a mother sitting in front of her home addresses the school director in Quechua as he approaches. Moreover, female community members may make different choices from males in the same setting, as for example in a women's association meeting where the women talk to each other in Quechua and a group of visiting men vaccinating the children give all their information in Spanish.

In trying to account for the variable choices made by Buang speakers in Papua New Guinea, we can make use of a model which views the selections made by speakers in terms of social and situational variables in the speech event, e.g. formality, addressee. Speakers have three languages to choose from: Buang, Yabem, and Tok Pisin. Fig. 2.1 shows the factors which serve to define certain types of situations in which particular choices are normally acceptable, appropriate, and likely.

I will now look at how the choices made by the individual may become institutionalized at the societal level in communities where bilingualism is widespread.

Diglossia

Often each language or variety in a multilingual community serves a specialized function and is used for particular purposes. This situation is known as 'diglossia'. An example can be taken from Arabic-speaking countries such as Egypt in which the language used at home may be a local version of Arabic. The language that is recognized publicly, however, is modern standard Arabic, which takes many of its normative rules from the classical Arabic of the Koran. The standard language is used for 'high' functions such as giving a lecture, reading, writing, or broadcasting, while the home variety is reserved for 'low' functions such as interacting with friends at home. The High (H) and Low (L) varieties differ not only in grammar, phonology, and vocabulary, but also with respect to a number of social characteristics, namely, function, prestige, literary heritage, acquisition, standardization, and stability. L is typically acquired

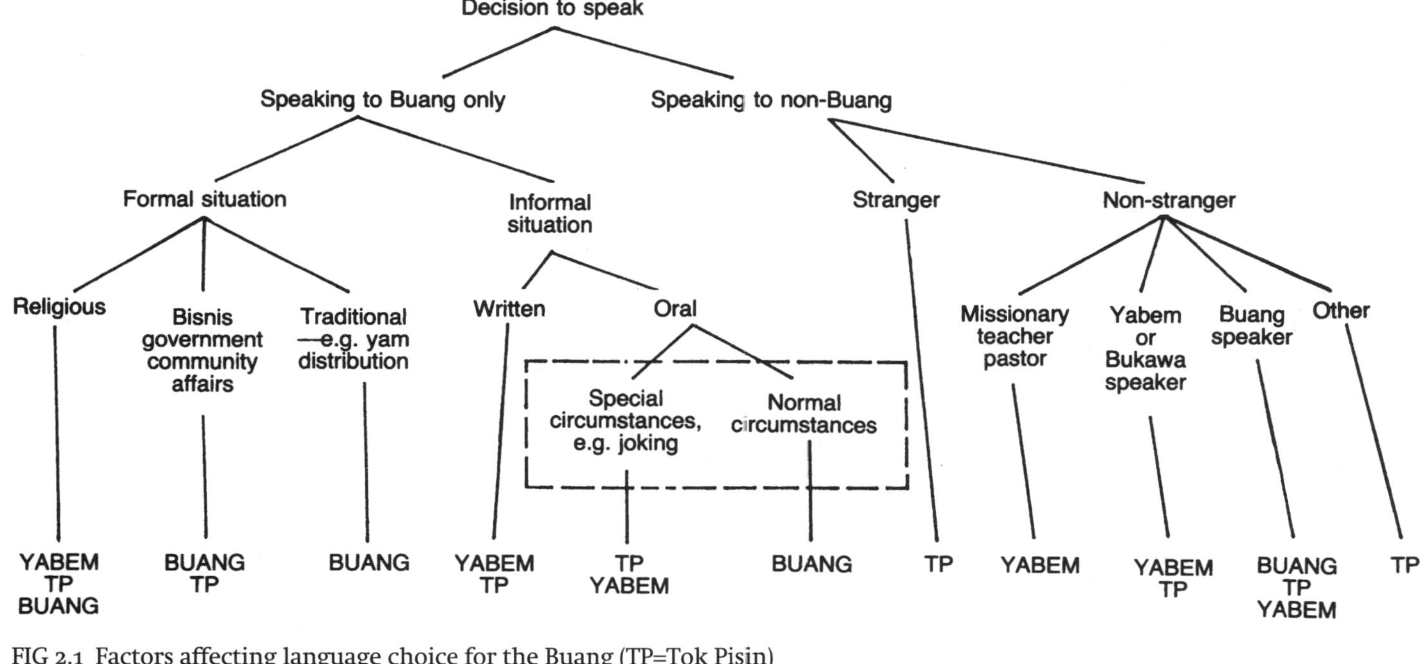

FIG 2.1 Factors affecting language choice for the Buang (TP=Tok Pisin)

at home as a mother tongue and continues to be used throughout life. Its main uses are in familial and familiar interactions. H, on the other hand, is learned later through schooling and never at home. H is related to and supported by institutions outside the home. The separate domains in which H and L are acquired immediately provide them with separate institutional support systems.

Diglossic societies are marked not only by this compartmentalization of varieties, but also by restriction of access. Entry to formal institutions such as school and government requires knowledge of H. The extent to which these functions are compartmentalized can be illustrated in the importance attached by community members to using the right variety in the appropriate context. An outsider who learns to speak L and then uses it in a formal speech will be ridiculed. Speakers regard H as superior to L in a number of respects. In some cases H is regarded as the only 'real' version of a particular language to the extent that speakers claim they do not speak L. Sometimes the alleged superiority is avowed for religious and/or literary reasons. For example, the fact that classical Arabic is the language of the Koran endows it with special significance. In other cases a long literary tradition backs the H variety, e.g. Sanskrit. There is also a strong tradition of formal grammatical study and standardization associated with H.

The analogy has been extended to other communities in which the varieties in diglossic distribution have the status of separate languages, such as Spanish and Guaraní (an indigenous Indian language totally unrelated to Spanish) in Paraguay. The situation is very similar to that just described for Quechua and Spanish in Peru. Spanish serves here as the high variety and is used for high functions. It is the official language of government and education, although 90 per cent of the population speak Guaraní, which has the status of national language. Diglossia and bilingualism have been stable there and recent attempts to use Guaraní as a medium of education have met with resistance, just as have similar efforts to use Quechua in rural schools in Peru. Opposition occurs despite the fact that studies have shown benefits to both pupils and teachers from the use of the indigenous languages. The use of indigenous languages in the schools, however, violates the community's expectations about education. They tolerate the existence of the school as an alien institution in their community precisely because they see it as a means for their children to acquire Spanish.

The notion of diglossia is also sometimes extended to include more than two varieties or languages which participate in such a functional relationship, e.g. in Tunisia, French, classical Arabic, and Tunisian Arabic are in triglossic distribution, with French and classical Arabic sharing H functions in relation to Tunisian Arabic, and French occupying the role of H in relation to the other two. The term 'polyglossia' has also been used to refer to cases such as Singapore where many varieties coexist in a functional relationship. English, Mandarin, Tamil, and Malay share co-official status, but each of these has local L variants. A child who speaks Hokkien at home may be schooled in Mandarin Chinese at school. English also functions as an H variety to the other three since it has more prestige.

The relationship between individual bilingualism and societal diglossia is not a necessary or causal one. Either phenomenon can occur without the other one. Diglossia both with and without bilingualism may be relatively stable, long-term arrangements, depending on the circumstances. As an example, we can take the old Order Amish (speakers of so-called Pennsylvania Dutch, a variety of German) and Hasidic Jews in the United States. Both groups maintain stable diglossia with bilingualism. They control their own schools. The utilization of the non-group culture is restricted to economic pursuits, and even these are tightly regulated. For example, the Pennsylvania Dutch use electricity for pasteurization of milk, as required by law, but they are not allowed to have it in their homes for refrigeration or for use with farm machinery. The degree to which the outside world is engaged is justified only to the extent that it contributes to the maintenance of the group. By not accepting or implementing the other culture in its entirety, it is kept in strict complementary distribution with their own. English is specifically excluded from home and religious use. It encroaches only in a limited way in economic domains.

Language shift and death

Stability, however, is a subjective notion. There are many bilingual situations which do not last for more than three generations. In some cases indigenous languages can be swamped by intrusive ones over a relatively short period of time. This is what has happened to the Aboriginal languages of Australia and the Celtic languages of the British Isles. In other places, immigrant languages have disappeared as their speakers have adopted the language of the new environment. This is true for many speakers of south Asian languages, like Gujarati and Bengali, in Britain. In cases such as these of bilingualism without diglossia, the two languages compete for use in the same domains. Speakers are unable to establish the compartmentalization necessary for survival of the L variety. In such instances language shift may be unavoidable.

Many attempts to increase the domains of use for a Low variety fail, as in Ireland, where there was no widespread knowledge of the classical written variety, and decreasing use of the spoken language. In Israel, however, the revival of Hebrew has been successful. There the task was to take a language which was widely known in its written form, and to add to it vernacular use and a native speaking community. Thus, in Ireland the problem was how to expand the language into H functions which had been taken over by English, and in Israel, how to add L functions to a High variety.

A number of researchers have commented on the extreme instability of bilingualism in the United States. Probably no other country has been host to more bilingual people. However, each new wave of immigrants has seen the decline of their language. In Australia the decline of non-English languages has been similarly dramatic. Only 4.2 per cent of the Australian-born population regularly uses a language other than English. This figure includes Aboriginal languages too. In Table 2.3 we can see major differences in the extent to which native languages are retained by the different ethnic groups. The figures show the extent of shift to use of English. Greek-Australians display the greatest maintenance, and Dutch-Australians the least.

This of course tells only part of the story of language diversity in Australia. The Aboriginal languages have been in decline since their speakers came into contact with Europeans in the eighteenth century. For example, the Aboriginal population of Tasmania (*c.* 3,000–4,000) was exterminated within seventy-five years of contact with Europeans. Some linguists predict that if nothing is done, almost all Aboriginal languages will be dead within the next decade. In North America native languages have also undergone extreme shift since first contact with Europeans.

From a global perspective, the trend is the same. Many smaller languages are dying out due to the spread of a few world languages such as English, French, or Chinese. It has been estimated that eleven languages are spoken by about 70

Table 2.3 Retention of languages by ethnic groups in Australia

Birthplace	% of respondents claiming to use English regularly
Germany	28
Greece	3
Italy	6
Malta	30
The Netherlands	44
Poland	20
Yugoslavia	10

Source: Adapted from Clyne 1982: 36, Table 14.

per cent of the world's population. In this respect, the majority of the world's languages are minority languages. Some linguists believe that the prospects for survival of the majority of these languages over the next century are very gloomy.

Choices made by individuals on an everyday basis have an effect on the long-term situation of the languages concerned. Language shift generally involves bilingualism (often with diglossia) as a stage on the way to eventual monolingualism in a new language. Typically a community which was once monolingual becomes bilingual as a result of contact with another (usually socially more powerful) group and becomes transitionally bilingual in the new language until their own language is given up altogether.

A detailed illustration of this is found in an investigation of the use of German and Hungarian in the Austrian village of Oberwart. Villagers, who were formerly Hungarian monolinguals, have over the past few hundred years become increasingly bilingual, and now the community is in the process of a shift to German. Oberwart is located near the present-day border of Austria and Hungary and has been surrounded by German-speaking villages for at least 400 years. After Turkish invasions in the sixteenth century forced most of the Hungarians in the surrounding villages to leave the region, the area around Oberwart was resettled by people who were ethnically and linguistically German. A further influx of German speakers came in the 1800s as Oberwart was transformed from a peasant village into a socially diverse commercial center linked by rail. At the end of the First World War the territory including Oberwart became part of Austria and German became the official language. The Third Reich banned the use of Hungarian in the schools. At the end of the Second World War, the Hungarian border was closed off.

It is only during this century, however, that Hungarian speakers have become a minority there. In 1920 Hungarian was spoken by three-quarters of the population, but by 1971 only one-quarter of the population could speak the language. All the Hungarian speakers are bilingual in German and are peasant agriculturalists or the children of peasants. By looking at the patterns of language choice made by different groups of speakers in the community and seeing which language was used for a given category of interlocutor, e.g. to grandparents, age-mates, government officials, it is possible to get a picture of the shift that is taking place. Table 2.4 shows the patterns of language choice for thirty-two speakers.

The difference in choice between German and Hungarian reflects the social contrast between modern urban worker and traditional peasant. The pattern of large-scale borrowing of German elements into Hungarian also reflected the greater prestige of German. Hungarian items were rarely found in German utterances. When faced with a potential interlocutor, the position of that

Table 2.4 Language choice patterns in Oberwart

Speaker	Age of speaker	Interlocutors										
		1	2	3	4	5	6	7	8	9	10	11
A	14	H	GH		G	G	G			G		G
B	15	H	GH		G	G	G			G		G
C	17	H	GH		G	G	G			G		G
D	25	H	GH	GH	GH	G	G	G	G	G		G
E	27	H	H		GH	G	G			G		G
F	25	H	H		GH	G	G			G		G
G	42		H		GH	G	G	G	G	G		G
H	17	H	H		H	GH	G			G		G
I	20	H	H	H	H	GH	G	G	G	G		G
J	39	H	H		H	GH	GH			G		G
K	22	H	H		H	GH	GH			G		G
L	23	H	H		H	GH	H		GH	G		G
M	40	H	H		H	GH		GH	G	G		G
N	52	H	H	H	GH	H		GH	G	G	G	G
O	62	H	H	H	H	H	H	GH	GH	GH	G	G
P	40	H	H	H	H	H	H	GH	GH	GH		G
Q	63	H	H		H	H	H			GH		G
R	64	H	H	H	H	H	H	H	GH	GH		G
S	43	H	H		H	H	H	H	G	H		G
T	35	H	H	H	H	H	H	H	GH	H		G
U	41	H	H	H	H	H	H	H	GH	H		H
V	61	H	H		H	H	H	H	GH	H		G
W	54	H	H		H	H	H	H	H	H		G
X	50	H	H	H	H	H	H	H	H	H		G
Y	63	H	H	H	H	H	H	H	H	H	GH	G
Z	61	H	H		H	H	H	H	H	G	GH	G
A1	74	H	H		H	H	H	H	H	H	GH	H
B1	54	H	H		H	H	H	H	H	H	GH	H
C1	63	H	H	H	H	H	H	H	H	H	GH	H
D1	58	G	H		H	H	H	H	H	H		H
E1	64	H	H		H	H	H	H	H	H	H	H
F1	59	H	H	H	H	H	H	H	H	H	H	H

Notes: Data are from interviews. Spaces indicate inapplicable questions.
Scalability = 97%. Number of speakers = 32 (both men and women).

Interlocutors: (1) God; (2) grandparents and their generation; (3) black-market client; (4) parents and their generation; (5) pals (*kollégák*), age-mate neighbours; (6) brothers and sisters; (7) spouse; (8) children and their generation; (9) government officials; (10) grandchildren and their generation; (11) doctor.

Key: G = German; H = Hungarian.

Source: Gal 1979: Table 5.1.

person on a scale of urbanness v. peasantness will determine the language used. An index was constructed to measure the extent of peasantness of the social networks within which different speakers interacted. It included factors such as the number and type of animals owned by a household, use of home-baked v. store-bought bread, type of employment. The more peasants a person had in his or her network, the greater the tendency to use Hungarian. Young women are spearheading the change from Hungarian to German. Although young people in general use more German than older people, young women use more German than men. Even young women with peasant networks were not constrained to use Hungarian. The women's choice of German can be seen as a linguistic expression of their rejection of peasant life. Because a woman's possibilities are largely determined by whom she marries, women increasingly were choosing non-peasant husbands, who tended to use German more. Because peasant men find it difficult to get wives, they have had to marry exogamously. I will say more about the effects of network on language choice in Chapter 3, and the role of women in linguistic change in Chapter 4.

Once the process of shift has begun in certain domains and the functions of the languages are reallocated, the prediction is that it will continue until the whole community has shifted to German. However, we cannot necessarily conclude that Hungarian will die out on the basis of a picture like this. The pattern could just represent a cyclical phenomenon related to the age of individuals. Thus, it could be that speakers regularly change their patterns of language choice as they get older, so that in each generation young people use more German and then switch to Hungarian when they get older. Or, it could be that people within one generation retain their patterns of language use throughout their lives, but each generation differs systematically from the previous one. Or, it is also possible that there has been a change from a pattern in which speakers used only one language throughout their lives to a new one in which young people use more German (but may or may not revert to Hungarian as they get older). Another follow-up study needs to be done at a later point in time to confirm whether language shift has progressed further (see Chapter 5 on linguistic change).

Freedom of choice has become restricted for Oberwarters. It used to be common practice for German businessmen to learn Hungarian, but this almost never happens now. Nowadays, it has become almost universal for bilinguals to speak only German in the presence of German monolinguals. Monolinguals often get annoyed at people who speak another language in their presence. If they are in a position to impose their own language in public encounters, either by official decree or by other pressure, this can result in a significant shift in the balance of power between the two languages.

In some cases shift occurs as a result of forced or voluntary immigration to a place where it is not possible to maintain one's native language, e.g. Italians in the United States, or as a result of conquest, e.g. the Gaels in Scotland and Ireland. The ultimate loss of a language is termed 'language death'. Many factors are responsible for language shift and death, e.g. religious and educational background, settlement patterns, ties with the homeland (in the case of immigrant bilingualism), extent of exogamous marriage, attitudes of majority and minority language groups, government policies concerning language and education. Where large groups of immigrants concentrate in particular geographical areas, they are often better able to preserve their languages, e.g. third-generation Chinese Americans who reside in China-towns have shifted less towards English than their age-mates outside China-towns. Often a shift from rural to urban areas triggers a language shift; e.g. in Papua New Guinea, where Tok Pisin (an English-based pidgin used as a lingua franca) is the language most used in the towns, many children grow up not speaking their parents' vernacular languages. When a language serves important religious functions, as German does among the Pennsylvania Dutch, it may stand a better chance of survival.

The inability of minorities to maintain the home as an intact domain for the use of their language has often been decisive for language shift. There is a high rate of loss in mixed marriages, e.g. in Wales, where if Welsh is not the language of the home, the onus for transmission is shifted to the school. Identification with a language and positive attitudes towards it cannot guarantee its maintenance. In Ireland the necessity of using English has overpowered antipathy towards English and English speakers. In some cases speakers may be forbidden to use their language altogether, e.g. the Kurds in Turkey. In a community whose language is under threat, it is difficult for children to acquire the language fully. Languages undergoing shift often display characteristic types of changes such as simplification of complex grammatical structures. These changes are often the result of decreased use of the language in certain contexts which may lead to a loss of stylistic options. In some Native American languages of the south-western United States complex syntactic structures have become less frequent because the formal and poetic styles of language are no longer used. The degree of linguistic assimilation may serve as an index of social assimilation of a group. It depends on many factors such as receptiveness of the group to the other culture and language, possibility of acceptance by the dominant group, degree of similarity between the two groups. Albanian speakers who emigrated to Greece have more readily given up their language and assimilated than have Albanian speakers in Italy, where attitudes towards diversity are more favorable.

Although the existence of bilingualism, diglossia, and code-switching has often been cited as a factor leading to language death, in some cases code-switching and diglossia are positive forces in maintaining bilingualism. Swiss German and Faroese may never emerge from diglossia, but are probably in no danger of death. In many communities switching between languages serves important functions.

Code-switching

Let us consider as examples the utterances in (1) to (7), which have come from a variety of bilingual or multilingual speakers. Although speakers in diglossic situations must know more than one code, only one code is usually employed at any one time.

1. *kio ke six, seven hours te school de vič spend karde ne, they are speaking English all the time* (Panjabi/English bilingual in Britain). 'Because they spend six or seven hours a day at school, they are speaking English all the time.'
2. *Will you rubim off? Ol man will come* (Tok Pisin/English bilingual child in Papua New Guinea). 'Will you rub [that] off [the blackboard]? The men will come.'
3. *Sano että tulla tänne että I'm very sick* (Finnish/English bilingual). 'Tell them to come here that I'm very sick.'
4. *Kodomotachi liked it* (Japanese/English bilingual). 'The children liked it.'
5. *Have agua, please* (Spanish/English bilingual child). 'Have water, please.'
6. *Won o arrest a single person* (Yoruba/English bilingual). 'They did not arrest a single person.'
7. *This morning I hantar my baby tu dekat babysitter tu lah* (Malay/English bilingual). 'This morning I took my baby to the babysitter.'

It can be seen that all of these utterances draw to differing extents on items which come from more than one language and which are combined in different ways. These kinds of utterances are normal everyday instances of language use for the individuals concerned. Indeed, I have deliberately drawn my examples from a diverse range of languages in order to show that they probably occur to some degree in the repertoires of most bilingual persons and in most bilingual communities. I have also intentionally included some examples from young children to draw attention to the fact that learning to speak more than one language often involves putting together material from two languages. This is a part of the normal process of growing up bilingually and acquiring competence in more than one language.

The early utterances of children growing up bilingually will often contain lexical items from both languages, as is the case in (5). The length of children's utterances (whether bilingual or monolingual) is severely constrained in the first stages of language acquisition, and the relationship between the child's and the adult's language is indirect. It is often difficult to say what the appropriate expansion is in any given case. Although the meaning of this child's statement is obviously a request for water, the adult equivalent in either Spanish or English would probably not make use of the verb *to have*. The closest equivalents would be: English: *I want water, please*, or Spanish: *Quiero agua, por favor*.

There seems to be no principled way to decide whether the child is speaking English, but with Spanish words inserted for particular items, or vice versa. All we can say is that the child's lexicon is drawn from more than one language, while the grammar is still in the early developmental stages. It follows the rules of neither monolingual Spanish nor English grammar. Thus, it would be misleading to describe it as a deviation from one language or another. In situations of intense language contact it is possible for a third system to emerge which shows properties not found in either of the input languages. Thus, through the merger or convergence of two systems, a new one can be created.

One can find analogous cases among the adult utterances given above, where even though we are dealing with a mature linguistic system, there does not seem to be any basis for assigning the speech event as a whole to a particular language. Examples (1) and (7) are good cases. While the second half of the utterance in (1) is clearly in English, the first half consists of elements from both languages. The English nouns *hours*, *school*, and the verb *spend* are inserted into what is otherwise a Panjabi syntactic structure, as can be seen, for example, by the fact that the verb occurs at the end of the clause, as it would in a Panjabi monolingual utterance. In this case, however, the verb is a mixed one, made up of English *spend* and the Panjabi auxiliary *karna*. In (7) elements from both Malay and English are juxtaposed in the same utterance, but since both languages share the same word order, it would be difficult to say that the utterance was basically English with some Malay words, or vice versa.

Examples (2), (4), and (6) present similar problems. Is it possible to say that the speaker is using one or the other language at a particular time? In the case of (4) we might be tempted to say that the language is basically English and that the speaker has temporarily 'borrowed' the Japanese noun for 'children'. However, when we look at (2), it becomes much more difficult to apply this kind of thinking. The first part of the utterance seems to be in English, except for the verb *rub* which has been given the Tok Pisin suffix - *im*, which marks transitive verbs. The second part also seems to be in English except for the noun phrase, which consists of the Tok Pisin plural marker *ol* and the noun *man*. Tok Pisin does not have a suffix like English - *s* to mark plurals; it simply uses the same form of the noun for both singular and plural. In (6) the pronoun, negator, and part of the verb phrase are drawn from Yoruba, while the rest of the utterance is in English.

We can see that example (3) is of a somewhat different type. A switch of languages occurs in the middle of the sentence, so that the first clause is in Finnish and the second in English. There is no mixing within the individual clauses. Instances where a switch or mixing of languages occurs within the boundaries of a clause or sentence have been termed 'intra-sentential' switches, to distinguish them from cases like (3), where the switching occurs at clause boundaries. The latter have been called 'inter-sentential'. However, since both these types of switches take place with no apparent change in topic or interlocutor, they call into doubt a common view of the ideal bilingual's behavior, which suggests that the ideal bilingual switches from one language to another according to appropriate changes in the speech situation (interlocutors, topics, etc.), but not in an unchanged speech situation. If we accept this view, we would have to conclude that these speakers are not ideal bilinguals and that they have less than ideal competence.

The kind of 'mixed' speech found in (1) is quite common in the Panjabi/English bilingual community in Britain, where contact with English is so intense, especially among the younger generation, that many fear the language will be lost in the future. This anxiety is widely shared by members of many other minority language communities. It has often been said that bilingualism is a step along the road to linguistic extinction. It has been said, for instance, that switching between Welsh and English and interference from English are signs of linguistic instability leading to death. Certainly, it is not hard to find cases where language death is preceded by bilingualism and extensive code-switching.

Nevertheless, there is increasing evidence to indicate that this mixed mode of speaking serves important functions in the communities where it is used and that it is not random. Despite this, in practically all the communities where switching and mixing of languages occurs it is stigmatized. In Nigeria, for example, instances of language use like (6) are described by community members as *amulumala* or *adalu ade* 'verbal salad'. In spite of the general negative reaction to it, there is a young generation of Yorubas growing up using this kind of mixed speech as their first language. My experience in working with bilingual children in urban areas of Papua New Guinea would suggest that much the same is happening there. Failure to recognize mixed speech as a legitimate mode of communication in its own right both within and outside the communities concerned has had a number of consequences, which I will look at in Chapter 7.

Recent studies of switching have tended to focus attention on different aspects of it. Within one approach the emphasis has been on trying to account for the grammatical constraints on where in utterances switching may occur. Are they language-specific? Or do they arise from an independently motivated principle of universal grammar? The other approach has investigated speakers' reasons for switching on the assumption that the motivation for switching is basically stylistic and that switching is to be treated as a discourse phenomenon which cannot be satisfactorily handled in terms of the internal structure of sentences.

Various grammatical principles have been proposed for switching such as the one called 'the equivalence constraint', which predicts that code switches will tend to occur at points where the juxtaposition of elements from the two languages does not violate a syntactic rule of either language. That is, switching should occur at points where the surface structures of the two languages map onto each other. This means that a language switch ought to take place only at boundaries common to both languages, and switching should not occur between any two sentence elements unless they are normally ordered in the same way. From a cross-linguistic perspective, this means that the more similar two languages are structurally, the more switching sites they should permit. The more different they are, such as Japanese and English, the fewer the places at which grammatical switches can occur. Incompatibilities will arise at any site where a switch involves any two adjacent constituents which are ordered differently in the two languages concerned.

In the case of Spanish/English, for instance, which are similar and related languages, this means that switches may occur between determiners and nouns, but not between nouns and adjectives in the noun phrase. Thus, noun phrases such as *his favorite spot/su lugar favorito* cannot be mixed because combination like **su favorito spot*, **his favorito lugar*, **his favorito spot* would result in ungrammatical combinations of constituents in either language. Thus, Spanish presumably has a phrase structure rule which expands the noun phrase so that most adjectives follow their nouns, i.e. NP → (det) N (adj), while English has one which places adjectives before nouns, i.e. NP → (det) (adj) N. Many other switch sites are, however, possible between Spanish and English, such as between a subject noun phrase and a verb phrase, between a verb and its object. The equivalence constraint was originally formulated using data from Spanish/English bilingual Puerto Rican communities in the United States, where it seemed to account well for observed switching patterns.

If we look at two languages which are as dissimilar as Panjabi and English and try to apply this principle to predict where switching will occur, it works less well. A switch within the prepositional phrase should be ruled out because English has prepositions and Panjabi postpositions. The equivalence constraint would predict the non-occurrence of either **parents te* or **te parents* 'on the parents', and similarly **family de nal* and **de nal family* 'within the family', because both violate the order of one or the other language. Panjabi presumably has a rule which would be violated by constructions like **te parents*, because it is a postpositional language (i.e. one in which what would correspond to prepositions in English would actually occur after rather than before the nouns they modify), while English has a rule which would be violated by constructions like **parents te*. Despite this lack of structural equivalence, however, there are cases where English nouns occur as the object of a Panjabi postposition, as in *family de nal* 'in/with the family'.

There are a number of reasons why the equivalence constraint does not work here. One may be that individual language pairs in contact impose specific additional rules on switching. Or it may be that the equivalence constraint has not been formulated precisely enough in the first place. Notions of what is grammatical switching will need careful evaluation.

Although most researchers stress the grammaticality of the majority of bilingual utterances, they assume that the grammatical norms of the two languages in isolation provide the basis for determining what is grammatical. But varieties of two languages in contact for a long time may become quite different from varieties of those languages spoken elsewhere. This has happened to the Austronesian languages of Papua New Guinea, as we saw in Chapter 1. Another factor which may affect switching behavior is the attitude of the participants concerned. In some Spanish/English bilingual communities, favorable attitudes to switching have been observed which has led to an increase in the use of switching as a marker of ethnic identity.

Many linguists have stressed the point that switching is a communicative option available to a bilingual member of a speech community on much the same basis as switching between styles or dialects is an option for the monolingual speaker. Switching in both cases serves an expressive function and has meaning. In an early study conducted in a rural Norwegian village called Hemnesberget, the concepts of 'metaphorical' and 'transactional' switching were introduced (sometimes referred to as non-situational v. situational code-switching). Transactional switching comes under the heading of the type of switching most commonly discussed as being controlled by components of the speech event like topic and participants, as already illustrated in Fig. 2.1. When residents in Hemnesberget step up to the counter at the post office, greetings and enquiries about family members tend to be exchanged in the local dialect, while the business part of the transaction, e.g. buying stamps, is carried out in standard Norwegian. This would be an example of transactional switching.

Metaphorical code-switching, however, concerns the various communicative effects the speaker intends to convey. For example, teachers deliver formal lectures in the official standard form of Norwegian, but lecturers shift to regional Norwegian dialect when they want to encourage discussion among the students. Thus, while the components of the speech event such as speaker, topic, listener, setting have not changed, the tone of the interaction has been altered by a switch in language.

There is a symbolic distinction between 'we' and 'they' embodied in the choice of varieties. Generally speaking, the tendency is for the minority language to be regarded as the 'we', and the majority language as the 'they' variety. The 'we' variety typically signifies in-group, informal, personalized activities, while the 'they' variety marks out-group, more formal relations. In this example from Panjabi/English switching, Panjabi serves to mark the in-group of Panjabi/English bilinguals, and English, the out-group: *esi engrezi sikhi e te why can't they learn?* 'We learn English, so why can't they learn [Asian languages]?' Here the speaker makes the point that Panjabi speakers are expected to learn English, but that English people are not required to learn their language. The switch from Panjabi to English emphasizes the boundaries between 'them' and 'us'.

A speaker may switch for a variety of reasons, e.g. to redefine the interaction as appropriate to a different social arena, or to avoid, through continual code-switching, defining the interaction in terms of any social arena. The latter function of avoidance is an important one because it recognizes that code-switching often serves as a strategy of neutrality or as a means to explore which code is most appropriate and acceptable in a particular situation. In many government offices in Canada, it is customary for employees to answer the telephone by saying 'Bonjour, hello' in order to give the caller the option of choosing either language to continue the conversation.

In some multilingual exchanges the question of code choice is not resolved because the parties involved do not agree on definition of the arena. We can take an example from western Kenya where a brother and sister are conversing in the brother's store. These siblings are used to conversing on home territory as family members and not as store owner and customer. In such cases where code choice has not been regularized, it must be negotiated on the spot. The sister wished to conduct the event on the basis of their solidarity as brother and sister because she wanted special treatment as a customer in her brother's store. Therefore, she chose their shared mother tongue, Lwidakho. The brother wanted to treat his sister as a customer and therefore used Swahili, which is an ethnically neutral choice in this speech community and the unmarked choice for service encounters of this type. The utterances in Lwidakho are italicized in this exchange. In some ways this conversation is like what happens in Hemnesberget, Norway, except that the sister does not switch to Swahili once the greetings are over, and the brother does not switch back to Lwidakho to accommodate his sister. The sister then goes away without everything she had hoped for.

Brother: *Good morning Sister.*
Sister: *Good morning.*
Brother: *Are you alright?*
Sister: *Yes, just a little.*
Brother: Sister, now today what do you need?
Sister: *I want you to give me some salt.*
Brother: How much do you need?
Sister: *Give me sixty cents worth.*
Brother: And what else?
Sister: *I would like something else, but I've no money.*
Brother: Thank you, sister. Goodbye.
Sister: *Thank you. Goodbye.*

The preference in market transactions in Jerusalem is for multilingualism, as this example shows, when four women soldiers walk up to look at bracelets outside a jewelry store:

Shopkeeper: You want bracelets?
Soldier 1: How much?
Shopkeeper: You want this one or this one?
Soldier 2 (in Hebrew): Those aren't pretty.
Soldier 1 (in Arabic): That's not pretty?
Shopkeeper (in Arabic, then Hebrew): Pretty. Like women soldiers.

The shopkeeper addresses the women first in English even though they are Israeli soldiers and obviously native speakers of Hebrew. Because Hebrew has a higher status than Arabic in Israel, for the Arab to use Hebrew would indicate a subordinate status. By choosing English, he downplays the nationalist dimensions of Hebrew, and opts for the even higher status associated with English. The first soldier accepts this choice of language, which permits the shopkeeper to continue in this more neutral language. The second soldier introduces Hebrew into the exchange to make a comment to her friend. This may be partly a bargaining ploy since she knows the shopkeeper will understand. The first soldier then switches to Arabic, making clear that she is not an English-speaking tourist or non-Arabic-speaking shopper who can be taken advantage of. The shopkeeper replies in Arabic and then Hebrew, establishing his own ability to speak Hebrew and reciprocating the soldier's accommodation to his language.

The speech functions served by switching are presumably potentially available to all speakers, whether bilingual or monolingual, as I will show in the next chapter when I consider style-switching. However, the ways in which they are marked linguistically or the degree to which they are accomplished successfully will depend on the resources available in any particular case. In some cases the resources may come from more than one language, while in others they may come from within what is regarded as one language; as in the case of Javanese registers discussed in Chapter 1. This is why many linguists use the term 'code-switching'; the term 'code', like 'variety', is a neutral one and does not commit us to taking a decision as to whether the varieties or codes concerned constitute languages or dialects.

It is easy to find code-switching behavior among monolinguals. The clearest cases involve instances of switching between dialects which are very different such as Black English Vernacular and standard English. Take the following example:

Well, i's long line, y'start off, an' y'shoot-y'shoot into skellies. An' 'en ef you make it in skellies, you shoot de onesies. An' den like IF YOU MISS ONESIES, de OTHuh person shoot to skelly; ef he miss, den you go again. An' IF YOU GET IN, YOU SHOOT TO TWOSIES. An' IF YOU GET IN TWOSIES, YOU GO TO tthreesies, An' IF YOU MISS tthreesies, THEN THE PERSON tha' miss skelly shoot THE SKELLIES an' shoot in THE ONESIES: An' IF HE MISS, YOU GO from tthreesies to foursies.

The parts of the passage in small capitals are in standard English. Since many items are shared by both systems, switch sites are often difficult to delimit.

The difference between the kind of approach advocated by those who see code-switching as a function of changes in setting, topic, etc. and those who see it as motivated by speakers' choices of discourse meanings is that in the latter approach, speakers play an active role in choosing the perspective and social framework in which they intend their discourse to be situated. Language choice is not imposed upon them by factors such as setting and topic. Because this approach is interpretive, there are a number of difficulties faced by analysts in describing members' perceptions of what count as instances of 'we' and 'they' codes. These difficulties cannot be as easily resolved empirically as can questions concerning the permissibility of certain types of switches and the validity of principles such as the equivalence constraint.

Most of the studies on bilingualism have been done in communities existing in modern societies, where a minority language is spoken at home which is different from the language used by the majority. Generalizations made about such communities may not be valid universally. Anthropologists working among Third World traditional people have questioned western notions about the intentionality and individuality of human behavior. It has been pointed out that in Samoa, for example, the meaning of someone's utterance emerges through communal negotiation. It may not be possible to attribute only one meaning to a particular switch since switches may accomplish a number of functions at the same time.

Linguistic diversity occurs in monolingual speech communities too. The most substantial body of work which is unequivocally thought of as sociolinguistic is the research on urban social dialects, particularly in the English-speaking world. However, that is the subject of the next chapter.

Annotated bibliography

Suzanne Romaine's book (1995) is a survey of issues in individual and societal multilingualism; see especially chapters 2 and 4 for discussion relating to this chapter. John Edwards's book (1994) is also a useful overview of multilingualism. The notion of 'acts of identity' has been taken from Robert Le Page and Andrée Tabouret-Keller's book (1985). For a discussion of the problems in using census data see J. de Vries (1985) and S. Lieberson (1969); for India, in particular, J. Das Gupta (1970), and V. Friedman (1996) on Macedonia. Nancy H. Hornberger's book (1988) describes the relationship between Quechua and Spanish in rural Peruvian communities. The example from Papua New Guinea in Fig. 2.2 is from Gillian Sankoff (1980). The notion of diglossia was first introduced in 1959 in an article by Charles Ferguson (and reprinted in 1972); see also Joshua Fishman (1967). A more recent and thorough discussion can be found in Ralph Fasold's textbook (1984), Francis Britto's book (1986), and Alan Hudson-Edwards's collection (1992). The Puerto Rican study is found in Joshua Fishman, Robert L. Cooper, and Roxanna Ma (1971). Reg Hindley's book (1990) provides a good overview of the status of Irish towards the end of the twentieth century. An overview of the Australian sociolinguistic situation can be found in Suzanne Romaine's book (1991) and the data in Table 2.3 are from Michael G. Clyne (1982). Nancy C. Dorian's book (1989) contains a survey of research on dying languages. Daniel Nettle and Suzanne Romaine's (2000) book examines some of the reasons why the world's languages are dying at an alarming rate.

The example from Oberwart comes from Susan Gal's study (1979). The Kenyan example is taken from Carol Myers-Scotton's book (1992). The Norwegian study is reported in Jan Petter Blom and John J. Gumperz (1972). For a discussion of the structural constraints on code-switching, see Shana Poplack and David Sankoff's article (1988), Carol Myers-Scotton (1993), and, for pragmatic motivations, see chapter 3 of John J. Gumperz's book (1982), and the papers in Milroy and Muysken (1995). The example from Jerusalem comes from Bernard Spolsky and Robert L. Cooper's book (1991). The example from Black English comes from William Labov's article (1971). An edited version of Rupert Murdoch's speech, the 11th annual John Boynthon lecture, appeared in the newspaper *Australian* (1994).

Chapter 3

Sociolinguistic Patterns

FIG 3.1 Vowel patriotism: the Norwegian language struggle has culminated for the time being in a bitter quarrel over whether one serves one's country best by saying *sne* or *snø* ('snow')

It has been known for some time that differences in language are tied to social class. In the 1950s, for example, it was suggested that certain lexical and phonological differences in English could be classified as U (upper class) or non-U (lower class), e.g. *serviette* (non-U) v. *table-napkin* (U), to take what was then one of the best known of all linguistic class-indicators of England. Notable pairs are *have one's bath* (U) v. *take a bath* (non-U), *writing paper* v. *note paper* (non-U), *pudding* (U) v. *sweet* (non-U), or what would be called 'dessert' in the USA. Previously, most studies of variability were concerned with regional variation or dialectology.

From the 1960s onwards, however, sociolinguists turned their attention to the language of cities, where an increasing proportion of the world's population lives in modern times. Indeed, major urban centers around the globe are likely to become even more fertile ground for sociolinguistic investigation in the future. The end of the twentieth century has witnessed an unprecedented change in patterns of human settlement worldwide, when for the first time in history more people will live in cities and towns than in rural areas. The effects of urbanization have spread unevenly, however, as I will show in two of the cases considered in this chapter—namely, Britain, one of the earliest places to be affected, and Papua New Guinea, where urbanization has become evident only in the latter half of the twentieth century.

By the latter half of the nineteenth century, for example, Britain had already become a largely urban nation. At the turn of the twentieth, 78 per cent of its population lived in towns. Thanks to the Industrial Revolution, which fuelled the growth of early metropolises like London, Britain became the first nation to have an industrial working class. Towns have typically attracted migrants from many rural areas, who speak different languages and regional dialects. The neighboring countryside of the counties of Essex, Kent, Suffolk, and Middlesex was depopulated as thousands of impoverished farm workers came to London's East End in search of work. We now know that a number of features made their way into working-class London speech from their regional dialects, and then eventually became part of middle-class usage.

The rise of urbanization is connected with an increase in social stratification which is reflected in linguistic variation. Again, the Industrial Revolution was a watershed because it opened up new avenues for the accumulation of wealth, prestige, and power other than those based on hereditary landed titles. As Jonathan Swift put it in the *Examiner* in 1710, 'Power, which according to an old maxim was used to follow Land, is now gone over to Money.' The combination of physical proximity yet vast social distance is a hallmark of urbanization. Within the confines of the city social segregation tended at first to operate vertically within buildings so that basements and attics might be divided into small flats or apartments, and the intermediate floors were occupied by the wealthier. In Edinburgh, for instance, which became an administrative and financial center in the eighteenth century, the inhabitants of a typical tenement in Dickson's Close included a fishmonger on the first floor, a lodging keeper on the second, the Countess Dowager of Balcarres on the third, Mrs Buchanan of Kellow on the fourth, and milliners and manteau makers on the fifth.

The socially distinct spaces modern city dwellers are accustomed to would emerge only later when the suburbs would be 'discovered' by the middle class as an ideal physical expression of their distance from the working class. In the suburb geographic distance became an icon of social separateness and class-consciousness. The spatial association of low-status residential districts with industrial areas prompted the more affluent to move to the suburbs, a move facilitated by the development of suburban railways. In the USA the flight to the suburbs was largely complete by the 1970s when more people lived in suburbs than elsewhere. The eventual segregation of cities into residential, manufacturing, and business areas took place in the context of the by now well-established social status of merchants and bankers, who played a considerable role in determining the pattern of migration to newer residential areas.

Overall, then, we can expect the sociolinguistic consequences of urbanization to be quite complex because urbanization tends to promote linguistic diversity as well as uniformity. Urban environments are often the sites of contact between languages as well as dialects. London, for instance, once provided a point of origin for the diffusion of standard English, but now it has become an increasingly diverse city through the influx of overseas migrants from the Caribbean and Asia. As many as fifty different languages may be spoken in parts of the city. Similarly, Melbourne, once primarily a monolingual town, now has the largest concentration of Greek speakers in the world.

This means that a person living in an urban environment typically has exposure not only to many more individuals from diverse social and cultural backgrounds, but also to a more diverse set of communicative situations occasioned by contact with the bureaucratic institutions of urban life. Most of these encounters no longer involve face-to-face interaction with people we know, but require the use of the telephone, fax machine, etc. with strangers. Urban residents are often members of larger, more numerous, and less dense social networks than rural dwellers, particularly those employed in service positions which bring them into contact with many people.

At the same time, however, languages of wider communication and standard languages serve to unify a diverse population in urban centers. Incoming migrants from rural areas often discard marked dialect forms as part of the process of accommodation to urban speech ways. The net result is dialect levelling, at present a major force across south-east England, and seen by some as a threat to the preservation of regional dialect more generally.

At first, dialectologists did not consider these newly emergent urban speech forms of interest, but concentrated their efforts instead on documenting the rural dialects which they believed would soon disappear. A study conducted in New York City in the 1960s was the first to introduce a systematic methodology for investigating social dialects and the first large-scale sociolinguistic survey of an urban community. Unlike previous dialectological studies, which generally chose one person as representative of a particular area, this survey was based on tape-recorded interviews with 103 informants who had been chosen by random sample as being representative of the various social classes, ages, ethnic groups, etc. to be found in New York City. This approach solved the problem of how any one person's speech could be thought of as representing a large urban area.

Previous investigations had concluded that the speech of New Yorkers appeared to vary in a random and unpredictable manner. Sometimes they pronounced the names *Ian* and *Ann* alike and sometimes they pronounced post-vocalic /r/ (i.e. *r* following a vowel) in words such as *car*, while at other times they did not. This fluctuation was termed 'free variation' because there did not seem to be any explanation for it. The New York study and subsequent ones modelled after it, however, showed that when such free variation in the speech of and between individuals was viewed against the background of the community as a whole, it was not free, but rather conditioned by social factors such as social class, age, sex, and style in predictable ways. Thus, while idiolects (or the speech of individuals) considered in isolation might seem random, the speech community as a whole behaved regularly. Using these methods, one could predict that a person of a particular social class, age, sex, etc. would not pronounce post vocalic /r/ a certain percentage of the time in certain situations. Through the introduction of these new methods for investigating social dialects by correlating sociolinguistic variables with social factors, sociolinguists have been able to build up a comprehensive picture of social dialect differentiation in the United States and Britain in particular, and other places where these studies have since been replicated.

Language and social class

In order to demonstrate a regular relationship between social and linguistic factors, we have to be able to measure them in a reliable way. The principal social dimensions sociolinguists have been concerned with are social class, age, sex, style, and network. Of these, social class has probably been the most researched. Many sociolinguistic studies have started by grouping individuals into social classes on the basis of factors such as education, occupation, income, and then looked to see how certain linguistic features were used by each group. The method used in New York City to study the linguistic features was to select items which could be easily quantified, in particular, phonological variables such as postvocalic /r/, which was either present or absent. This was one of the first features to be studied in detail by sociolinguists.

Varieties of English can be divided into two groups with respect to their treatment of this variable: those that are *r*-pronouncing (rhotic) and those that are not *r*-pronouncing (non-rhotic). Today in Britain accents that have lost postvocalic /r/ as a result of linguistic change generally have more prestige than those, like Scottish English, that preserve it. In many parts of the United States the reverse is true, although this has not always been the case (see Chapter 5).

Table 3.1 compares the pronunciation of postvocalic /r/ in New York City with that of Reading, England. The results show that in New York City the lower one's social status, as measured in terms of factors such as occupation, education, and income, the fewer postvocalic /r/s one uses, while in Reading the reverse is true.

Like many features investigated by sociolinguists, the pronunciation of postvocalic /r/ shows a geographically as well as socially significant distribution (see Chapter 5). This difference among dialects of English is the result of a linguistic change involving the loss of /r/ following a consonant, but not a vowel, which began centuries ago in south-east England and spread north and west. The distribution of postvocalic /r/ in the United States reflects the history of settlement patterns of colonists from different parts of Britain and Ireland. Because the relevant linguistic factor for this change was the presence or absence of a consonant in the immediately following word (cf. e.g. *car engine* v. *car key*), a so-called 'linking /r/' appears in non-rhotic accents before words beginning with a vowel. Subsequently, this pattern seems to have been restructured and generalized so that /r/ is inserted in many contexts before a vowel where historically it was never present, e.g. *the idea of it* becomes *the idear of it* and *Shah of Iran* becomes *Shar of Iran*. This phenomenon is known as 'intrusive *r*'.

Just as the diffusion of linguistic features may be halted by natural geographical barriers, it may also be impeded by social class stratification. Similarly, the boundaries between social dialects tend for the most part not to be absolute. The pattern of variation for postvocalic /r/ shows 'fine stratification' or continuous variation along a linguistic dimension (in this case a phonetic one) as well as an extralinguistic one (in this case social class). The indices go up or

Table 3.1 Percentage of postvocalic /r/s pronounced

New York City	Reading	Social class
32	0	upper middle class
20	28	lower middle class
12	44	upper working class
0	49	lower working class

down in relation to social class, and there are no sharp breaks between groups. A major finding of urban sociolinguistic work is that differences among social dialects are quantitative and not qualitative.

There are many other variables in English which show similar sociolinguistically significant distributions, such as those studied in Norwich in the 1970s in an urban dialect study modeled after the New York research. Three consonantal variables which varied with social class were investigated. Table 3.2 shows the results for (*ing*), (*t*), and (*h*). The numbers show the percentage of non-RP (received pronunciation) forms used by different class groups. The variable (*ing*) refers to alternation between alveolar /n/ and a velar nasal /ŋ/ in words with *-ing* endings such as *reading*, *singing*. Table 3.2 shows that the lower a person's social status, the more likely he or she is to use a higher percentage of alveolar rather than velar nasal endings. This is often referred to popularly as 'dropping one's gs'. It is a well-known marker of social status over most of the English-speaking world.

The variable (h) refers to alternation between /h/ and lack of /h/ in words beginning with /h/ such as *heart*, *hand*. Unlike RP, most urban accents in England do not have initial /h/ or are variable in their usage of it. For these speakers who 'drop their *hs*', *art* and *heart* are pronounced the same. Again, the lower a person's social status, the more likely he or she is to drop *hs*. Speakers in the north of England, Scotland, and Ireland retain /h/, as do speakers of American English. The variable (*t*) refers to the use of glottal stops instead of /t/, as in words such as *bottle*, which are sometimes stereotypically spelled as *bot'le* to represent the glottalized pronunciation of the medial /t/. Most speakers of English glottalize final /t/ in words such as *pat*, and no social significance is attached to it. In many urban dialects of British English, however, glottal stops are more widely used, particularly by younger working-class speakers in London, Glasgow, etc.

By comparing the results for the use of glottal stops in Norwich with those for

Table 3.2 Percentage of non-RP forms in Norwich

Social class	(*ing*)	(*t*)	(*h*)
Middle middle class	31	41	6
Lower middle class	42	62	14
Upper working class	87	89	40
Middle working class	95	92	59
Lower working class	100	94	61

(*ing*) and (*h*), we can draw some interesting conclusions about the way language and social class are related in this English city. Looking first at frequency, even the middle class in Norwich uses glottal stops very frequently, i.e. almost 50 per cent of the time, but this isn't true of (*h*). There is of course no reason to assume that every instance of variation in language will correlate with social structure in the same way or to the same extent. Most sociolinguistic variables have a complicated history. Some variables will serve to stratify the population more finely than others; and some cases of variation do not seem to correlate with any external variables: the variation between /i/ and /ɛ/ in the first vowel of *economic* is probably one such instance. Phonological variables tend to show fine stratification and there is more socially significant variation in the pronunciation of English vowels than in consonants. In the case of glottal stop usage, what is socially significant is how frequently a person uses glottal stops in particular linguistic and social contexts. The use of glottal stops is particularly socially stigmatized in medial position, e.g. *bottle*, *butter*. A hierarchy of linguistic environments can be set up which seems to apply to all speakers. Glottal stops are more likely to occur in the following environments:

most frequent	word final + consonant	e.g. *that cat*
	before syllabic nasal	e.g. *button*
	word final + vowel	e.g. *that apple*
	before syllabic /l/	e.g. *bottle*
least frequent	word medially	e.g. *butter*

Although all speakers are affected by the same internal constraints in the same way, they apply at different frequency levels, depending on social class membership and other external factors. Table 3.3 shows the incidence of glottal stops in relation to social class in Glasgow for all environments compared with that occurring only in medial position. Class I is the highest and contains professional people, while Class III is the lowest and contains unskilled workers. The results show that glottal stops are the norm for this community (74.3 per cent), if we look at all the environments. Even the highest social class uses glottal stops nearly half the time, and the lowest class almost all the time. However, if we look at medial position, the highest social class use no glottal stops in this environment, while the lowest class use them 68.8 per cent of the time.

The view of language which emerges from the sociolinguistic study of urban dialects is that of a structured but variable system, whose use is conditioned by both internal and external factors. The use of other variables, however, can be more sharply socially stratifying. That is, a large social barrier between the middle class and the working class may be reflected in the usage of some linguistic feature. In English such features are more likely to be grammatical or

Table 3.3 Incidence of glottal stops in all environments compared to medial position

	Class				Average
	I	IIa	IIb	III	
All environments	48.4	72.9	84.3	91.7	74.3
Medial position	0.0	7.2	42.5	68.8	29.6

syntactic, such as the use of multiple negation (e.g. 'I do*n't* want *no* trouble'), than pronunciation variables.

Table 3.4 shows the results of a study of a grammatical variable in Detroit and Norwich. The variable concerns the use of non-standard third person singular present tense verb forms without *-s*, e.g. *he go*. Only working-class speakers use these forms with any great frequency and this is more so in Norwich than in Detroit. The gap between the middle- and working-class norms is also greater in Norwich than in Detroit, reflecting the greater social mobility of the American social system. There are also other varieties of British English, e.g. in parts of the north, south-west, and south Wales, where the present tense paradigm is regularized in the opposite direction and all persons of the verb take *-s*, i.e. *I goes, you goes, he goes*, etc.

There is a close relationship between regional and social dialect in both the United States and Britain. More specifically, it appears that working-class varieties are more localized. This is especially true in Britain, where those who are at the top of the social scale speak RP, an accent which does not betray the local origin of the speaker, only his or her social status. There is nothing like RP in the United States, where regional standards exist in different parts of the country.

Table 3.4 Verbs without *-s*

Class	Detroit	Norwich
Upper middle class	1	0
Lower middle class	10	2
Upper working class	57	70
Middle working class		87
Lower working class	71	97

George Bernard Shaw's *Pygmalion* and the popular musical made from it, *My Fair Lady*, attest to the far greater preoccupation in Britain with accent (and its power for social transformation). The Cockney flower seller Eliza Doolittle is trained by the phonetics professor Henry Higgins to speak like a 'lady' with an RP accent. Like many others both before and after her, Eliza Doolittle submits to remodelling her social and linguistic persona. As long as she pronounces her vowels and consonants correctly, Eliza Doolittle does not betray her working-class east London origins and is indeed received in the best of society, no matter how 'vulgar' her vocabulary or grammar are.

Henry Sweet (on whom Shaw's character Higgins was based) described all too well the anxiety bound up with validating one's social place through accent when he wrote:

> The Cockney dialect seems very ugly to an educated Englishman or woman because he—and still more—she—lives in a perpetual terror of being taken for a Cockney, and a perpetual struggle to preserve that *h* which has now been lost in most of the local dialects of England, both North and South.

It is clear from other commentators that *h*-dropping was tantamount to social suicide. Even today, it may be the single most powerful pronunciation shibboleth in England, as suggested by the results of the Norwich study where *h*-dropping shows the sharpest stratification of any of the phonological variables, with a large gap between middle- and working-class speakers. Indeed, it functions more like some grammatical variables which are generally more sharply stratifying in the English-speaking world than phonological ones.

In the USA, by contrast, it is quite possible for highly educated speakers to have marked local accents as can be seen, for instance, in the fact that former President John F. Kennedy spoke with a recognizable east coast New England variety, and former President Jimmy Carter with a non-coastal southern one. Both in fact were non-rhotic, while the majority of Americans speak with rhotic accents. The idea of the 'President's English' then is not one Americans would find interpretable in the way Britons would make sense of the notion of the 'Queen's' or 'King's English'. Of course, educated speakers in both countries would tend not to use non-standard grammatical features. I will examine more closely the gender dimensions of this and other variables to which Sweet alludes a bit later in this chapter.

The nature of the relationship between social and regional varieties needs further investigation since it is likely that it varies considerably in non-western societies, where differences in social status may be organized quite differently. For instance, in India we might expect sharp stratification of linguistic features to correlate with caste differences since the castes are named groups, highly stable and rigidly separated from one another. There is little mobility because

'By gum, tha's got a reet rum session ahead o' thee, an' as I were only saying t' Bishop o' Sheffield t'other day. . . .'

(GUARDIAN · 6. November 1984. P.1.)

FIG 3.2 The Queen's English?

membership in a particular caste group is hereditary. Some evidence for this can be seen in Table 3.5, which shows some regional and caste differences in lexicon and grammar from two regional and social dialects of Kannarese, a Dravidian language spoken in south India.

The regional dimension of variation can be seen by looking at the different forms in two towns, Bangalore and Dharwar, which are about 250 miles apart. The social dimension can be illustrated by comparing the Brahmins, who are the highest caste, with non-Brahmins. For the non-Brahmin castes the forms are the same, regardless of region. This is not true for the highest caste, the Brahmins, who show more variation. Not only is their speech different from that of the non-Brahmins, but Brahmin speech in Dharwar is also different from that of Bangalore (compare especially the first three items). Thus, in Kannarese, unlike English, the forms typical of the higher social group are more localized than those used by the lower social group. Social distance is more important than geographical distance.

Style

Not only do some of the same linguistic features figure in patterns of both regional and social dialect differentiation, but they also display correlations with other social factors. The intersection of social and stylistic continua is one of the most important findings of quantitative sociolinguistics: namely, if a feature occurs more frequently in working-class speech, then it will occur more frequently in the informal speech of all speakers. Table 3.6 shows this for the

Table 3.5 Regional and caste differences in Kannarese

	Brahmin		Non-Brahmin	
	Dharwar	Bangalore	Dharwar	Bangalore
'It is'	*ədə*	*ide*	*ayti*	*ayti*
'Inside'	*-olage*	*-alli*	*-āga*	*-āga*
Infinitive affix	*-likke*	*ōk*	*-āk*	*-āk*
Participle affix	*-ō*	*-ō*	*-ā*	*-ā*
'Sit'	*kūt-*	*kūt*	*kunt-*	*kunt-*
Reflexive	*kō*	*kō*	*kont*	*kont*

Source: Trudgill 1974*a*: 36, Table 2.

Table 3.6 Percentage of forms without final *g*

Social class	Style	
	Casual	Formal
Middle middle class	28	3
Lower middle class	42	15
Upper working class	87	74
Middle working class	95	88
Lower working class	100	98

variable (*ing*) in Norwich, whose social class distribution we have already looked at. The behavior of each social class group varies according to whether its style is casual or formal. Style can range from formal to informal depending on social context, relationship of the participants, social class, sex, age, physical environment, and topic. Although each class had different average scores in each style, all groups style shift in the same direction in their more formal speech style, that is, in the direction of the standard language. This similar behavior can also be taken as an indication of membership in a speech community. All groups recognize the overt greater prestige of standard speech and shift towards it in more formal styles.

Language and style

Some deviations in this pattern have been observed, however, as in Fig. 3.3, which shows the stylistic distribution of postvocalic /r/ in New York City. The highest and lowest groups have the shallowest slopes, but the second highest group in the social hierarchy, the lower middle class, shows the most radical style shifting, exceeding even the highest-status group in their use of postvocalic /r/ in the most formal style. This has been called the 'crossover pattern' and is taken to be a manifestation of 'hypercorrection'. The behavior of the lower middle class is governed by their recognition of an exterior standard of correctness and their insecurity about their own speech. They see the use of postvocalic /r/ as a prestige marker of the highest social group. In their attempt to adopt the norm of this group, they manifest their aspirations of upward social mobility, but they overshoot the mark. The clearest cases of hypercorrection occur when a feature is undergoing change in response to social pressure

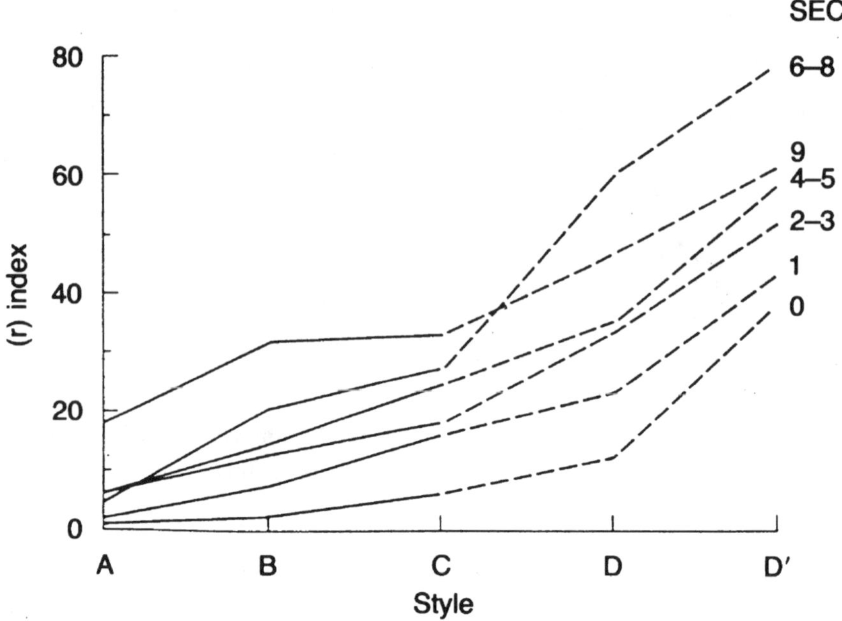

SEC (socio-economic class) scale:	Style:
0–1: lower class	A: casual speech
2–4: working class	B: careful speech
5–6, 7–8: lower middle class	C: reading style
9: upper middle class	D: word lists
	D′: minimal pairs

FIG 3.3 Social and stylistic stratification of postvocalic /r/ in New York (class stratification of a linguistic variable in process of change: /r/ in *guard, car, beer, beard, board*, etc.)

from above, i.e. a prestige norm used by the upper class. In New York City the new /r/-pronouncing norm is being imported into previously non-rhotic areas of the eastern United States (see Chapter 5). Hypercorrection by the lower middle class accelerates the introduction of this new norm.

By contrast, (*ing*) shows no such hypercorrection and is not undergoing any linguistic change. It is a stable social and stylistic marker and has been for centuries as far as we can tell.

Another type of hypercorrection actually results in the production of forms which are incorrect. In New York City highly stigmatized pronunciations such as 'toity toid street' (for 33rd Street) are popularly associated with the so-called Brooklyn accent (although in fact are more widespread throughout working-class speech of the city). Speakers who wish to dissociate themselves from this way of speaking often 'correct' forms which contain the sound < oi >, so that *toilet* becomes *terlet* and *boil* becomes *berl*. Speakers alter these sounds because they are aware of the 'toity toid' stereotype, which to them suggests that < oi > is an incorrect pronunciation of < er >, so they correct all cases where < oi > occurs to < er >. In cases like *terlet*, this produces a form which is not only hypercorrect, but also in fact non-existent in the more prestigious form of speech which these speakers are trying to emulate. These hypercorrections often become so common that they too have now become stereotypes.

Although speakers no doubt pay attention to their speech in some circumstances more than others, they also make adjustments depending on whom they are talking to. In choosing which speech forms to use, they assess not only the relative formality or informality of the context, but also the audience to whom their talk is directed. The accommodations speakers make towards their audiences may of course depend on the social status of the participants, as we saw in the Javanese example in Chapter 1 used to illustrate the concept of register, which is closely related to style.

In some cases the accommodations speakers make involve adopting forms similar to those used by the person(s) being spoken to. This is called 'convergence' because one person's speech forms become similar to those of another. For instance, in the sociolinguistic study of Norwich the linguist who interviewed Norwich residents found on listening afterwards to the recordings that he had varied his own use of glottal stops according to that of his interviewees. Convergence is a sign of solidarity. This result is not surprising since the linguist who conducted the study was himself from Norwich and positively identified with the town and its inhabitants.

In a different kind of study done in a travel agency in Cardiff, assistants also varied their speech in relation to that of their clients. These results would be difficult to explain solely in terms of the amount of attention paid to speech. In another study done in New Zealand, radio announcers who broadcast on more than one station made accommodations in their speech style according to the type of audience (defined in terms of social status) a particular station was aimed at. As in the Cardiff travel agency, such style switches were made quite rapidly. At off-peak hours a single newsreader might alternate between news broadcasts for two different stations with as few as ten minutes in between, while in the travel agency many of the clients were dealt with in person and on the telephone during the day.

There are, however, also occasions on which readers choose to adopt a divergent style. This has the effect of distancing the speaker from the hearer. A particular style (or even a whole language) can be used as a boundary marker. In this example from a provincial government office in Montreal, a man who has come to take a French proficiency test required for members of certain professions insists that the receptionist address him in English. Although he is able to speak some French, and presumably the receptionist is able to speak some English, neither accommodates to the other. This strategy serves to maintain the boundaries between anglophones and francophones.

Man: Could you tell me where the French test is?
Receptionist: Pardon?
Man: Could you tell me where the French test is?
Receptionist: En français (in French?)
Man: I have the right to be addressed in English by the government of Quebec according to Bill 101.
Receptionist (to a third person): Qu'est-ce qu'il dit?
[What's he saying?]

In a similar fashion, some young British-born blacks of Caribbean ancestry who identify with black culture have deliberately adopted a way of speaking which diverges considerably from that of their white peers. It draws heavily on West Indian creole forms of speech. When they use this speech style, they are dissociating themselves from white mainstream society and its values.

Speakers have at their disposal a range of forms (or languages) which they can use to influence how their message is to interpreted, how they view the context or topic, and how they align themselves with their audience. These examples show that style is a multidimensional phenomenon.

Gender

There are also strong correlations between patterns of social stratification and gender. A number of sociolinguistic studies have found that women tend to use higher-status variants more frequently than men. This pattern was found, for example, with both postvocalic /r/ and (*ing*). An example can be seen in Table 3.7, which shows the results for multiple negation, e.g. *I don't have no money*, for male and female speakers in Detroit. Women of each social class group use the more standard variants more often than men of equal status. The variable is more sharply stratifying for women than for men, and the biggest gaps occur in the lower middle class and lower working class. Women tend to hypercorrect more than men, especially in the lower middle class.

Similar results have been found in other places, such as Sweden, Britain, and

Table 3.7 Multiple negation in Detroit

Class	Men	Women
Upper middle class	6.3	0.0
Lower middle class	32.4	1.4
Upper working class	40.0	35.6
Lower working class	90.1	58.9

the Netherlands. In fact, one sociolinguist has gone so far as to say that this pattern of sex differentiation is so ubiquitous in western societies today that one could look at women's speech to determine which forms carry prestige in a community, and conversely, at men's to find out which are stigmatized. Among the explanations put forward for the finding that women use more prestige forms and are more concerned with politeness than men is that using non-standard forms of speech carries connotations of masculinity. When asked to say which forms they use themselves, Norwich women, for instance, tend to 'over-report' their usage and claim they use more standard forms than they actually do. Men, however, are likely to under-report their use of standard forms. From these findings it has been suggested that for men, speaking non-standardly has 'covert' prestige, while the 'overt prestige' associated with speaking the standard variety is more important to women.

Women may be using linguistic means as a way to achieve status denied to them through other outlets. Since women have long been denied equality with men as far as educational and employment opportunities are concerned, these are not reliable indicators of a woman's status or the status she aspires to. Thus, the market-place establishes the value of men in economic terms, but the only kind of capital a woman can accumulate is symbolic. She can be a 'good' housewife, a 'good' mother, a 'good' wife, etc., with respect to the community's norms for appropriate behavior.

In the Victorian era 'speaking properly' became associated with being female, and with being a lady in particular. That is why Sweet, for instance, considers it far worse for a woman to drop /h/s than a man. Fig. 3.4 shows the title-page of a popular elocution book of the day devoted to the topic, where a woman is caught in the act of dropping an /h/, thereby losing her claims to respectable social status.

The Victorian cultural construction of women as 'ladies' was grounded in prescriptions about language as much as it was in sanctions on dress and behavior. Talking properly was very much like putting on the right sort of

FIG 3.4 Woman caught in the act of /h/ dropping

clothing and make-up, or having gloves that fit. Not coincidentally, the early twentieth-century BBC radio announcers were required to wear dinner jackets for their evening broadcasts, while disseminating the news in their correct BBC English. Yet whatever was required of gentlemen was even more mandatory for ladies. Sarah Ellis, for instance, wrote quite bluntly in 1839 that '[a lady] cannot—positively cannot—dare not—will not do anything that the world has pronounced unladylike'.

The equation between proper dress and proper speech is made explicitly in Victorian etiquette manuals, where proprieties of language are spoken of as if they were cosmetics. Conversely, slovenly forms of speech were referred to as 'blemishes'. A lady's dropping of an /h/ is a 'fatal blot', according to one conduct book. Another source declared that 'ladies' were 'more susceptible of external polish than Man is'. Moral Purity, a lady's cardinal virtue, went hand in hand with purity of accent: 'Her accent is not provincial.' The purest ladies spoke with the purest accents. Similarly, another piece of advice warned that:

> A young man may talk recklessly of 'lots of bargains', 'lots of money', 'lots of fellows', 'lots of fun' &c, but a lady may *not*. Men may indulge in any latitude of expression within the bounds of sense and decorum, but woman has a narrower range—even her mirth must be subjected to the rules of good taste. It may be naive, but must never be grotesque. It is not that we would have *primness* in the sex, but we would have refinement. Women are the purer and the more ornamental part of life, and when *they* degenerate, the Poetry of Life is gone.

Such standards of behavior informed the cultural attitudes of the day and provided the context in which the identity of young girls was formed. Female education as it was construed then placed significance on elocution and voice training for women. Accurate pronunciation could be obtained only by constant practice and vigilance. Authors of conduct manuals saw elocution as a skill to enhance the home, for reading aloud was regarded as an activity well suited to the woman's role in the domestic sphere. There was no place like home. Women such as Sarah Ellis, however, observed how deficient was the education given to women with its concentration on manners rather than matter, on show rather than substance. Gentlemen's wives were ladies of leisure, not to be engaged in baking, brewing, tending the chickens and garden. In commenting at the end of the nineteenth century on the considerable waste of talent and energy directed towards becoming a lady in this constrained sense, Margaretta Grey noted that 'A lady, to be such, must be a mere lady, and nothing else.'

Because a woman aspirant to the status of lady could not attain it independently, but only through marriage, it was incumbent on her to behave and speak like a lady. One advice book recommended, moreover, that couples should be

/h/ compatible: 'So important indeed is the question of the use of h in England ... that no marriage should take place between persons whose ideas on this subject do not agree.' It goes on to relate how a newly married woman wrote to the *Lancashire Evening Post* to complain that her husband had asked her at the dinner table, 'Where are your h's?'

Language and age

Sociolinguistic patterns are acquired quite early in some communities. Gender, style, and social class differentiation can be found among Scottish schoolchildren as young as 6. Many of these children also were aware of the social significance of variants (see further in Chapter 4). In other communities such awareness may develop later. Table 3.8 shows the results of sociolinguistic research done in Sweden, which indicate that the variable (*t*) is a marker of social class membership among the adult and school-age population. The highest group (I) uses the most standard forms, e.g. more final /t/s, which in Swedish indicate either the neuter singular definite article as in *huset* 'the house' or the past participle of certain verbs such as *kastat* 'thrown'. The use of /t/ in such forms is in general increasing throughout Sweden under the influence of the written language. The adult pattern also appears in the two younger age groups. In fact, the youngest speakers between the ages of 7 and 16 use more standard forms than the young adults between the ages of 16 and 20.

The age distribution of a variable may be an important clue to ongoing change in a community, but that will be the subject of Chapter 5.

The trends I have been describing up to this point in the chapter are often referred to collectively as *sociolinguistic patterns*, i.e. regular, recurrent correlations between language and external factors such as social class, style, age, sex. For many, this aspect of sociolinguistics is synonymous with the whole

Table 3.8 Percentage of /t/ forms in the speech of Eskilstuna schoolchildren and adults in relation to social class

Social group	Age 7–16	Age 16–20	Adults
I	39.5	15.7	78
II	31.3	12.9	52
III	20.5	2.8	37

field which goes by that name. From this work we can state a number of generalizations about the relationship between linguistic variables and society. A number of types of variables have been identified, e.g. 'indicators', which show regular distribution over socio-economic, ethnic, or age groups, but are used by each individual more or less in the same way in any context; 'stereotypes', socially marked forms stereotyped by society such as Brooklyn 'toity toid' and 'terlet', which may or may not conform to any objective reality; and 'markers', such as (*ing*), which are stable reflectors of social class and style.

Language and social network

There has been some dissatisfaction with class-based approaches to variation because many studies have taken for granted that individuals can be grouped into social classes. Once these groups are established, variables are correlated with them and there is generally no mention of the extent to which these social groups are linguistically homogeneous. In other words, investigators have generally ignored variation within these groups on the assumption that those in the same group will behave similarly. Some have argued, however, that we should start instead with the individual and see what patterns emerge regardless of social class. This kind of sociolinguistic study has emphasized the nature of contacts and networks in a society. We have already seen in Chapter 2 how the kind of people in an individual's network has an effect on language choice. In the village of Oberwart, the fewer peasant contacts a person has, the greater the likelihood that German will be used. The speech habits of young women with social aspirations have been fueling a shift away from Hungarian towards German.

Contact between groups in urban society may also accelerate the use of nonstandard features and in some cases inhibit change towards the standard. In a study of Puerto Rican speakers in New York City, it emerged that Puerto Ricans who were in contact with black speakers deleted final *-t/d* more often (e.g. *fas' train, gol' watch*) than blacks or whites or Puerto Ricans who did not socialize with blacks. This makes it clear that the people with whom we interact are a powerful source of influence on speech. We will take a closer look at the linguistic aspects of this variable in Chapter 5.

The concept of 'social network', adopted from anthropology into sociolinguistics, takes into account different socializing habits of individuals and their degree of involvement in the local community. The use of network as an analytical construct does not require grouping individuals into social classes.

Networks may cut across social class boundaries and they may also reveal differences within social classes.

Network analysis was applied to the study of three working-class communities in Belfast, Northern Ireland. The different types of networks within which individuals socialized were examined and network strength was correlated with linguistic variables. A measure of network strength was devised which took into account the extent of the density and multiplexity of different network types. For example, a dense network is one in which the people whom a given speaker knows and interacts with also know each other. A multiplex network is one in which the individuals who interact are tied to one another in other ways. Thus, if two men in a network interact both as workmates at the same factory and as cousins, there is more than one basis to their relationship with one another.

The results in Table 3.9 show how two women, Hannah and Paula, who live in the same type of housing in the same area of Belfast and have similar employment, nevertheless behave quite differently from one another linguistically. Hannah is much more standard in her speech than Paula. Scores for only two of the eight variables of the study are given here: (*th*) refers to the absence of intervocalic *th* in words such as *mother*, and (*e*) refers to the frequency of a low vowel in words such as *peck*, which then merges with *pack*. Higher scores indicate a more localized or non-standard usage.

The explanation lies in their socialization patterns which are clearly very different. Paula, whose speech is more non-standard, is a member of a local bingo-playing group and has extensive kin ties in the area. Hannah has no kin in the area and does not associate with local people. In fact, she stays at home a lot watching TV. In general, those with high network scores indicating the strength of association with the local community used more local, non-standard forms of speech. Those whose networks were more open and less locally constrained used more standard speech. Networks in which individuals interact locally within a well-defined territory and whose members are linked to each other in several capacities, e.g. as kin, neighbor, workmate, act as a powerful influence on the maintenance of local norms. If these networks are

Table 3.9 Two Belfast women compared

	(*th*)	(*e*)
Hannah	0.0	66.7
Paula	58.34	100.0

disrupted, then people will be more open to the influence of standard speech. Speakers use their local accents as a means of affirming identity and loyalty to local groups.

There is, however, a broad link between network and social class to the extent that middle-class speakers tend to have looser networks than the working class. However, dense networks may also be found at the upper levels of society, as in Britain, where the so-called 'old boy network', whose members have usually been educated at English public schools and at Oxford and Cambridge, gives rise to an equally distinctive speech variety, RP. More men than women had dense networks in Belfast, which suggests an explanation for some of the patterns of sex differentiation other sociolinguists have found. The network approach has also been applied in non-western settings such as Africa and Brazil. In Brazil, for example, it was used to study the extent to which rural migrants to urban areas assimilated to urban standard speech norms. Change has been slower for migrant women, who have fewer social contacts than men.

The notion of network is thus more useful than social class and it applies equally well to multilingual and monolingual settings. As illustrated in the last chapter, where the Austrian study was discussed, an understanding of network structure leads to insight into the process of language shift in a bilingual community. At a more general level, we can say that the same kinds of processes must operate on speakers of different cultures. Dense networks can be found at any level of society, whether it be among working-class Belfast or upper-class British RP speakers, to produce a focused set of linguistic norms. Speakers whose norms are more diffuse participate in networks whose members are geographically and socially more mobile, e.g. women in Oberwart and Belfast.

The relationship between female speech and social dialects also needs reexamination from a new non-class-based standpoint because men's and women's relations to the class structure are unequal. From a Marxist perspective, it is obvious that women do not have the same relationship to the means of production that men have. Women are concentrated in specific occupations, particularly poorly paid white-collar work, and of course housework, generally unpaid and unrecognized as related to the prevailing economic structure. In France until quite recently bakers' wives who sold bread all day long were classified as 'unemployed' and received no pension (see Chapter 4 for discussion of some of the linguistic consequences of this). Their labor was expected as part of their wifely duties and therefore did not officially count. However, as feminists have pointed out, it is precisely housework which makes the modern capitalist economy feasible since it frees the man to work in the public sector by relieving him of domestic work which has to be done and would otherwise have to be paid for. According to the United Nations, women perform nearly two-thirds of the world's work, for which they receive one-tenth of its income and own one-hundredth of its property.

It is only within the last few decades since the modern feminist movement that government departments and academic disciplines such as sociology have come to see women's relationship to social classes as a political issue and a technical problem for official statistics. Censuses and other surveys rely on a patriarchal concept of social class, where the family is the basic unit of analysis, the man is regarded as the head of a household, and his occupation determines the family's social class. Women disappear in the analysis since their own achievements are not taken into account and their status is defined by their husband's job.

Most of the sociolinguistic surveys of urban dialects I have discussed in this chapter have simply adopted notions of social status uncritically. Based on the 1971 British census, however, it is actually the case that more than half of all couples have discrepant social classes. The concept of the traditional nuclear family of man, woman, and children is also outdated. Studies in both the UK and USA have shown that already by the late 1960s the majority of families were not of this type in both countries, and over the past few years government inquiries have been mounted expressing concern that the break-up of this family structure has serious consequences for society.

This means that not only do sociolinguistic patterns between language and gender need to be re-examined, but also the explanations that have been put forward for them. If men and woman of the so-called working class do not really have equal status, then comparisons drawn between the classes do not have equal validity for men and women. The network approach shows that some patterns of social class stratification are actually better accounted for as gender differences. In the Belfast study there was in fact one group of working-class women who had tighter and denser networks than all the other men and women and also used more non-standard forms than men. And, of course, we have already seen that women such as Hannah and Paula may behave quite differently.

In a large-scale survey of around 200 married couples from the upper working and lower middle class in the Netherlands, most of the women in the sample were actually better educated than their husbands. Nevertheless, more of these Dutch women who worked were in lower-status part-time jobs. Since level of education correlates well with degree of use of standard language, if there were similar discrepancies in the other surveys I mentioned, then this could easily account for the finding that women are closer to the standard than men. In non-western societies women are often further removed from the norms of the standard language, as indeed were women in general in western societies before they were given access to education, and other institutions and contexts where standard or prestigious forms of speech can be acquired.

Another factor seldom considered is the effect of children, with respect both to employment patterns as well as to language use in families. The Dutch study found that when a couple had children, both parents used more standard language. One of the reasons why women may adopt a more prestigious variety of language is to increase their children's social and educational prospects.

Standardization

The sociolinguistic patterns I have examined in this chapter have for the most part been derived from studies of urban speech in western industrialized societies. It is largely on the basis of these findings that most sociolinguists now take as their starting point the notion that social stratification will be an important dimension in accounting for linguistic variation in all speech communities. A basic premise is that inequalities in society will be reflected in the distribution of social dialects (also called sociolects).

In many other parts of the world village-based societies which were formerly stratified along traditional lines of kin and other social networks have now assumed the kind of class-based hierarchy commonly found in industrialized nations. Papua New Guinea is a case in point, where social class stratification has just begun to emerge, and the distribution of varieties of language has come to reflect the incipient class divisions. How did this come about? Are there any egalitarian societies where we do not find such sociolinguistic patterns? A closer examination of such cases can help us to understand the sociolinguistic patterns of present-day urban western societies.

In order to answer questions such as these, we need to examine the process of standardization, which is one of the main agents of inequality. What we see reflected in sociolinguistic patterns is the uneven distribution of access to the standard variety. In Chapter 1 I introduced the notion of a standard language as a highly codified variety of a language, which has been developed and elaborated for use across a broad range of functions. The process of standardization converts one variety into a standard by fixing and regulating its spelling, grammar, etc. in dictionaries and grammars, which serve as authorities in prescriptive teaching to both native speakers and foreign learners. Standardization is not an inherent, but rather an acquired or deliberately and artificially imposed characteristic. It is helpful to draw an analogy between language standardization and standardization of coinage, weights, measures, etc. In all these cases, the aim is to remove variation and establish only one system to serve as a uniform one for a group.

Standard languages do not arise via a 'natural' course of linguistic evolution or suddenly spring into existence. They are created by conscious and deliberate planning, which may span centuries. Indeed, the process can never be regarded as complete. As I noted in Chapter 1, by the eighteenth century a single, unified standard for English had ceased to exist, as speakers of new varieties of English such as American English began to codify their own standards in their own dictionaries and grammars. That process continues today as new varieties of English such as Australian and even Indian English assert their autonomy.

It can be argued with some justification that standardization and standard languages are European inventions. Most of the present-day standard languages of Europe emerged within a climate of intense political nationalism. They were developed in part out of the need to create prominent ideological symbols of shared purpose, nationhood, etc. The models selected for codification were those current in capitals like Copenhagen, Paris, and London—seats of the court, centers of trade and finance, and breeding places of the aristocracy. The spread of these new standard languages was made successful by the printing press, and the rise of the newly literate middle classes, who adopted them eagerly as a means of social advancement and mobility.

In England, it was the east Midlands dialect which emerged as the standard since the region in which it was used was the most important in the country in terms of its wealth and population, containing, for instance, London, already an important commercial center, and Oxford and Cambridge Universities. This variety had also been used by Chaucer and other literary figures. So what is now a social dialect was once a regional variety of English.

The spread of what one historian of the English language called 'the new-fangled English' was at first very uneven. The nouveau riche London merchants were particularly eager to adopt it as a sign of their status. The standards of the highest class of speakers were not necessarily those of the new self-constituted authorities on correctness of the seventeenth and eighteenth centuries, such as Samuel Johnson's dictionary of 1755 which aimed to fix a standard for English based on the usage of the best authors. Still, there was much variation. Even Johnson himself used two 'standards' of spelling, one in his dictionary and another in his private writings.

There was even more variation in the spoken language, with the aristocracy still using what would now be called provincial accents. One historian assures us that modern English speakers would no doubt consider that educated persons of that period spoke in a 'reprehensible' manner. Dropping of final - *t*/*d*, for instance, was widespread among all classes of speakers in the seventeenth and eighteenth centuries. Although the term 'King's English' was used by the end of the sixteenth century to label normative forms of English, not all royalty have been considered good exemplars of it. Actor John Kemble, for instance, advised King George IV when he was Prince of Wales that 'it would become your royal mouth much better to pronounce the word oblige, and not obleege'. By 1864, however, Henry Alford warned of the open and merciless laughter which awaited 'any unfortunate member [of Parliament] if he strews the floor with his "aitches"'. Elocution became a public and private pursuit as sixpenny manuals such as the Honourable Henry H's book sold thousands of copies. Five times as many works on elocution appeared between 1760 and 1800 as had done so in the years before 1760. As I noted earlier, women were particularly targeted for such advice on how to speak properly.

Until modern times it was largely only the gentry who were educated. The introduction of compulsory schooling in England in 1870 eventually made the majority of people literate and the newfangled English available to an increasing portion of English society. Sarah Ellis commented on the metamorphosis in the meaning of the social label *lady* brought about by modern schools:

> Amongst the changes introduced by modern taste, it is not the least striking, that all daughters of tradespeople, when sent to school, are no longer girls, but young ladies. The linen-draper whose worthy consort occupies her daily post behind the counter, receives her child from Mrs. Montagu's establishment—a young lady. At the same elegant and expensive seminary, music and Italian are taught to Hannah Smith, whose father deals in Yarmouth herrings; and there is the butcher's daughter, too, perhaps the most ladylike of them all.

In the modern society to emerge as a result of the Industrial Revolution, even the daughter of a herring seller could call herself a lady, once a title referring only to the aristocracy, if her father could afford to send her to an elegant and expensive school where she would learn to read and write, and to speak like a lady. Note too that the daughters of the butcher, the herring seller, and other categories of tradespeople mentioned would all belong to the upper working class and lower middle class, precisely those levels in the social hierarchy where modern sociolinguistics finds the greatest differentiation in male and female speech.

In the English-speaking world dictionaries such as the *Oxford English Dictionary* (*OED*) and Webster's became surrogates for the language academies of other countries such as France with its Académie Française, which has responsibility for and control over linguistic matters. The academy defines what counts as 'correct', i.e. standard French. It is not sufficient, however, for a language to have de facto norms or grammars and dictionaries. Probably all communities evaluate certain kinds of language as 'good' or 'bad'. Jamaican Creole, for instance, has grammars and dictionaries as well as de facto norms, but there is no standard Jamaican Creole. The same is true of the languages of north-west New Britain I discussed in Chapter 1. The grammars and dictionaries of Jamaican Creole were written by linguists for other linguists. They have no official recognition and play no role in teaching. Standard British English is the only variety approved for use in Jamaican schools.

No other variety has the resources and prestige of the written standard. The fact that it exists as an object described in grammar books engenders the notion that it is somehow the 'real' language or the language as it 'should be' and that other varieties of it are degenerate or corrupt versions of it. But it is a false 'reality' which has been consciously engineered. I showed in Chapter 1 how English speakers believe that the 'true' meanings of words can be found in the dictionaries, despite the fact that our assessments of whether an utterance is true depend on context.

There is usually a great deal of resistance to changes in a standard language, as can be seen by looking at newspapers and magazines, where people often write in to complain about new usages. In recent years, some English speakers have complained that many people use *disinterested* incorrectly to mean 'uninterested'. Their decision to condemn this as incorrect is based on the fact that formerly it meant 'impartial' and this is still the meaning recorded in most dictionaries. Nearly all the members of the usage panel of *The American Heritage Dictionary* (1975), for instance, who include authors, critics, publishers, and academics, reject the new meaning of *disinterested* as non-standard. Similarly, *hopefully* has changed its meaning. Formerly, it meant 'with hope', 'in a hopeful manner', but now for many it has come to mean 'it is hoped that'. However, nearly half the panel accept the new meaning.

Over time, the differences between the written standard and the spoken forms may become substantial. The norms enforced by dictionaries, grammars, publishing houses, etc. are 'prescriptive' rather than 'descriptive' in the sense that their intention is to tell people what to do rather than describe what actually occurs, much as etiquette books tell people it is impolite to eat peas with a knife. Nevertheless, it is a descriptive fact that some people do eat peas with a knife, just as many speakers of English do not follow the rules of prescriptive grammars.

Standardization and literacy go hand in hand since the acquisition of literacy presupposes the existence of a codified written standard, and standardization depends on the existence of a written form of language. When a language is written, linguistic matters can be subject to regulation in a way they cannot be when a language exists in spoken form only. The possibility of prescribing certain usages as right and proscribing others as wrong assumes the availability of a means of recording language so that it can be taken apart. Linguistic matters can then be governed by a superimposed 'logic' which is derived from the way in which items are arranged in print. It is this kind of artificial logic that prescriptive grammarians apply in their campaign against non-standard forms such as 'dangling modifiers'. English speakers are taught that a sentence such as *Lincoln wrote the Gettysburg address while riding in a train on the back of an envelope* is incorrect because it means that the train is riding on an envelope. Of course, everyday common sense tells us that a train is bigger than an envelope and no one would misinterpret the meaning of this sentence. Nevertheless, the process of writing allows us to juxtapose words such as *train* and *envelope* and analyze them in such a way that a 'problem' is created. The political novelist Norman Mailer won a battle with his publishers, who edited out a dangling modifier from one of his novels. Mailer protested that the original sentence better conveyed what he wanted to say.

Using language successfully at school and later in public life involves a way of thinking about language which has to be taught explicitly. For instance, pupils are questioned by teachers in the classroom and on tests about things such as the author's purpose in writing a story, as in the following, which has been used in New Zealand to test reading comprehension:

Mr Brown liked animals. He had a duck, a pig and a bear. They liked Mr Brown. He was kind to them. Why was this story written?

1. to tell about someone.
2. to tell something funny.
3. to tell how to do something.

Those who designed the test have decided that the only correct answer is the first one. However, children who chose other answers were able to give equally reasonable accounts of their choices. One child who picked the third answer, for instance, explained that if you had one of those pets, Mr Brown told you how to take care of them by being kind. Another child, who said it told something funny, pointed out that it would be funny to have a duck, a pig, and a bear together as pets. This child has obviously not learned one important characteristic of the written text; namely, that objects which would never appear together in the real world can occur together in print, just as in my earlier example of the train on the back of an envelope.

Similarly, grammarians and teachers apply a kind of quasi-algebraic logic in correcting students for using multiple negation. The argument goes that two negatives make a positive, so *I don't have no money* must mean, 'I have some money'. Of course, no English speakers interpret such sentences in this way. Languages do not obey logical rules of this type. Many languages in fact require multiple negation, and earlier in the history of English this was customary too. It has, however, become a social convention that multiple negation is no longer seen as part of standard English. What we see reflected in the sociolinguistic pattern shown in Table 3.7, which depicted the use of multiple negation in the speech of men and women of different social classes in Norwich and Detroit, is the uneven diffusion of this prescriptive ideology associated with standard English.

Another example of the artificial logic of standard languages can be taken from syllogistic reasoning, which is often assessed on IQ tests. Syllogisms typically contain three statements. The first establishes general premises; the second states a specific fact, and the third requires a conclusion to be drawn about a specific case from the general premises. Thus,

all men are mortal $a = b$
Socrates is a man $c = a$
Socrates is mortal $c = b$

The syllogism is self-contained and conclusions are to be derived only by reference to the premises and not by anything outside it. The mathematical argument is such that if $a = b$ and $c = b$, then c must also equal a. In mathematical equations, however, the numbers do not represent anything beyond values in a closed system. In language, the words we deal with do have referential meaning which extends beyond this closed logical system. We can see this if we substitute the following:

Nothing is better than heaven. $a = b$
Anything is better than nothing. $c = a$
Anything is better than heaven. $c = b$

In this case the syllogism is rendered paradoxical by the meanings of the words representing a, b and c. While it was once thought that this kind of reasoning was universal, we now know that it is derived from schooling in particular kinds of literacy. Preliterate peoples have difficulty in solving these kinds of puzzles because they have not been taught to divorce language from its social context.

Standardization and its effects in Papua New Guinea

It is instructive to look at preliterate societies, where literacy and standardization have been more recently introduced, to see how different languages begin to acquire prestige and others are devalued. Once writing has been introduced into a speech community, the balance of power shifts. The literate become a powerful minority who try to impose their norms of language on others. I observed in Chapters 1 and 2 that European societies have been based on the notion of one nation–one language, a characteristically European mode of sociolinguistic organization. Multilingualism was seen as a threat to the integrity of the state, and a common language critical for unification. Linguistic diversity is still seen as an obstacle to development. An essential feature of linguistic stratification in Europe is an ideology of contempt. Subordinate languages are despised languages. From the sixteenth century the label 'barbarous' was applied by speakers of dominant languages to those who spoke subordinate languages. The word *barbarian* comes to us from Greek *barbarus* meaning 'one who babbles'. The Greeks called others 'barbarians' if they could not speak Greek or pronounced it improperly.

In their role as colonizers, Europeans transported this ideology with them to the New World, where they used it to justify their policy of spreading their own languages as a means of socioeconomic control. For the most part, the colonizers had languages which had already figured prominently in the political movements which fueled the establishment of their own nation-states. They had been consciously manipulated and standardized to play a role in the dissemination of state ideology. France is a case in point, where unity of language was seen as integral to the Revolution at a time when most of the population were native speakers of varieties other than French. Moreover, the Revolution attacked the linguistic distinctions employed by the aristocracy, thereby trying to create a classless French. The Revolution called for universal primary education in which all citizens were to be trained in French. The literary variety of French chosen for standardization was, however, reserved for secondary schools and higher levels of education and government. Thus, the new standard diffused unequally through society and created a new linguistic hierarchy.

Where colonizers tolerated some plurality of language use, they established hierarchical relations among languages. In Papua New Guinea, for instance, colonial rule altered the traditional egalitarian relationship among languages to produce a situation in which indigenous languages are devalued in relation to Tok Pisin (an English-based pidgin) and English, which are languages of wider currency and thus have a higher value in the linguistic market-place. In one village school I encountered a particularly telling indicator of the present linguistic hierarchy. In one of the classrooms a notice was posted advising pupils about activities which were categorized under the heading of 'good', 'bad', and 'worst'. Among them was one relating to language. To speak English was considered good; to speak Tok Pisin was bad, but to speak *tok ples* (literally 'talk place' or village language) was worst. All the schools I visited had signs reminding pupils that English was the language of the classroom.

Missionaries were essential to colonization efforts. Their involvement in language policy and the spread of literacy was not coincidental because the aim of colonization was control of the populace. Education was seen as the main instrument for disseminating the colonizers' culture. Providing education to indigenous peoples was also regarded as part of the white man's burden and was used to justify the legitimacy of colonial rule. Language standardization and the choice of language(s) used as media of education are not disinterested academic exercises. Preferences for particular language varieties are always articulated within the context of an ideology which reflects society's view of itself. In the case of Papua New Guinea, indigenous views of language and society clashed with those of the colonizers. In precolonial Papua New Guinea linguistic diversity was greater than in Europe, but there were no rigidly stratified societies, no far-reaching empires, and no nationalistic consciousness, so this horizontal linguistic diversity was not accompanied by any vertical sociolinguistic stratification of the type commonly found in western industrialized societies today.

Ideas about which languages were suitable for teaching reflected Europeans' beliefs about their own cultural and racial superiority. Many believed the natives were mentally inferior and it was therefore pointless to give them more than enough training to be the servants of white men. The determination of the white community to maintain its prestige and upper position in the colonial hierarchy was reflected in the token educational facilities provided for 'natives' in the early years. There were no government-run schools in these days, only mission schools which could use whatever languages they liked. The various missions were not always agreed on which languages to use in their schools. While almost all of them agreed that the indigenous languages were primitive and inferior to European languages, one justification used by the Lutherans for their policy of vernacular education was based on the assumption that English was too sophisticated a language for the natives. Even though they did not have a high opinion of it, other missions used Tok Pisin because they recognized its usefulness as a lingua franca. Many of the potential converts who gathered at the mission stations already spoke it.

One of the first steps of the missionaries, who set up the first schools, was to choose and codify one variant of a language as a mission standard. This meant creating an orthography for it and vocabulary for the expression of new Christian concepts. The missionaries chose the Wemo dialect as the standard for the Kâte language in 1892. Today the other main dialects have all but disappeared. The same is true for the 'non-standard' dialects of Yabem, an Austronesian language used as a mission lingua franca. Tok Pisin was also standardized for use in mission schools. In contrast with other cases of standardization, where the varieties of the elite in capital cities like London and Paris provided the basis for the codification of a standard, in Papua New Guinea it has been rural

Tok Pisin which has set the standard. This kind of Tok Pisin can be found in *Nupela Testamen* (The New Testament). People were at first eager to learn Tok Pisin, often in the erroneous belief that it was the white man's language.

In the small, remote village of Gapun, roughly midway between the Sepik and Ramu rivers, Tok Pisin is still seen as the key to development and modernity. Most of the hundred or so villagers support themselves through hunting and agriculture. Villagers who do not speak Tok Pisin are regarded as pagan and uncivilized. The only people in Gapun who are not fluent speakers of Tok Pisin or who prefer not to use it are women. Long before that, Tok Pisin had male connotations because it was a language of plantation and other forms of indentured labor done by male villagers for white men. Women in general lag behind men in shifting to Tok Pisin, exhibiting a pattern that is often the reverse of that found in cases of language shift in Europe such as in the case of Oberwart examined in the last chapter.

By shifting their language from Taiap to Tok Pisin, however, Gapun people are attempting to gain symbolic association with, and entry into, the sphere of the developed economy, much in the same way that young women in Oberwart, Austria, chose German over Hungarian because they perceived the former to be of greater economic value. For Gapuners, however, this economy is as yet a mere idea, something they encounter through occasional visits to towns (several days distant by canoe), through migrants and the things they bring back, and through information which filters back to them. As yet, there is virtually no market economy in this isolated village surrounded on all sides by rainforest and mangrove swamp, and almost no out-migration. Knowledge of Tok Pisin does not confer any economic advantage, as there is virtually no socio-economic differentiation among villagers.

Although all villagers agree that their own language, Taiap (spoken nowhere else in the country and not related to any other language), is desirable to know, they are at a loss to understand how it is that their children do not speak it: by 1987 no child under the age of ten actively used Taiap. They prefer Tok Pisin. Yet the values of the parents are transmitted almost unconsciously through the patterns of language choice they make. Because they code-switch so much between Taiap and Tok Pisin, they don't appreciate that the bulk of children's input is in Tok Pisin. The vernacular is tied to the past they now devalue. Just as in Europe, where the newfangled standard languages became symbols of prestige and modernity, Tok Pisin, and then English, became desirable acquisitions. In remote Gapun, however, English plays almost no role in villagers' perception of development.

Once the government took over responsibility for schooling for Papua New Guinea in the 1950s, it set out to establish universal primary education in English and it gave assistance only to those mission schools which taught in

English. Now, in the post-war years, fluency in English and English literacy are sought after for the almost magical access that they give to jobs in town. As in many developing countries, there is a relationship between education and migration with propensity to migrate rising markedly with educational level. Correlations have also been established between migration and size of village of origin, which in turn reflects the relationship between access to educational facilities. The more distant villages are less affected by education and other socio-economic changes and are therefore less likely to have formal employment opportunities. The introduction of a cash economy has had a stratifying impact, dividing the people into wage earners and non-wage earners. The existence of a dual economy based on subsistence agriculture on the one hand and on formal wage labor centred in towns on the other has led to the formation of social classes and stratification.

The towns are recent innovations and they are first and foremost a province for Tok Pisin. Just as Tok Pisin is nobody's first language, the town is no man's land. It does not belong to any one group and everyone has access to it. The hallmark of urban areas in Papua New Guinea is the presence of a significant concentration of non-indigenous people (and hence different language groups needing a common lingua franca). More than 85 per cent of townspeople in the major urban areas speak Tok Pisin. In towns, Tok Pisin has become the ethnic vernacular for Melanesian in-group communication, particularly for the youngest generation, who often have no other language. Western-style education in English has created an indigenous urban elite and given rise to a dichotomy between rural and urban areas, which is reflected in language use. Social mobility, wealth, prestige are almost exclusively related to education. The urban elite are, above all, well educated and fluent in English as well as in Tok Pisin and sometimes in one or more vernacular languages. Their children often attend English-speaking playgroups and schools run largely for the children of European expatriates rather than the local community schools.

The economic value of knowing Tok Pisin and now English in town as opposed to knowledge of a vernacular language was illustrated in one study which, while not about religion or language, serves to emphasize the fact that church affiliation is associated with people's educational opportunities and aspirations for development. Of all the church congregations in Lae, the second largest town, the Catholic Church and the Seventh Day Adventist Church both have high percentages of English and Tok Pisin speakers and they also show a preponderance of skilled over unskilled workers. The four churches with the highest proportions of members in skilled occupations are also the churches with the highest proportions of English speakers. The Anglicans have the greatest number of English speakers (87 per cent), while the Lutherans have the fewest (22 per cent). No Anglicans are found in domestic employment (e.g. as *hausbois* 'houseboys' or *hausmeris* 'housegirls'), and 50 per cent of them are in skilled employment, as compared to only 15 per cent of the Lutherans. By contrast, 24 per cent of the members of Immanuel Hall, a new fundamentalist church which attracts a large number of newly immigrant Highlanders, are employed as domestics and only 4 per cent have a knowledge of English. These statistics reflect the linguistic aspect of social stratification in urban Papua New Guinea, which has its roots in the language policies pursued by mission schools. The Anglicans have a long history of using English in their schools in Northern Province where most of the Lae Anglicans originate. In the context of a developing country like Papua New Guinea, where more than 86 per cent of the population still have no formal schooling at all, education can quickly create vast inequalities. School outcomes create categories of literate and non-literate. Schooling and literacy create a division between those whose credentials give them access to town as opposed to those who have no negotiable skills on the wage market. English is a kind of cultural capital with a value in the linguistic market-place. Villagers became distrustful of missions which taught in the vernacular in the belief that they withheld the truth.

In traditional society illiteracy and lack of access to particular languages of course posed no problem. In town, however, standard English, English spoken as a second language with varying degrees of fluency, highly Anglicized Tok Pisin, more rural Tok Pisin of migrants, and the nativized Tok Pisin of the urban born coexist and loosely reflect the emerging social stratification. Almost ironically, however, Anglicization is now seen to undermine the integrative function of Tok Pisin and its perceived value as a national language. Rural Tok Pisin is now perceived as the 'real' or 'pure' variety and urban varieties are 'impure' because they are mixed with English. Although the competence of most urban speakers includes rural Tok Pisin, the reverse is not true. Many of the items which are found in the media and commonly used in town speech are not intelligible to the average rural adult speaker.

Complaints about Anglicized Tok Pisin have become more frequent since the 1970s. If rural and urban speakers no longer speak mutually intelligible varieties, the gap between rural and urban life and language grows larger. These tensions are played out at other levels in the linguistic hierarchy because in some areas Tok Pisin is seen as a threat to the purity of vernacular languages. Purism is now being used by some groups at both the village and elite levels to constitute part of an ideology for resisting exogenous language norms.

This is not an infrequent phenomenon in other parts of the world during periods of national resistance, authentification, and ethnic and class conflict. Language is often manipulated as a conscious symbol in a people's attempts to identify themselves in social and historical terms and purification may be an important component of validating and preserving uniqueness. An extreme case of the role of purism in the expression of nationalistic and racial conscience can be seen in Nazi Germany. The Académie Française has felt threatened by the spread of English and has tried to legislate against the use of foreign borrowings. Francophonie, an international language movement led by government and non-government elites in more than thirty countries where French is used, has as one of its goals the purification of the language from English borrowing. This can be seen as a reaction to France's diminishing role as a world power, which is reflected in the decline of French as an international language. Another kind of purification can be seen in the attempt to spread Nynorsk ('new Norwegian') as the national language of Norway in opposition to Danish, which had functioned as Norway's written language between 1380 and 1814 when Denmark ruled Norway.

Given the complex of social, cultural, and political variables which transformed the linguistic ecology of pre-contact Papua New Guinea to its modern state, it is unrealistic to expect that a change in language policy alone can undo the effects of colonial strategies of development. One sociologist of language has observed that every liberation not accompanied by a defeat of the linguistic superstructure is not a liberation of the people who speak the dominated language. It is instead a liberation of the social class that continues to speak the dominant language. It is not easy to win a linguistic revolution. In India, for instance, the decision to replace English with Hindi as the national language originally met with riots. It is probably impossible to overthrow the present linguistic hierarchy without far-reaching socio-political reform. While the colonial struggle was between Europeans and those whom they colonized, the role of the foreign colonizers has now been transferred to the English-speaking elite who have perpetuated the colonizers' language and lifestyle. Any attempt to reduce the role of English will be seen as a threat to the political status quo. Unless Tok Pisin is politicized, it will be difficult to increase its status.

I have shown here how competition between traditional concerns and pressures of European cultural origin aimed at integrating Melanesian village societies into western-style models of centralized government, wage economy, development, and education have created a social hierarchy which is now reflected in language use. The processes responsible for this were of the same type as those found previously in Europe: the introduction of literacy and universal schooling, standardization of languages, etc. In fact, one could argue that they were simply exported to other parts of the world from Europe. In raising the question of whether linguistic hierarchies are inevitable, we must ask ourselves whether egalitarian speech communities are possible in the modern industrialized societies in which most of us live today.

The Norwegian attempt to legitimize Nynorsk resulted in its acceptance as one of two official standards, making Norway the only European nation with such a linguistic state of affairs. Created by the schoolteacher Ivar Aasen as a common denominator of rural dialects, it claimed to be a more democratic and more Norwegian norm. Attempts to fuse the two varieties have foundered since the replacement of the older, more prestigious variety associated with the Oslo upper class is resisted by the politically powerful. To establish a linguistic order is to declare a social order. In the cartoon at the beginning of this chapter two Norwegians obstinately cling to their differing pronunciations of 'snow' as *sne* or *snø*. In the next chapter, I will look at another case where linguistic differences reflect social differences, and how male-dominated patterns of communication have excluded women from equal access to society's institutions.

Annotated bibliography

The notion of U and non-U speech can be found in Alan Ross's article, first published in 1956 and reprinted in 1980. The example of the Edinburgh tenant is described by Gordon (1970), and the quotation by Jonathan Swift is cited in Corfield (1991: 106). Bengt Nordberg's (1994) book deals with urbanization in the Nordic countries.

The New York City study was done by William Labov and described in his book (1966), and in Labov (1972 *a*). The Reading and Norwich data are from Peter Trudgill's (1974 *b*) research in England; see also Trudgill (1972). The Glasgow data are taken from R. K. S. Macaulay's study (1977); Macaulay (1991) looks at a range of syntactic and discourse variables in Scottish English. The Detroit data are based on the Detroit dialect survey by Walt Wolfram (1974). Lesley Milroy's (1987) study contains a critical overview of sociolinguistic methodology. Further discussion of sociolinguistic patterns among younger speakers can be found in Suzanne Romaine (1984 *a*). The Swedish sociolinguistic research was done by researchers at FUMS at the University of Uppsala, most of which has appeared in Swedish in a series of FUMS reports; see Nordberg (1990) for a bibliography. The Belfast study is described in Lesley Milroy's (1980) book and James Milroy's (1992) book. An example of the network approach applied to Africa can be found in Joan Russell's (1982) article, and to Brazil in Stella Bortoni-Ricardo's (1985) book. The notions of focusing and diffusion are discussed in R. B. Le Page and Andrée Tabouret-Keller's (1985) book. The Dutch study was done by Dedé Brouwer and Roeland van Hout (1992). The notion of language hierarchy is developed in Ralph D. Grillo's book (1989). A good overview of the standardization process can be found in John E. Joseph's (1987) book, and James and Lesley Milroy's (1985) book. Another source is Louis-Jean Calvet (1974).

The quotation from Henry Sweet is from his book (1890: vi–vii). H. C. Wyld (1920) used the term 'new-fangled English'. The quotation about King George IV is from Bailey (1991: 3), as is the quotation about young men being able to use expressions such as 'lots of bargains' (1991: 259). Lynda Mugglestone's (1995) book provides a good account of how accent became so important in Britain. The quotation from Margaretta Grey is cited in Butler (1894: 288). Hill's book (1902: 14–15) is the source of the story about /h/ compatibility in marriage. Vandenhoff (1862) is the source for /h/-dropping being a 'fatal blot'; *Etiquette for Ladies and Gentlemen* (1839) is the source of the advice about 'polish' and purity of accent. The source for Sarah Ellis's statements is her book (1839: 107, and 309–10). Suzanne Romaine's (1998) article discusses the rise of standard English in the eighteenth and nineteenth centuries. A critique of social stratification theories applied to women can be found in Ann Oakley's book (1982).

The example of Lincoln writing the Gettysburg address on the train comes from Dwight Bolinger's (1980) book. The example from the New Zealand reading test comes from research conducted by Barbara Horvath. Don Kulick's (1992) book is a study of language shift in Gapun, Papua New Guinea. The study of language use and religious affiliation is in Lucas (1972). Suzanne Romaine's article (1992 *a*) provides a fuller account of the present status of Tok Pisin and English in Papua New Guinea. The Norwegian situation is discussed in Einar Haugen's (1966) book.

A critique of structuralist social class-based approaches to sociolinguistics from a Marxist perspective is contained in Glyn Williams's book (1992); see also John Rickford's (1986) article, and the papers in Norbert Dittmar and Peter Schlobinski's collection (1988). Lesley and James Milroy's (1992) article attempts to reconcile social class-based and network-based studies.

Alan Bell's article (1984) accounts for style in terms of the accommodations speakers make to their audiences, drawing on the model of Howard Giles (1984) and others. The Cardiff study was done by Nicholas Coupland (1980), and the example from Montreal is in Monica Heller's (1992) article. For information on British Black English, see Viv Edwards's (1986) book. The collection of papers in Finegan and Biber (1994) is illustrative of renewed interest among sociolinguists in questions of style, genre, register, and the relationship between spoken and written varieties.

Chapter 4

Language and Gender

> The first non-sexist Bible to be published in Britain was launched yesterday. The revisers have systematically changed expressions such as 'any man' to 'anyone', but have kept the masculine, especially for God, on the grounds that this is faithful to the original.
>
> (*Guardian*, 4 October 1985)

IN Chapter 3 we saw that one of the sociolinguistic patterns established by quantitative research on urban social dialects was that women, regardless of other social characteristics such as class, or age, use more standard forms of language than men. Although many reasons, such as women's alleged greater status consciousness and concern for politeness, have been put forward to try to explain these results, they have never been satisfactorily accounted for.

For the most part, however, women's speech has just been ignored until recently. Although one widely quoted linguist writing in the early part of this century actually devoted a chapter of his book on language to 'The Woman', in his view women had a debilitating effect on language and there was no corresponding chapter on 'The Man'. He believed there was a danger of language becoming languid and insipid if women's ways of speaking prevailed. Although practically all linguists would regard these ideas as sexist, even some of the early work of the 1970s prompted by the women's movement proposing the existence of a 'women's language' has been recently criticized by feminists for its circularity of argumentation.

Much of the early research on language and gender devoted a great deal of energy to addressing the issue of 'women's language' using laundry lists of specific linguistic features such as hedging (e.g. *it's* ***kind of*** *late*, ***you know***), the use of tag questions (e.g. *we're going at 6 o'clock,* ***aren't we***?), the use of a high rising tone at the end of an utterance, especially when making statements, which makes it sound as if a question is being asked, etc. These features were believed to be tied to women's subordinate status, and made women seem as if they were tentative, hesitant, lacking in authority, and trivial.

Because many researchers simply counted the number of tag questions used by men and women without paying attention either to the function or context in which they were used, the results were inconclusive on the issue of whether tags showed gender-differentiated usage. Out of a number of studies done between 1976 and 1980 on tag questions, six found that women used more tag questions than men, while five found that men used more than women. One study found no differences between men and women. Not surprisingly, the studies which found that men actually used more tag questions than women did not conclude that men might be lacking in confidence.

This approach is doomed to naivety and circularity unless it acknowledges that the same linguistic features can, when used by different persons in different contexts and cultures, often mean very different things. Some tags facilitate contributions from hearers, e.g. one friend to another, *you've bought a new house, haven't you*?, while others more aggressively force replies or challenge the hearer, e.g. police officer to a teenager caught shoplifting, *you're not ever going to do that again, are you*?

Much of language is ambiguous and depends on context for its interpretation, a factor far more important than gender. On closer examination, there are few, if any, context-independent gender differences in language. The same words can take on different meanings and significance depending on who uses them in a particular context. Imagine the words 'How about meeting for a drink later, honey?' said by a male customer to a waitress he does not know or said by a woman to her husband as they talk over their schedules for the day. Such examples suggest that we need to seek our explanations for gender differences in terms of the communicative functions expressed by certain forms used in particular contexts by specific speakers. They also point to the complexity involved in reforming sexist language. We cannot simply propose to ban words like *sweetie* or *honey* from public communication because they can be construed as offensive in some contexts.

This shows that the way in which research questions are formed has a bearing on the findings, as I pointed out in Chapter 2. If men's speech is taken to be the yardstick for comparison, then women's speech becomes secondary or a deviation which has to be explained. Similarly, because monolingualism has been taken as a societal norm, bilingualism is seen as problematic and in need of explanation, if not remediation and intervention (see Chapter 7). A new cottage industry of assertiveness training courses aimed at teaching women to express their needs and wants directly is based on the 'women as problem' view of gender differences, and the assumption that it is women who do not fit into the public sphere and therefore have to change.

If men's greater success in business lies not in the way they act and speak, but is due instead to their gender and society's endorsement of male behavior as 'normal', then the advice being given to women is self-defeating. The cosmetic nature of such makeovers offered in elocution and other forms of self-improvement is evidence of their futility. Women are still women at the end of it. Quite often women who make extreme attempts to accommodate to male norms are then made fun of or criticized for trying to be one of the boys. When politician Geraldine Ferraro tried to talk in the way accepted by men, it prompted then First Lady Barbara Bush to refer to her as 'the word that rhymes with rich'.

Those in a position of authority define the world from their perspective and so it is not surprising that academic disciplines are not only male centric but Eurocentric too since European males have defined the world's civilization in their own terms. Because modern linguistic theory is essentially a product of nineteenth-century European scholarship, some notions basic to linguistic analysis such as the arbitrariness of the linguistic sign and theories of markedness are also embedded in this master narrative of masculinist science.

Women occupy what might be called a problematic or negative semantic space. They are seen as derivative of men, or inferior versions of men. In practically all fields of research, it is women's differences from men and masculine norms which are seen as standing in need of some explanation. Because women (and other minority groups in society) are devalued, so is their language. But how much of what is believed to be characteristic of women's speech actually is? Some of the features thought to be part of 'women's language' can be found in use by males when those males are in a subordinate position. Thus, maybe women's language is really the 'language of powerlessness'? Women typically use the speech style they do because they are in less powerful positions in relation to men. Nevertheless, many feminists now argue that languages such as English have been literally 'man-made' and are still primarily under male control. In their view, only radical reforms can create a situation in which women are not obliged to use a language which forces them to express themselves only as deficient males rather than in their own terms. Thus, women's liberation requires a linguistic liberation. The question of language and gender seen from a feminist perspective must address not only the question of how women speak, but also, how women are spoken about. In this chapter I will look at some of the research findings related to these issues in more detail.

Sex and gender

I have called this chapter 'language and gender' rather than 'language and sex' to draw attention to the fact that what concerns me here is the socio-cultural dimension of the division of humans into male and female persons (i.e. gender), rather than its biological determinants (i.e. sex). While the distinction between sex and gender is well established in usage, it presupposes that we can distinguish between innate and environmental differences, and that is far from the case at present. Again, part of the problem is that even in biology, society's views about the cultural position of women dictate that men should be regarded as genetically superior to women. The innatist position is summed up very well by John Stuart Mill when he wrote: 'What it is to be a boy, to grow in the belief that without any merit or exertion of his own, by the mere fact of being born a male he is by right the superior of all of an entire half of the human race.'

Much of the early research on female/male differences was undertaken primarily to try to validate this assumption. Women stand to lose much from such research because it tried to prove scientifically that certain characteristics such as a societal division of labor which confined women to their roles as housewives were 'natural', i.e. biologically based, and therefore, inevitable and beyond questioning. For instance, the size and volume of women's brains were measured and when they were found to be smaller than men's, this was taken as a sign of genetic inferiority (see also Chapter 7). As late as 1873, it was argued that higher education for women would shrivel their reproductive organs and make them sterile. Even in the early part of this century it was suggested that allowing schoolgirls to play hockey would impair their ability to breastfeed in later life. Thus, men have used the observed differences between the sexes to justify their dominance and priority in the human scheme of things.

From a biological point of view, however, the development of the fertilized egg is basically female. For the first seven weeks of the life of a fetus internal and external genitalia look the same. Biological maleness is brought about when the embryonic gonads, glands which later become either male testes or female ovaries, start to produce the male hormone testosterone. This causes the genitals to assume male form and later is responsible for the appearance of secondary sexual characteristics. Whether the gonads become ovaries or testes is determined by the chromosomes received from the parents at the time of conception. All female eggs contain one of the sex chromosomes, X. Male sperm may be either X-chromosome (female) or Y-chromosome bearing (male). Some have, in fact, described the Y chromosome as an incomplete X. It is one of the smallest chromosomes and seems to carry no information other than maleness.

Many feminists have concluded from evidence such as this that the basic human form is female and that maleness represents an addition to this basically female groundplan. Of course, all this flies in the face of received wisdom handed down culturally, which suggests women are derivative of men, such as the biblical account of God's creation of the two sexes, in which Adam is made first and Eve is formed later by God's taking of a rib from Adam. Interestingly, this idea that women are appendages to men finds a counterpart in many languages such as English, where many feminine occupational terms are formally derived from the male version, e.g. *manager/manageress*, and many women's names are diminutives of men's, e.g. *Henrietta*, *Georgette*, *Pauline*, etc. Significantly, God also gave Adam the right and power to name and domesticate the animals. Who names, has power, as I will argue when I talk about naming practices. These are but a few of the linguistic ways in which women are constructed as Other.

The biological evidence for female basicness and superiority can also be strengthened by the fact that there are some species such as the whiptail lizard in the south-western United States which have only females. There are no all male species. In a few species the males are eaten after they have fulfilled their role in reproduction. If we were to apply the logic often used by men that culture simply mirrors the natural state of affairs between the sexes, then really it is surprising that we refer to 'mankind' instead of 'womankind' and that it is women who are labelled as *manageresses*, *poetesses*, etc. But naming practices are social practices and symbolic of an order in which men come first, as can be seen in the conventions followed in expressions going back to *Adam and Eve*, such as *man and woman (wife)*, *husband and wife*, *boys and girls* (a notable exception being *ladies and gentlemen*). Women are the second sex.

Some evidence of how much is learned through socialization as a male or female child rather than part of genetic inheritance can be obtained from cases such as the one in which one of a pair of identical male twins was raised as a female. At the age of 7 months the twins were circumcised by electrocautery and the penis of one of the boys was burned off by an overly powerful current. A consultant plastic surgeon recommended raising 'him' as a girl. When the child was 17 months old they changed 'his' name, clothing, and hairstyle and four months later 'he' underwent surgery to reconstruct 'his' genitals as female. When the twins were 4 years old, the mother remarked of the girl that she was amazed by how feminine she was. She said, 'I've never seen a little girl so neat and tidy as she can be . . . She is very proud of herself, when she puts on a new dress, or I set her hair. She just loves to have her hair set; she could sit under the drier all day long.' Thus, in the words of one feminist, 'One is not born, but rather becomes, a woman.' I will have more to say later about how girls learn to talk like ladies.

Another area where biology and culture interact in a complex way can be seen in features of speech such as pitch. On average, men have lower-pitched speaking voices than women. This difference is at least partly anatomical. Men have larger larynxes and their longer and thicker vocal cords vibrate at lower fundamental frequencies. Fundamental frequency is the main (though not the only) determinant of perceived pitch. It has also been observed that women use a wider pitch range than men. This is what gives rise to the stereotype that women are more excitable and emotional than men.

However, male–female differences in pitch cannot be fully accounted for without reference to social factors. Adult Polish men, for instance, have higher-pitched voices than American men. Speakers can also be taught to use pitch levels which are not appropriate to the size and shape of their larynx. A well-known case is Margaret Thatcher, whose female voice was considered a liability to the public image of her the media wanted to project. In fact, one source noted that 'the selling' of Margaret Thatcher as a politician had been set back years by the mass broadcasting of Prime Minister's question time since she had to be at her 'shrillest' to be heard over the din. She undertook training both to lower her average pitch and reduce her pitch range and was advised to try to maintain a steady pitch to carry her voice through rather than over the noise.

All speakers raise their pitch somewhat in public speaking to make themselves heard, but because most women's voices are already higher pitched than those of men, they have less leeway to raise their pitch before listeners start to perceive them as shrill and emotional. Women have been typically excluded from media positions as announcers and broadcasters because it was thought that their voices lacked authority. Women were therefore seen as unsuitable for conveying information about serious topics such as the news. Apparently, it is still difficult to convince the BBC to let women produce commentaries or voice-overs.

Significant differences between male and female pitch do not appear to emerge until puberty, but it has also been shown that the voices of adult deaf males who have never heard speech do not 'break' at puberty. All these things indicate that pitch is at least partly a matter of cultural convention. There may be a biological element to it too. Over time, human as well as animal males have developed low-pitched voices to sound dominant and aggressive, probably in order to compete with one another for access to female mating partners. When animals fight, the larger and more aggressive one wins. It was thus advantageous from an evolutionary point of view for males to try to alter their pitch to signal large body size.

Man-made language?

If you accept my arguments in Chapter 1 that what we call society, or even more grandly 'reality' itself, is largely constructed through language, and the feminist argument that language is 'man-made', then our history, philosophy, government, laws, and religion are products of a male way of perceiving and organizing the world. Because this knowledge has been transmitted for centuries, it appears 'natural', 'objective', a 'master' discourse beyond question. In this man-made world view women are seen as deviant and deficient. Language thus holds the key to challenging and changing male hegemony.

Sexism in language can be demonstrated with many different kinds of evidence. Words for women have negative connotations, even where the corresponding male terms designate the same state or condition for men. Thus, *spinster* and *bachelor* both designate unmarried adults, but the female term has negative overtones to it. Such a distinction reflects the importance of society's expectations about marriage, and, more importantly, about marriageable age. A spinster is more than a female bachelor: she is beyond the expected marrying age and therefore seen as rejected and undesirable. Like the old grey mare in the song, 'she ain't what she used to be'. She is an 'old maid', an image popularized in a children's card game which carries that very name. No one wants to be stuck holding the card with the picture of the old maid.

These cultural stereotypes about old maids being losers in card games and the marriage market also affect the term *maiden*, as in *maiden aunt* or *maiden lady*, and notably even expressions such as *maiden horse* to refer to a horse that has not won a race. The *Oxford English Dictionary*'s entry on figurative uses of the term *maiden* defines them as sharing the meaning of 'yielding no results'. Woman who have not caught a man have lost the race. Other figurative uses such as *maiden voyage*, *maiden speech*, *maiden flight*, etc. referring to the first occasion or event of a kind relate to the stereotype that women should be virginal, inexperienced, intact, untried, and fresh in worldly as well as sexual matters. Containers of olive oil claiming to be 'virgin', i.e. from the first pressing of the fruit and therefore of the highest quality, often show young maidens.

Although some have speculated that the word *spinster* may be dying out, women such as Mary Daly have been trying to revive it in its original meaning of a woman engaged in spinning. Because these women spinners were often unmarried, this connotation eventually ousted the original meaning and became the primary sense of the word. In the seventeenth century the term *spinster* became the legal designation of an unmarried woman. While there are no instances of the word in the Brown Corpus of American English (the first computerized collection of texts compiled in the 1960s), it appears to be still in common use in British English, as can be seen in the British National Corpus (released in 1995), where I found 156 instances in a sample of 100 million words of text. By comparison, the word *bachelor* occurs 479 times, indicating the general tendency I will discuss later, whereby men and their activities are

FIG 4.1 Old maids and old butlers

more talked about than women and theirs. Interestingly, the term *bachelor girl* (presumably a young spinster?) occurred three times.

If anyone has any doubt about the negative connotations of *spinster*, all they need to do is look at the range of words with which it is used, or what linguists call its 'collocations'. Although there are some neutral descriptive adjectives used with the word, such as *66 year old*, *disabled*, or *American*, the majority of words collocating with *spinster* are negative. They include the following: *gossipy*, *nervy*, *over-made up*, *ineffective*, *jealous*, *eccentric*, *love-/sex-starved*, *frustrated*, *whey-faced*, *dried-up old*, *repressed*, *lonely*, *prim*, *cold-hearted*, *plain Jane*, *atrocious*, and *despised*. By comparison, the collocations of *bachelor* are largely descriptive or positive, with the exception of one occurrence of *bachelor wimp*!

This example shows how the meanings of words are constructed and maintained by patterns of collocation. Collocations transmit cultural meanings and stereotypes which have built up over time. If the problem lies not with words themselves, but how they are used, this poses considerable problems for reform which targets the elimination of sexist language. Seemingly gender-neutral terms such as *aggressive* and *professional* have different connotations when applied to men and women. To call a man a professional is a compliment, but to be a woman and a professional is perhaps to be a prostitute, in English as well in other languages as diverse as Japanese and French, where *une professionelle* is a euphemism for prostitute.

This sort of bias in the connotations of words for women is far-reaching and applies even to our associations of the basic terms *man* v. *woman*, *boy*, and *girl*. No insult is implied if you call a woman an 'old man' (if indeed this makes any sense), but to call a man an 'old woman' is a decided insult. Again, it is revealing to look at some of the collocations of these basic terms. Not surprisingly, words with negative overtones are still more frequently used together with *girl/woman* than with *man/boy*. The figures in Table 4.1 indicate the number of times words such as *silly* or *hysterical* are found together with the basic terms *man*, *woman*, *boy*, and *girl* in a sample of 3 million words of text.

Men are more likely to be referred to with positive adjectives such as *honest* and *intelligent*, while only women are described as *silly* and *hysterical*. Negative terms such as *frigid*, *neurotic*, *loose* relating to sexuality occur predominantly with the female terms, as do terms such as *blond(e)* and *ugly* describing appearance.

Where similar terms exist such as *mother* or *father*, their collocations create worlds of different meanings. To say that a woman *mothered* her children is to draw attention to her nurturing role, but to say that a man *fathered* a child is to refer only to his biological role in conception. The notion of mothering can be applied to other people, and children other than one's own, whereas fathering cannot. More recently, the term *surrogate mother* has been used to refer to a

Table 4.1 Collocations with *man/woman* and *boy/girl* in the British National Corpus

	Woman	Girl	Man	Boy
Blonde	25	28	1	1
Frigid	2	0	0	0
Honest	11	2	68	1
Hysterical	14	1	0	0
Intelligent	17	9	44	3
Loose	3	2	1	1
Neurotic	2	2	2	0
Silly	16	35	0	10
Ugly	6	4	0	0

woman in her biological role as mother. As I was writing this book, such a surrogate mother was the first woman to give birth to her own grandchildren. Now there are many kinds of mothers, e.g. *biological mother*, *surrogate mother*, *unwed mother*, *single mother*, *birth mother*, *working mother*, and even *natural mother*. The fact that these notions vary from our cultural stereotype of housewife-mother is signalled linguistically by the use of special terms to refer to them. We make inferences from such terms and use them in our thinking about men and women. There is no term *working father* because it is redundant.

The Virginia Supreme Court in 1995 ruled that Sharon Bottoms was an 'unfit parent' because she was a 'lesbian mother'. She had to surrender custody of her 5-year-old son to her mother. We generally only single out for special emphasis or marking things which are unusual or unexpected such as the *working mother*. There is a women's magazine carrying the title *Working Mother*, but not surprisingly no new men's magazine called *House Husband* or *Working Father*.

The paradox of housework not counting as 'real' work and the myth of the 'happy housewife' are at the heart of what Betty Friedan, founder of the National Organization for Women (NOW), called 'the problem that has no name'. Because housework doesn't count, it is possible to say that a woman at home doesn't 'work'. She is included among the 'unemployed', a 'dependant' for tax purposes, although everyone else in the household is in fact dependent on her. 'She's just a housewife' is a familiar refrain, despite the fact that many housewives with children work ninety-hour weeks. In 1979 a newspaper article about men who were full-time 'homemakers' was headed 'The Non-Workers', further reinforcing the misconception that work done at home is not 'real' work. A 'working mother' does her 'work' outside the home. Here we see a double bias against women; a woman who works is marked as deviant with a special name, as is a mother who works.

We do not normally talk of *single* or *unwed/unmarried fathers*, for example, because there is no stigma attached to this status for men. The British National Corpus, for instance, contains 153 instances of the phrase *single mother* and only 2 instances of *single father*. There are 68 occurrences of *unmarried mother* (plus 2 of *unwed mother*), but only 6 of *unmarried father* (and none of *unwed father*). We can also compare 59 occurrences of *teenage mother* with only 2 of *teenage father*. Similarly, there are 81 cases of *working mother* and none of *working father*. New gender-neutral terms such as *caretaker/giver*, *parenting*, are more recently being used to try to avoid the stereotypical association of women with child care. Yet even the magazine called *Parenting* which claims to address contemporary parents displays mothers almost exclusively.

Because the word *woman* does not share equal status with *man*, terms referring to women have undergone pejoration. If we examine pairs of gender-marked terms such as *lord/lady*, *baronet/dame*, *Sir/Madam*, *master/mistress*, *king/queen*, *wizard(warlock)/witch*, we can see how the female terms may start out on an equal footing, but they become devalued over time. *Lord*, for instance, preserves its original meaning, while *lady* is no longer used exclusively for women of high rank. *Baronet* still retains its original meaning, but *dame* is used derogatorily, especially in American usage. *Sir* is still used as a title and a form of respect, while a *Madame* is one who runs a brothel. Likewise, *master* has not lost its original meaning, but *mistress* has come to have sexual connotations and no longer refers to the woman who had control over a household. There is a considerable discrepancy between referring to someone as an *old master* as opposed to an *old mistress*.

Mary Gauerke
5-5
"Are you the house person who advertised for a cleaning person?"

FIG 4.2 House persons and cleaning persons

Due to differences in social structure between the USA and Britain, terms like *dame*, *lady*, and *mistress* have somewhat different connotations in the two countries. The use of terms *mistress* and *master* as titles in the British educational system made Geoffrey Warnock's (former Vice-Chancellor of Oxford University) remark so witty (at least by male standards) when his wife, a philosopher who held the title Dame of the British Empire, became head of Girton College, Cambridge: "Once I was married to a Dame; now I have a Mistress." The remark sounds much less witty to American women.

Both *hussy* and *housewife* have their origin in Old English *huswif*, but *hussy* has undergone semantic derogation. *King* has also kept its meaning, while *queen* has developed sexual connotations. *Wizard* has actually undergone semantic amelioration, or upgrading; to call a man a wizard is a compliment, but not so for the woman who is branded (or in medieval times burned) as a witch.

Words like *biddy* and *tart* have changed dramatically since they were first used as terms of endearment. *Tart* meant a small pie or pastry and was later extended to express affection. Then it was used to refer to a woman who was sexually desirable and to a woman of the street. In general, it seems that English and other languages have many more terms to refer to a sexually promiscuous female than to a sexually promiscuous male. According to one count, there are 220 words for such women, but only 20 for men. Some of the more common derogatory terms applied to men such as *bastard* and *son of a bitch* actually degrade women in their role as mothers. Because it is men who make the dictionaries and define meanings, they persistently reserve the positive semantic space for themselves and relegate women to a negative one.

The prevailing world view that everyone is male unless otherwise designated is manifested in various ways in language as well as in models of linguistic analysis. Some analyses assume maleness is the more basic semantic category and that females are therefore to be described as [-male]. Thus, if we were to break down nouns such as *man* and *woman*, *boy* and *girl* into their semantic primitives, we would analyse them as shown in Table 4.2.

Table 4.2 Semantic feature analysis of *man*, *woman*, *boy*, and *girl*

Man	Woman	Boy	Girl
[+animate] [+human] [+adult] [+male]	[+animate] [+human] [+adult] [-male]	[+animate] [+human] [-adult] [+male]	[+animate] [+human] [-adult] [-male]

All the terms share the feature of [animacy] which distinguishes them from inanimate objects such as tables and chairs, and the words *boy* and *girl* are distinguished from *man* and *woman* in terms of sex as well as age. We also need the feature [human] to distinguish between human beings and other animate beings such as cats and dogs which would be marked for [-human]. Again, we see a bias expressed in the distinction [-human] and [-adult], which suggests that the adult human life form or state is more basic, and that children are in a sense regarded as deficient adults, while animals are not on a par with humans. One could of course argue precisely the opposite from a biological point of view since all adults were once children, and, pushing the argument further, humans are evolutionarily later life forms than animals. While such a feature analysis may seem elegant since it captures a number of semantic contrasts with a minimum of binary features, it is sexist and one can easily see that the cards are stacked against women, who have one negative feature, and little girls, who have two strikes against them. Is it surprising that grown women have objected to being called 'girls'?

However, if the feature [adult] adequately distinguished the meanings of *girl* and *woman*, we ought to find a logical contradiction in this next sentence: 'Practically no adults were using it [a reformed number system in Norway SR], including the girls in the telephone exchange, and schoolchildren appeared to drop it when they became adults.' Here the author's use of *including* makes it clear that 'the girls at the telephone exchange' are adult females, who are contrasted with 'schoolchildren', who are not adults.

As another linguist put the problem more bluntly: 'a female never grows up.' His remark was prompted by an examination of job ads in the *Los Angeles Times* in the 1980s: ninety-seven used the term *gal* or *girl*, while only two used *boy*. Neither education nor social status spares a woman from being called a girl. In a 1989 letter to the *Sunday Gleaner* newspaper in Jamaica, eminent jurist Morris Cargill referred to Dr Carolyn Cooper, an academic at the University of the West Indies, as a "very clever girl". This dismissive and patronizing remark served to underline the negative force of his attack on her for having criticized an earlier letter he wrote to the newspaper. What do girls know about anything, even if they have Ph.D.s?

It is not hard to see why women have been especially sensitive to gender differences in naming practices and forms of address since these are a particularly telling indicator of a person's social status. To answer Shakespeare's question of 'what's in a name?', we could reply, a person's social place. To be referred to as 'the Mrs' or 'the little woman' indicates the inferior status to which men have allocated women. For many men in particular, feminism has been equated with what is perceived as a pointless and at times amusing or irksome insistence on the replacement of titles such as *Mrs* and *Miss* with *Ms* and other gender-marked terms such as *busboy* with *busperson*. Many articles and cartoons such as the one in Fig. 4.3 appear in the press about this, and most have a jocular tone to them, suggesting that somehow the proposed gender-neutral terms are ridiculous and preposterous. One press item, for instance, had the title 'Death of a salesperson', another from New Zealand 'Gone like the melting snowperson' and still others created terms such as *one upspersonship*. One male humorist suggested *Mush* (abbreviated *Mh*) as a title for unmarried men.

When I first began teaching in Britain, I was puzzled by the fact that males and females were indicated on student lists by using the initials and last names for the men, while women had the title *Miss* (or *Mrs*) added to their names. When I asked a colleague why this was the case, he replied that it was done so that we would know which students were male and female. He had no answer to my next question, which was why on a class list it was even necessary to know, or why the women were singled out to have titles indicating their marital status. That was simply the way it had always been done, and it had never occurred to him that we should abandon this as a sexist practice.

This system of marking the females is still used at all levels of society. At the time I was appointed to my chair at Oxford, there were only 3 women holding

"I love being a partner Mr. Jenkins!
There's just one problem."

FIG 4.3 Why women don't want to be called by their first names

the rank of full professor out of a total of more than 200 professors. (There are not many more women in such positions now!) In the diaries printed for academic staff, and various other official lists of the University and the different colleges, the names of men are still given in this way or with a title, followed by a list of degrees and where they were obtained, so that, for instance, a man named John Smith who is professor of modern history would be listed as J. Smith, MA, Ph.D. (Edinburgh), Professor of Modern History. I and my women colleagues are given a title, either *Miss* or *Mrs*, rather than simply 'Professor' before our names. The term *Ms* is still not as widely used in Britain as it is in the United States (where since 1973 it has been sanctioned as an optional title), as can be seen in sporting events such as the Wimbledon tennis matches, where women players are referred to as *Miss/Mrs*, but men are referred to with last name only. The men are also just 'men', but the women are always 'ladies'.

Many feminists have pointed out that it is difficult even to trace the history of women because the history of most countries, as Virginia Woolf said in talking about England, is 'the history of the male line'. The opening of the Gospel according to St Matthew gives an impressive list of thirty males successively begetting one another from the Patriarch Abraham down to Christ. Only once is a woman mentioned, not because she plays the role of begetter, but because she is a non-Jewish Moabite. Men are seen as the creative force. Fathers pass their names on to both male and female children, and when women marry they have traditionally taken the names of their husbands, abandoning their 'maiden names', and becoming, as Una Stannard put it, 'Mrs Man'. In Greece, a married woman takes the possessive form of her husband's name, indicating that she belongs to him. In Arabic a married woman is usually not referred to by name, but by the title 'wife of X'. In China adult women may have no proper names but only names which refer to them in some role, e.g. 'third daughter', 'little sister'. *The Book of Common Prayer* pronounces a man and a woman 'man and wife'. His status as a person remains the same, while she exchanges her person for a role. Even though some churches have changed this line in the marriage service to read 'husband and wife', they have often retained the traditional order of male before female.

Only men have a right to the permanency of their names. Traditional Scandinavian naming practices call attention to the importance of the male heir line since both the female and male children in a family would carry names such as *Johansson*, literally 'Johann's son', and even in Iceland, where names such as *Johannsdottir* 'Johann's daughter' were used, the female child is still seen as a possession of the father. A common practice among some feminists has been to replace the father's last name with the name of a female friend or relative, or to drop the father's name. In this way, Julia Stanley became Julia Penelope. Similar motivations are behind the change in designations witnessed among newly independent countries such as Vanuatu (formerly the New Hebrides) and Zimbabwe (formerly Rhodesia), and the practice among certain black Muslims to take new names. In his autobiography Malcolm X makes the point that the names of blacks were appropriated by their white masters. In changing their names, women and other minorities are asserting their right to be called by a name of their own choosing rather than one given by an oppressor.

Nothing is more personal or as closely related to our identity as our names. A rose by any other name does not smell as sweet. This is why one of the struggles in the women's movement has centered on the legal right to name or rename ourselves. The issue was prominent at the 1848 convention on women's rights when women signed the Declaration of Sentiments with their own first names. When Lucy Stone tried to vote in 1879 in Massachusetts using her birth name, she was prevented from doing so, even though there was no law requiring wives to use their husbands' names. Stone proclaimed, 'My name is a symbol of my identity which must not be lost.'

Non-reciprocity of address to women is a feature of many societies. Javanese women use more deferential speech levels to their husbands than they receive in return. I mentioned in Chapter 1 that there were four different Japanese pronouns for 'I'. When used by women, the terms represent a lesser degree of deference than when used by men. Traditionally, only men used the terms *boku* and *ore* to refer to themselves, although now some feminists have begun to use *boke*. To take some examples from western societies, women teachers in some schools in Italy tended to be addressed as *signora* 'Mrs' or *signorina* 'Miss', but men received a title plus their last name. Some women did not regard this as unfair since they thought of *signora* as a term of respect and valued their role as women more than the role of professional. In one school, the headmaster announced a policy specifying that he would address the women by *signora* or *signorina* plus last name and the men by their first name. The male teachers could also address him by first name, but women were expected to call him *headmaster* or *Mr Headmaster*. Women in many non-English-speaking countries have proposed titles similar to *Ms*, such as the Danish *Fr*, to replace *Fru* 'Mrs' and *Fröken* 'Miss', and the French *Mad.* to replace *Madame* 'Mrs' and *Mademoiselle* 'Miss'.

Women are also more likely than men to be addressed by their first names. Women often protest that male doctors call them by their first names even on the first consultation. Men, however, are more likely to be addressed by a title plus last name. It would, however, break the rules of address if women were to call their doctors by their first names. Patients are subordinate to doctors, but it seems that female patients are even more so. Doctors interrupt female patients and female doctors are interrupted more by male patients than male doctors, which suggests that to be a woman is to be a subordinate, no matter what professional level she attains. Some feminists recommend that women should begin using their male doctors' first names to draw attention to sexist practices.

The use of reciprocal first names in English-speaking countries and many other places too is indicative of intimacy and familiarity, while non-reciprocal use is indicative of unequal power (see Chapter 5). Again, it is not the linguistic forms themselves which discriminate, but the way in which they are used in particular contexts to particular persons. If I call a student by her first name but expect and insist on being called *Professor* in return, it is the asymmetry itself, not the particular forms of address, which can be considered discriminatory.

Another example of the marking of women can be seen in the use of titles such as *lady/woman/female doctor*. It is assumed that a doctor is a man, so a woman who is a doctor must somehow be marked as such, which conveys the idea that she is not the 'real' thing. In the British National Corpus, for instance, I found the following usages: *lady doctor* (125 times), *woman doctor* (20 times), *female doctor* (10 times), compared to *male doctor* (14 times). There were no occurrences of *gentleman doctor* and only one case of *man doctor*. Conversely, we have terms such as *male nurse*, where the male has to be marked because the norm is assumed to be female. The British National Corpus has 20 instances of *male nurse* and only one of *female nurse*.

Consider also the *career woman* (or even *career girl*, as I heard Sarah Ferguson, the Duchess of York, referred to on the BBC news in 1992), but not the *career man*. Men by definition have careers, but women who do so must be marked as deviant. A man can also be a *family man*, but it would be odd to call a woman a *family woman*. Women are by definition family women. We can check my intuitions against the British National Corpus, where the expression *family man* occurs 94 times, and the corresponding *family woman* only 4 times. Similarly, *career woman* occurs 48 times, *career girl* 10 times, and *career lady* once, but *career man* only 6 times, and *career boy* or *career gentleman* not at all. Expressions such as *career woman/lady/girl* count as two strikes against women. On the one hand, they suggest that as women, females can't be real professionals, while on the other, they suggest that as professionals, females can't be real women, unless of course, they are prostitutes! Not surprisingly, the term *business girl* used to be a slang term for a prostitute.

In my college at Oxford, which was formerly all male, I am often referred to as the college's 'lady professor'. Even after I became the college's first woman fellow, it was common for speakers at college meetings to begin their remarks by saying, 'Gentlemen', and I routinely received announcements about events such as the annual fellows' wives dinner (since abolished!) asking me to indicate if I would be bringing my wife. I cannot count how many times when I was present among the still primarily male gatherings at my college it was assumed I was either someone's wife or a junior research fellow. Not surprisingly, a lady fellow who is also a professor is marked by her presence in a context where all fellows are assumed literally to be fellows.

The use of *lady* as a polite euphemism for *woman* is far more common in Britain than in the USA, and American feminists have been rather more insistent on its replacement. The term *lady* is not simply the polite equivalent of *gentleman*, as men like to claim when women protest at being called ladies. We can see this from the fact that *lady* is used in circumstances where *gentleman* would not be. We say, for example, *cleaning lady* but not **garbage-gentleman*. When a woman becomes president of the USA, it will be interesting to see how her husband is referred to. I predict that he will not be called the *first gentleman*!

The expression *lady of the house* is not matched by *gentleman of the house*, but contrasts instead with *man of the world*, another indication of the linguistic mapping of the division between the public and private spheres onto male and female, respectively. Indeed, the French equivalent of 'woman of the world' (*femme du monde*) carries the meaning of 'prostitute'! Looking at the British National Corpus, for instance, we find 25 cases of *lady of the house*, 3 of *woman of the house*, none of *gentleman of the house*, and only 8 of *man of the house*. By contrast, there are 29 occurrences of *man of the world*, but only 12 of *woman of the world*.

In a 1982 speech about the economy President Ronald Reagan blamed the recession on the increase in women in the workforce: 'It is the great increase of the people going into the job market, and — ladies, I'm not picking on anyone but . . . because of the increase in women who are working today.' By pointing the finger at 'ladies', while disclaiming that he was 'picking on anyone', he drew attention away from his own economic policies. His use of the term *lady* is a double whammy here. It is polite, in keeping with his claim that he's not 'picking on anyone', but it's also intended to suggest that ladies should be ladies of the house and have no place in the workforce. Ladies don't work (unless of course they are doing housework, which is not 'real' work). Thus, there are no working ladies, only working women.

I explained in the last chapter how in Victorian England the term *lady* came to refer to middle-class females and *women* to females of the working class. Female students at Owens College in Manchester, for instance, were divided between 'ladies' (taking a single course, presumably for pleasure only since ladies would not need to do real work) and 'women' who were registered for examinations, which they needed for career purposes. This suggests at least one reason for the finding that there are no *ladies of the world*, but only *women of the world*, and conversely that the woman who stays at home is overwhelmingly referred to as the *lady of the house* rather than the *woman of the house*.

Language has helped to gender the way we think about space; men's space is public, in the workplace, while women's place is private and in the home. This difference is encoded discursively in expressions such as *working mother*, *businessman*, *housewife*, making it easier to accept as 'natural' the exclusion of women from public life. In Japanese these views are embodied in the terms used by husbands and wives to refer to one another. A married woman is called *Okusan* 'Mrs Interior', signifying that her place is in the home. Japanese men call their wives *kanai* 'house insider'. Women speak of their husbands as *shujin* or *danna* or the more informal *teishu* which means 'master of an inn or tea house'. These terms of address reflect the traditional wisdom embodied in the English proverbs *A man's home is his castle*, and *A woman's place is in the home*. Traditional norms dictate that the husband is breadwinner, while the wife is the bread baker. This is reflected historically in the Old English words *hla:fweard* 'loaf-keeper' and *hlæfdige* 'loafkneader', which became modern English 'lord' and 'lady', respectively.

Other examples which show the markedness of females in relation to males can be found in the many cases where female terms are formed from the male terms by adding endings such as - *ess*, e.g. *actor/actress*, *major/majorette*. We can compare other terms such as *salesman/saleswoman/saleslady*, and *salesgirl* (though not *salesboy*). This is found in other languages too such as German, where *der Student* 'the student' is male and *die Studentin* 'the student' is female. We can see in this example a significant difference between English and many other languages. English does not require the use of gender-differentiated forms of the definite article and other similar words. Other European languages have two or three so-called 'genders', masculine, feminine, and neuter. All nouns, not just those referring to males and females, must be either masculine or feminine and the articles, adjectives, or other modifiers that go with them must be marked accordingly, as in French *la semaine dernière* 'the past week' (feminine) v. *le bureau nouveau* 'the new office' (masculine). Women use forms such as *je suis contente* 'I am happy' and *je suis allée* 'I went', while men say *je suis content* and *je suis allé*.

In these languages, however, gender is a grammatical category similar to the four-way classification system for Dyirbal nouns which I discussed in Chapter 1. The fact that a noun is feminine, for instance, is no guarantee that the entities it refers to are feminine. A noun that is classified as feminine in one language might be masculine in another. For instance, French *la voiture* 'car' is feminine while German *der Wagen* is masculine. English, on the other hand, is a language which is said to have 'natural' gender; items which are referred to as 'she' are in fact (with a few exceptions to be noted below) feminine in the real world.

The contrast is humorously illustrated in this extract from one of Mark Twain's stories, where he confuses natural and grammatical gender in his suggestion that 'a young lady has no sex, while a turnip has' because the word for young woman is *das Mädchen*, or neuter in gender.

Gretchen: Wilhelm, where is the turnip?
Wilhelm: She has gone to the kitchen.
Gretchen: Where is the accomplished and beautiful English maiden?
Wilhelm: It has gone to the opera.

The traditional distinction between 'natural' v. 'grammatical' gender, however, is fraught with problems since there is 'leakage' from society even into languages with so-called grammatical gender. While German speakers do not, of course, conceive of a tree as male, its leaves as sexless, and its buds as female simply because the corresponding words belong to the masculine, neuter, and feminine gender categories respectively (cf. *der Baum* 'the tree', *das Blatt* 'the leaf', *die Blume* 'the flower'), nevertheless, insulting terms for males often take the feminine article, e.g. *die Memme* 'male coward', *die Tunte* 'gay male' (but *der Zahn* 'sexually desirable young girl'). In English, which is supposed to be a language with 'natural' gender, ships, boats, cars, and, until recently, hurricanes are referred to as 'she'. Such usages reflect the male point of view which dictates that effeminate men are not masculine and that cars, boats, like women, are generally owned and controlled by men, while hurricanes are destructive and irrational forces, akin to Dyirbal's fire and dangerous things.

As I pointed out in Chapter 1, we must be careful not to make simplistic equations between categories of the mind and categories of grammar. I showed how the Dyirbal classification drew on perceived as well as culturally derived similarities and associations which resulted in a grouping of women, fire, and dangerous things into one category. Fire belongs to this category since it is associated with the sun, and recall that the sun is a member by virtue of a Dyirbal myth in which the sun is the wife of the moon. But can we conclude that Dyirbal speakers are induced by this linguistic schema to see a motivation behind these associations? Actually, there is some evidence to support this because one male speaker consciously linked fire and danger to women in saying, 'Buni [fire] is a lady. Ban buni [class II fire]. You never say bayi buni [class I fire]. It's a lady. Woman is a destroyer. 'e destroys anything. A woman is a fire.' However, this requires further systematic testing, which is problematic since Dyirbal is a dying language and the classification system has been dramatically simplified or is no longer used by younger speakers.

Now we can ask what some of the consequences are of the linguistic fact that certain male terms include females. Where gender-differentiated pairs of words exist, such as *dog* and *bitch*, the male term can be taken to include the female. This has been applied to pronouns too. Grammarians tell us that the male pronouns and certain other terms such as *mankind*, *manpower*, *man-made*, and, of course, even *man*, as in *prehistoric man*, encompass women. Feminists argue that if such terms were truly generic, we would not find sentences such as this one odd: *Man, being a mammal, breastfeeds his young*. French feminists have seized upon the shock value associated with such unexpected usages in their slogan *un homme sur deux est une femme* 'One man out of two is a woman'. Male terms used to include females are called 'androcentric generics'.

Prescriptive grammarians also tell us that *everyone should get his hat* is supposed to refer to both men and women, despite the use of the masculine pronoun *his*. In informal English, of course, the alternative, *everybody should get their hat*, exists even though it has been condemned as non-standard. However, many people have seen it as a more elegant replacement for masculine pronouns than using both *he* and *she*, i.e. *everyone should get his or her coat*. Some feminists have suggested new gender-neutral singular pronouns such as *tey* to replace *she* and *he*, or combining them as *s/he*. But do androcentric generics actually influence the way we conceive of the entities they refer to?

Experiments have shown that women feel excluded when they read texts with generic *he*. When people are asked to make drawings to go with such texts, they tend to draw men. Results such as these show that the structure of language can affect thought processes. They point to the psychological cost many women experience at being non-persons in their own language. Women are at the margins of the category of 'human beings', just as when we think of a prototypical bird, the chicken does not readily come to mind. It is somehow less of a bird than a robin or sparrow. Still, we must exercise caution because there are some Aboriginal Australian languages in which the unmarked gender is female. Unfortunately, we do not have adequate information about the social groups in which these languages are spoken. There are also some languages where a mixed group of people is referred to with a feminine plural pronoun, but in at least one of them, the feminine form is used because the presence of even one woman in a male group is enough to contaminate it and therefore, a marked pronoun must be used! From all these examples we can conclude that grammatical categories may lead us to perceive things in certain ways, so that women are in effect contaminated by their association with fire and dangerous things in Dyirbal, as well as in English, where terms marked as female maybe used to express or create negative views of women. My quotation at the beginning of this chapter drew attention to the way in which our mental imagery associated with God is masculine. After all, God made man in *his* own image!

If the perception of women is culturally derived, then we might expect anthropological research to reveal some interesting cross-cultural differences in the position of men and women. While this is true, it must also be pointed out that for the most part, anthropologists also ignored women until recently. Men were seen as a more legitimate object of study if one wanted to understand a culture. Indeed, until the 1990s one of the most important journals in anthropology still carried the title *Man*! One of the earliest studies which set the tone for much of the discipline and established a working method which is still widely practised today by anthropologists was devoted to an explication of the kula, a trading system organized across great distances in the south-western Pacific whereby bracelets went in one direction, and necklaces in the other. The kula network, a male activity, was seen as fundamental to all aspects of the culture, while women's gathering and trading of brown leaves was not noticed until recently. Now, however, it has been seen to play a crucial role in the community's life-stage rituals, which were run by women.

Nevertheless, there were some intriguing mentions in some of the early anthropological literature of cultures with male and female languages. In Yana, a Native American language, most words have distinct male and female forms. The male forms are used exclusively by males speaking to other males, but the female forms are used not only by females speaking to other females, but also by females speaking to males and males speaking to females.

Learning to talk like a lady

Recently, much less attention has been focused on individual words used by men and women, and more on their conversational styles. We are all familiar with the stereotype that women 'gossip' and 'chatter' while men 'talk shop', but actual research reveals that men talk much more than women across a wide range of contexts, e.g. in husband–wife interaction, TV discussions, meetings. Women are expected to remain silent, so when they do talk, it is noticed and commented upon negatively. The topics that women discuss are different from those of men and typical female topics such as child-rearing and personal relationships are seen as trivial when compared with male topics such as sports, politics. However, these judgments reflect the differing social values we have of men and women which define what men do as more important. A British newspaper carried the headline 'girl talk' to describe a meeting between Margaret Thatcher and Indira Gandhi when the two were prime ministers in their respective countries. One study showed that women did not in fact talk more about topics which were independently rated as trivial by both men and women. Actually, nearly half of all the discussions undertaken by all-male, all-female, and mixed-sex groups were on topics that had been independently judged as trivial.

Studies have revealed quite different patterns of verbal interaction in all-male and all-female groups, which begin in early years when children play in same-sex peer groups. Boys tend to have a larger network than girls, who usually have one or two girlfriends with whom they play regularly. To some extent the size of these groups may be determined by the different types of activities they engage in. It takes only three girls to skip rope or two to play house, while more boys are needed for team sports such as football. Extensive interaction in single-sex peer groups is probably a crucial source of the gender differentiation patterns found by sociolinguists.

Although much less attention has been paid to girls' networks than those of boys, there are observable differences in the way in which language is used in boys' v. girls' play. Girls use language to create and maintain cohesiveness, and their activities are generally cooperative and non-competitive. Differentiation between girls is not made in terms of power. When conflicts arise, the groups breaks up. Bossiness tends not to be tolerated, and girls use forms such as 'let's, we're gonna, we could' to get others to do things instead of appealing to their personal power. When they argue, girls tend to phrase their arguments in terms of group needs rather than in personal terms.

Boys, on the other hand, tend to have more hierarchically organized groups than girls, and status in the hierarchy is paramount. In boys' groups speech is used to assert dominance, to attract and maintain an audience when others have the floor. They issue commands to other boys rather than suggest what should be done. Certain kinds of stylized speech events such as joking and storytelling are valued in boys' groups. A boy has to learn how to get the floor to perform so that he can acquire prestige. Some of the most extensive sociolinguistic work on the verbal skills of male peer groups has been done in black communities in the United States, where there are a number of competitive speech events such as 'sounding' or 'playing the dozens' in which insults (usually about mothers) are exchanged. Some of these are in the form of rhymed couplets and some are more like taunts or challenges, e.g. 'Your mother wears high heeled sneakers to church'. The winner in these contests is the boy with the largest store of sounds and the best delivery. High value is placed on obscene language and swearing.

Some of these differences can be found in the following examples of talk in single-sex peer groups among black working-class children between the ages of 8 and 13. In the first extract the boys are making slingshots from coathangers, and in the second the girls are making rings from old bottle tops.

Michael: Gimme the pliers.
All right. Give me your hanger Tokay.
Huey: Get off my steps.
Get away from here Gitty.
Michael: Get out of here Huey.
Huey: I'm not gettin out of nowhere.

Sharon: Let's go around Subs and Suds.
Pam: We could go around looking for more bottles.

Terry: Maybe we can slice them like that.
Pam: We gotta find some more bottles.

Evidence such as this does not support one of the explanations sometimes given by sociolinguists for gender differentiation; namely, that both boys and girls first learn 'women's language' at home and school since their primary caretakers are mothers and female teachers. Later, usually during adolescence under the influence of peer pressure, the boys shift towards more non-standard speech, while the girls retain their more standard speech. Certainly, there is a lot of evidence that boys talk more in classroom interaction and get more attention from teachers than girls, but this pattern can be found in the home too. Moreover, we have already seen from Chapter 3 that patterns of gender differentiation in language are already present in the early school years. This suggests children receive some exposure to different gender-appropriate norms even before they come to school. Mothers pay more attention to their male infants. Books for both preschool and school-age children typically depict boys and men in more active roles and a greater variety of them. Children's cartoons are also very much male-dominated.

Even 6-year-olds I worked with in Edinburgh were aware of differences between girls' and boys' speech. They said that girls spoke more politely and boys roughly, and that boys used more slang and swear words. There is also some explicit coaching by mothers and schoolteachers (and even neighbors!), who tell children what is polite speech. A case is reported where a woman vividly recalls being corrected as a child for using a local dialect word, *ken* meaning '(you) know': her mother slapped her in the face so hard that she lost a tooth as a result. This is perhaps an extreme example of the pressure young children can be put under to conform to adult ways of speaking. One 10-year-old told me in answer to the question of whether her mother ever told her to speak politely:

Girl: If there's somebody polite in. Like see, some people come in. There's new people in the stair we've moved up to and they come in and I'm always saying 'doon' [the local way of pronouncing *down*] Shep, cause it's my wee dog, so I say 'doon'. My mum says, 'That's not what you say'. She says, 'It's sit down'. Ken, cause she doesn't like me speaking rough.
SR: Why do you think she doesn't like it?
Girl: Well, if I speak rough, she doesn't like it when other people are in because they think that we're rough tatties in the stair.
SR: Does your Mum ever speak polite?
Girl: She doesnae really speak polite, but she corrects all her words.
SR: How about your teachers, do they ever say anything to you about the way you speak?
Girl: I've never actually said 'doon' to the teacher.

It is clear from this passage that this girl knows a lot about the social significance of the options open to her, i.e. using the local Scots form of speech, as opposed to speaking in a more standard-like English. She evaluates these ways of speaking in the same terms that local adults use, namely, speaking local Edinburgh Scots is 'rough', whereas more standard speech is 'polite'. Moreover, she is aware that the way one speaks is an important part of the impression one conveys to others and that others make judgements about social character on the basis of speech. She has also learned that there are at least two contexts for polite speech, i.e. in front of strangers and the teacher in the classroom. She can also identify the local pronunciation 'doon' as an inappropriate one for contexts requiring polite speech. This is the form she would most likely use consistently at home among family members, and, as she says, when addressing her dog. When used in the home and with in-group members, speaking this way is the normal unmarked way of talking, but outside this domain it becomes 'speaking rough'.

There are also competing pressures on children from their peers. Boys, in particular, feel they have to talk rough with other boys in order not to be ridiculed. While girls are under the same pressure to fit in with a group, they have to be careful not to go too far or people will judge them negatively. These conflicting patterns were expressed by one girl in a study of peer influence on girls in Birmingham, who said, 'You always try to be the same as everyone else. You don't sort of want to be made fun of . . . sort of posher than everybody else. Then you get sort of picked on. But then if you use a lot of slang and that, people don't think very much of you.'

In a French study, girls put pressure on each other to use standard speech, as can be seen in this extract:

Girl 1: Moi, j'ai un oncle qui s'appelle Gérard.
[I've got an uncle called Gerard.]
Girl 2: Ah, bon.
[Oh really.]
Girl 1: ouais.
[Yes (with non-standard pronunciation).]
Girl 3: On dit pas 'ouais'. On dit 'oui'.
[One doesn't say ouais. One says 'oui' (with standard pronunciation).]
Girl 1: Moi, j'sais dire les deux.
[But I know how to say both.]
Girl 3: Ici, on dit 'oui'.
[Here we say 'oui'.]

Some of these peer groups, however, exert powerful pressure on their members to conform to norms which are at odds with those approved by the family and school. The group's influence can even extend to levels of acceptable academic achievement and reading ability. In one school in Edinburgh, where I interviewed some children, a group of boys operated a system of fines which they levied against those who were seen to cooperate too much with the teachers. What makes a boy successful in school is irrelevant to prestige in the peer group. Some boys are less well integrated into the group's activities than others and are 'lames' because they do not know the rules for these events. It is these boys who used more standard-like forms of speech. Those who are most integrated reject the ethic of the school and speak more non-standardly. This is of course what some of the network studies described in the last chapter have found; namely, that certain types of group structure may have an effect on linguistic behavior.

Most of the early sociolinguistic studies were in fact done by men and many of the questions asked of both men and women reflected a masculine bias. For example, in the New York City study discussed in the last chapter, a male investigator asked both men and women to read a passage ending with a very unflattering comparison between dogs and a boy's first girlfriend, i.e. 'I suppose it's the same thing with most of us: your first dog is like your first girl. She's more trouble than she's worth, but you can't seem to forget her.' In other parts of the interview men and women are asked about their words for different things. Women are asked about childhood games, while men, among other things, were asked about terms for girls and even, on occasion, terms for female sex organs. Naturally, researchers have since questioned the nature of the relationship established between male sociolinguists and the women they interviewed. It is not likely that a discussion of hopscotch would established the same kind of rapport between the male interviewer and a female interviewee as talk about obscene language would between two men.

Gossip v. shop talk

Looking at adults, we can see some continuity between adolescent ways of speaking and the management of social interaction later in life. There are common elements in the speech styles of boys and men such as storytelling, verbal posturing, and arguing. Men tend to challenge one another. Women, on the other hand, do not value aggressiveness and their conversations tend to be more interactional and aim at seeking cooperation. They send out and look for signs of agreement and link what they say to the speech of others. In all-female groups women often discuss one topic for more than half an hour. They share feelings about themselves and talk about relationships. Men, however, jump from topic to topic, vying to tell anecdotes about themselves. They rarely talk about themselves or their personal problems.

There are also differences in how conversations are managed. Women are careful to respect each other's turns and tend to apologize for talking too much. They dislike anyone dominating the conversation. Men compete for dominance with some men talking a lot more than others. They do not feel a need to link their own contributions to others. Instead, they are more likely to ignore what has been said before and to stress their own point of view.

What happens in talk between men and women? The existence of these different discourse patterns indicates a potential for miscommunication. A best-selling book on this subject claims that communication between men and women is similar to cross-cultural communication. In fact, lack of communication is one of the most frequently given reasons for breakdown of marital relations leading to divorce in the United States. Wives commonly complain to their husbands, 'Why don't you ask me how my day was?' or 'Why don't you listen to me?' We are all familiar with cartoons which depict the silent husband behind his newspaper at the breakfast table. Women want their partners to be like their best friend from school days—someone to whom they can tell secrets. Women value details in conversation because they represent a sign of involvement with others, but men are not socialized to be concerned with taking care of others, and do not use talk in this way. Women do what has been called the 'shitwork' of conversation. The responsibility of initiating conversations on topics likely to be of interest to men and keeping them going has been traditionally seen as women's work. But all the work that women do towards maintaining conversation still leaves them at a disadvantage because men end up dominating conversations.

In mixed-sex conversations men interrupt women more with the result that women are less able to complete their turns at talk and tend to talk less. Not surprisingly, this means that men can dominate the topics of conversation. In fact, we can even go so far as to say that for men, the point of conversation is to be the speaker. Women value listening much more than men. It is a common experience of many women to have their own contributions ignored, but once a man makes the same point, it is seen to be important and worth further consideration by the group.

Language reform: a msguided attempt to change herstory?

We have seen how language reflects women's status, but does this mean that society has to change before the language can? Or can linguistic change bring about a social reform? Language is clearly part of the problem, but how can we make it part of the solution? As one feminist says, male superiority should not be confused with male power. Male superiority is a myth which can be exposed by education and a change in consciousness, but male power has to be challenged in a more radical way in order to effect change. Some feminists maintain that as long as women must use a language which is not of their own making, change is impossible. That is why some of them not only want to rid language of its male bias, but also want to use terms such as *spinster* or *hag* positively. To insist on being called *Ms* is to undermine men's power in a visible way. Many women authors deliberately use *she* as the generic pronoun to shock their readers. One feminist writes that if there are men who feel uncomfortable about being excluded, they should think of how women feel within minutes of opening most books. A reform in usage is required to promote a positive self-image. One can compare the case of women to that of other minorities such as blacks, who have pointed out how the term 'black' has negative connotations, as can be seen in terms such as 'black market', 'black sheep', 'blackball'. By adopting the name 'black' to refer to themselves (in place of negro or colored) and asserting that black is beautiful, they attempt to create a positive image for blackness.

Women have complained that there are systematic gaps in the lexicon of English to refer to female experience. For instance, English has no expression corresponding to *virility* to refer to female potency, and likewise no counterpart to *emasculate*. The term *gynergy* has been proposed as the opposite of *virility*. Other terms such as *phallustine* and *testeria* have also been created and used by feminists. As indicated in my heading for this section of the chapter, some men have regarded some of these changes as ridiculous.

Probably all deliberately proposed innovations are laughed at initially. When, for instance, *Frau* was proposed to replace *Madame* in German many years ago, one historian actually rashly predicted that *Frau* would never be accepted, but in fact it has been. Indeed, as a German male colleague confided to me in an amused manner, his young female research assistants were nowadays quite adamant they should be called *Frau*. Of course, traditionally, as young unmarried women, they would have been called *Fräulein*, where the ending - *lein* is diminutive. There is, however, not surprisingly, no corresponding male term of address, *Herrlein*, for young unmarried men. The reason for the replacement of *Madame* with *Frau* had nothing to do with feminism, but was part of a purification effort to rid German of foreign, especially French, borrowings. Now some German feminists are suggesting that *frau* should replace the indefinite *man*, which is an androcentric generic when used in contexts such as *man soll das nicht machen* 'one shouldn't do that'.

I noted some resistance, particularly in Britain, to accepting the title *Ms*. I had quite an argument with my bank before they allowed my full name to be printed on my checks without any title. Of course, some professional women have the option of using their titles to avoid being addressed as *Miss* or *Mrs*. I once had the experience of giving my title as *Dr*, to which I got an aggressive reply, 'but is it *Miss* or *Mrs*?' An argument resulted because I refused to give it since I took the question to be aimed at putting me in my place. The use of *boy* to refer to adult black men, particularly in colonial contexts, is obviously insulting in a similar way, as can be seen in Dr Poussaint's account of being stopped by a white policeman in a southern United States town. The policeman puts him in a subordinate place by refusing to address him by his proper title.

'What's your name, boy?', the policeman asked.
'Dr Poussaint. I'm a physician.'
'What's your first name, boy?'
'Alvin'.

Many arguments have been put forward against some of the changes proposed by feminists. For example, some object to *Ms* because its pronunciation cannot be determined from the spelling, but then this is true for *Mrs* and *Mr* too, and for a great many other English words. The reasoning put forward by some men against changing such male-dominated naming practices often amounts to no more than resentment at a change in the status quo. As one man said, it makes it 'jolly difficult to work out whether women were married these days because of the ridiculous practice of not taking their husbands' names'. This is, of course, precisely the point. One's marital status is irrelevant and is marked only for men's convenience. Practices such as taking a man's family name or using titles such as *Mrs* or *Miss* are symbolic of women's position as men's property and represent their status as sex objects, whose availability or non-availability due to ownership by another male has to be marked in a conspicuous way.

In a rape case which went to trial in the USA, the victim's status as an unmarried mother was made prominent through the defense attorney's use of the address term *Miss*. This was done despite the fact that during pretrial motions it had been agreed that the defense was not allowed to broach the subject of her marital status. Here the address term functioned as a convenient and acceptable symbol to mark the woman in a way which would not have been possible if the defendant had been a man.

While many women have argued that all sexist words in the English language should be eliminated, this is not feasible. It would be necessary to eliminate not only almost all words referring to women, but also most referring to men too since the enhanced positive image of men in relation to women would also have to be ousted from the language in order for linguistic parity to be achieved. This makes it clear that society's perceptions of men and women must change in order for linguistic reform to be successful. But language is not simply a passive reflector of culture, it also creates it. There is a constant interaction between society and language. Thus new terms which are introduced will become incorporated into the existing semantic bias in favor of males. We can see this happening already with some of the supposed sex-neutral terms.

The United States Department of Labor and other government bureaucracies have made some attempts to eliminate sexist language in their documents. The Department of Labor, for instance, revised the titles of almost 3,500 jobs so that they are sex-neutral. Thus, *steward* and *stewardess* are 'out' and *flight attendant* is in. The Australian government even has a linguist who acts as an adviser on sexism in its publications.

Studies have shown that some of the new neutral terms are used in such a way as to perpetuate the inequalities expressed by the old sex-marked terms they are supposed to replace. Thus, for example, women are much more likely than men to be referred to as a *chairperson* or *salesperson* or even *Madame Chairperson*, or *Madame Chairman*. My examination of the titles *chairman*, *chairperson*, *chairwoman* in the British National Corpus revealed that *chairman* was still the most frequently used title (1,142 occurrences in a 3 million-word sample). The title *chairperson* was used only 130 times, for both men and women, though more often for women. The title *chairwoman* was used only 68 times. Thus, the intended gender-neutral term *chair* or *chairperson* has become in effect a marked term in opposition to *chairman*, which still remains the neutral and unmarked term, an androcentric generic. It is the woman occupying the position referred to by the title who gets singled out by the new term. This raises the question of how successful such reforms are likely to be. At the moment, sex-neutrality is not a recognized category.

The reinterpretation of the feminist term *Ms* is a good example of how women's meanings can be appropriated and depoliticized within a sexist system. The title *Ms* has not entirely replaced the marked term *Mrs*, as was intended. Instead, it has been added as a new term of address alongside the conventional *Mrs* and *Miss*, or is seen as a replacement for *Miss* and thus is used more often than not in connection with unmarried women. One study in Canada indicated that many people used *Mrs* for married women, *Miss* for women who have never been married, and *Ms* for divorced women. For some people *Ms* also carries the connotation that a woman who uses the title is trying to hide the fact that she is single. These examples make clear that the introduction of the new term *Ms* has not altered the underlying semantic distinction between married and unmarried. Only the title used to mark the unmarried distinction has changed.

Another study even noted a directive sent out to public information officers in the state of Pennsylvania which instructed them, 'If you use Ms. for a female, please indicate in parentheses after the Ms. whether it's Miss or Mrs.' Thus, the title *Ms* is being used in ways its proposers never intended, to maintain the very distinctions it was supposed to replace. This indicates the high premium that dominant institutions still place on defining women in terms of their relationships with men. Thus, the category of gender gets reconstituted and implemented in a different way with a different set of terms.

Some evidence on the effect of another type of language reform comes from experiments examining whether those who have reformed their use of male androcentric generics have also changed their mental imagery. Are those who appear more egalitarian in their language actually more so in their thoughts too? Groups of undergraduate students at Harvard University who either had or had not reformed their usage in their written work were asked to draw pictures to go with sentences such as *an unhappy person could still have a smile on his/her (or her/their) face*. The findings showed that there were still more male images than female ones, regardless of the pronoun used, and regardless of whether the subject had reformed his or her written usage. However, only women who had reformed their usage produced more female images, and they did so for all three pronouns. Thus, even the men who had ostensibly reformed their usage had done so only superficially and were still androcentric in their thought patterns. In some respects, this shows that language reforms have had only limited success. Proposed for the most part by women, not surprisingly, it is women for whom they seem to have the greatest effect. Men take more convincing, but then they stand to lose more, and women to gain more, from such reform.

In another sense, however, the change is significant if seen from the perspective of earlier experiments in the 1970s in which people were given journal articles to evaluate. Some received articles which had the name of a woman author, while others received exactly the same articles but men's names were given as authors. Both men and women judged the same articles as better and more scientific when they thought they had been written by a man than by a woman. Women did not of course need experiments to tell them of this bias. It was partly for this reason that Emily Brontë published *Wuthering Heights* under the male pseudonym of Ellis Bell. Studies have since shown how differently the novel was interpreted when it became known that a woman was the author.

Men have interpreted experimental results such as these as an indication that women shared the negative image assigned to them by men and even went so far as to express surprise that 'women were prejudiced against women'. This is part of the process of being in a subordinate position. It is because the superordinate are more powerful that they impose their own way of thinking (and their language) as the only valid one. The behavior of these women was reminiscent of that of black children who in experiments conducted in the late 1940s expressed preferences for white over black dolls, and non-RP speakers who rate RP speakers as more intelligent, successful, etc. Such studies are often used to support the status quo, as for instance with the producers of children's cartoons who claim that both boys and girls prefer to see male characters in more prominent roles. Later attitudinal studies on accent preference have, however, indicated a reversal of some of these negative attitudes. As far as television is concerned, once females are depicted in more positive roles, it is likely that a better image for women will be created.

Women who work in professional positions often have a hard time competing on an equal basis with men. They are at a disadvantage if they do not adopt some features of male interactional style, but when they do they are seen as less feminine and criticized by both men and women. This is of course the double standard. It has been applied to women such as Margaret Thatcher, and probably most women who have to speak in public, though, interestingly, experiments have shown that British women who speak RP are perceived as more androgenous. Until recently, women have been denied access to the registers needed for success in society. Similar phenomena can be observed in other cultures, where it is men who control the high ritualistic language and written language. In most developing countries men have much higher literacy rates than women because fewer women get to go to school.

Requiring women to be 'one of the boys' in order to succeed treats symptoms of women's inequality rather than its causes. Many would argue that some aspects of women's conversational style with its emphasis on cooperation and solidarity rather than competitiveness are more desirable for everyone. In fact, this style has been adopted by feminists for their meetings. In principle, there is no reason why the negative connotations and stereotypes associated with women could not be changed by language planning. After all, drinking lager was once regarded as effeminate in England, but the advertising industry has transformed it into a macho enterprise.

There are some signs that change has taken place to rectify some of the linguistic imbalances in English and other languages. Many government agencies, newspapers, and publishing houses have style manuals prohibiting the use of sexist terminology. An examination of newspaper articles will reveal that women used to be more often referred to as 'girls', where in a similar context males would be referred to as 'men'. The tendency to comment on women's appearance, but not men's, was something I experienced personally when an article appeared about me in the British national press not too long after my appointment in 1984 to my position at Oxford. A male reporter wrote that a 'fussy silk blouse pokes from under a casual striped sweater'. It also described my hair as being center-parted and as 'neat as a doll's house curtains'. I was annoyed at these references not just because I thought them irrelevant to the point of the article, but also because they were inaccurate. I have never parted my hair in the center, and I didn't own any silk blouses at the time, 'fussy' or otherwise. The only shirts I own and wear are completely plain, all without ruffles or frills of any kind—in fact, I would have thought they were totally indistinguishable from men's shirts. Very seldom would a man's way of dressing be commented on as routinely as a woman's would.

There is evidence that public norms for language use are changing. The *Washington Post*'s *Deskbook on Style*, for instance, says that last names alone are to be used on second reference to both men and women in newspaper articles and that expressions such as 'the comely brunette', 'weaker sex' are to be avoided. Androcentric generics have declined dramatically over the past decade in the *Washington Post* and the use of women's middle initials on first reference has become more frequent since the style manual was introduced.

In conclusion, we can say that the study of gender differentiation is much more complicated than it at first appears. The next chapter will show how the influence of gender will differ from culture to culture and it may interact with many other social characteristics of speakers such as social class, age, context, to varying extents in language change. The existence of sexist language is not simply a linguistic but a social problem. As such, any remedy will require change in both society and language.

Annotated bibliography

Otto Jespersen's (1922) book contains a chapter on women and their language. One of the most influential early studies (but now criticized) arguing for the existence of 'women's language' was Robin Lakoff's book (1975). Arguments for the biological superiority of women can be found in Ashley Montague's book (1968). The concept of 'man-made language' is discussed in Dale Spender's (1980) book and Mary Daly's (1978) book. Good overviews of the connections between language and gender can be found in Jennifer Coates's book (1988), Deborah Cameron and Jennifer Coates's collection (1988), David Graddol and Joan Swan's book (1989), and Suzanne Romaine's (1999 *a*) book. For discussion of the masculine bias in linguistic theory, see Deborah Cameron

(1985). For some specific studies, see Betty Lou Dubois and Isobel Crouch (1975) on tag questions; Pamela S. Kipers (1987) on topic choice; Candace West (1985) on doctor/patient communication, and the papers in Bergvall et al. (1996). The quotation from John Stuart Mill is taken from his book (1869).

The semantic analysis of the terms *man/woman, boy/girl* can be found in Geoffrey Leech's textbook (1974: 96–102). The example of the 'girls' at the telephone exchange in Norway is from Haugen (1966: 188), and the quote about females never growing up is from Bolinger (1980: 100). Julia Stanley (1977) is the source of the count for terms referring to sexually promiscuous women and men.

The study of girls' speech in Birmingham was done by Jane Cullum and is reported in her MA thesis (1981). The example from boys' and girls' peer groups comes from Marjorie Harness Goodwin's (1980) study and the French example from Claudine Dannequin's (1977) book. See also Goodwin's book (1990) and Carole Edelsky's (1977) article. Roger Brown and Albert Gilman's (1972) article is the standard source for rules governing forms of address. Annette Schmidt's book (1985) documents the death of Dyirbal. The study of changing perceptions of usage of generic pronouns is in Fatemeh Khosroshashi's (1989) article. Deborah Tannen's (1990) book is a highly readable study of the conversational styles of men and women, although it has been criticized for not paying enough attention to fundamental differences in power between men and women: see the review by Senta Troemel-Ploetz (1991) and Tannen's (1992) reply, and Aki Uchida's (1992) article. On the subject of language reform, see Stefan Kanfer's (1972) article. Donna Atkinson (1987) did the Canadian study on the use of *Ms*, and Ehrlich and King (1994) examined the ways in which titles for women are reinterpreted in line with sexist ideology. Marlis Hellinger's (1990) book contains an overview of the efforts of German feminists.

Chapter 5

Language Change in Social Perspective

As I was writing this book in Sweden, an interesting case of linguistic change came to my attention. It seems that young people in Sweden have begun using the word *nörd* (from American English *nerd*) to refer to someone who is stupid. There is also an adjectival form *nördig* 'nerdy'. This new usage has been commented on by the newspapers and the radio, and some of my Swedish colleagues began noticing it over the summer of 1991. After some discussion, my colleagues and I concluded that *nerd* probably crossed the Atlantic to Sweden via the American film *Revenge of the Nerds*, which was translated in Swedish as *Nördarna kommer* 'The nerds are coming'. Some young people have apparently also picked up the word through visiting the United States. It has now been noticed in Denmark too. The influence and prestige of American pop culture on youth everywhere has no doubt been responsible for the introduction of a number of new English words into other languages.

The possibilities for change of this type are indeed potentially enormous nowadays considering how much more mobile most people are, and how much exposure people get to speech norms outside their immediate community through mass media, and via the internet in particular, popularly called the 'information superhighway', on which we can transcend great distances without leaving home or the office. In this chapter I will examine some of the mechanisms of linguistic change and its social motivations.

Dialectology and language change

Linguists have long been interested in language change. In the nineteenth century the discipline of linguistics was understood in a historical sense and the main preoccupations of the field were to study the development of languages over time. Since those beginnings in the nineteenth century historical investigations of dialects have made contributions of both theory and methods to the study of language change. This work, which sees the spread of linguistic forms primarily in terms of geographical space, provides a foundation for historical sociolinguistics. The early studies done in Germany and France provided a basis for interpreting the linguistic significance of the patterning of isoglosses.

An isogloss represents the boundary of any linguistic feature or set of features which separate one speech variety from another. Most importantly, however, from a theoretical perspective such research seriously challenged prevailing views of sound change. Ironically, early studies of dialects had set out to support the hypothesis that sound change took place according to sound laws that admitted no exceptions. In the case of the so-called second Germanic sound shift, an important test case, this principle would predict, among other things, that all instances of /p/ in early Germanic would become /f/ all over the High German territory, regardless of the words these sounds occurred in. Investigations, however, showed that the second Germanic sound shift did have exceptions.

This can be seen in the set of isoglosses in Fig. 5.1, which separates the so-called Low variety of German from High German. The isoglosses run from east to west across Germany (slightly north of Berlin) and Holland. The features comprising the isoglosses include the pronunciation of final consonants such as *p*, *t*, and *k* in words such as *dorp/dorf* ('village'), *dat/das* ('that', 'the'), and *ik/ich* ('I'). The first member of each of these pairs is the Low German variant, as found in modern standard Dutch, and the second is the High German variant, as found in modern standard German. The isoglosses for *machen* cross the Rhein near Benrath, slightly south of the point where the isogloss for *ich* crosses the Rhein at Urdingen. This is one of the most important dialect boundaries in German, called the Benrath–Urdingen line, which divides Low from High German. As one moves eastward, the isoglosses for the two words and also for *dat/das*, *dorp/dorf*, etc. are the same. The point at which the isoglosses meet the Rhine is marked by a fanning out of the isoglosses. For this reason the isogloss has been called the Rhenish fan. In villages along this area speakers may have some Low German features and some High German features, for example, both *dat* and *dorf*.

In practice, most changes are not completely regular because all innovations diffuse through time and space at different rates. Many of the variables studied by sociolinguists today actually have a considerable time-depth and represent ongoing long-term changes which have not yet been completed or may never be so in all varieties of a language. This is often not fully appreciated because the histories of languages are usually written from the perspective of the

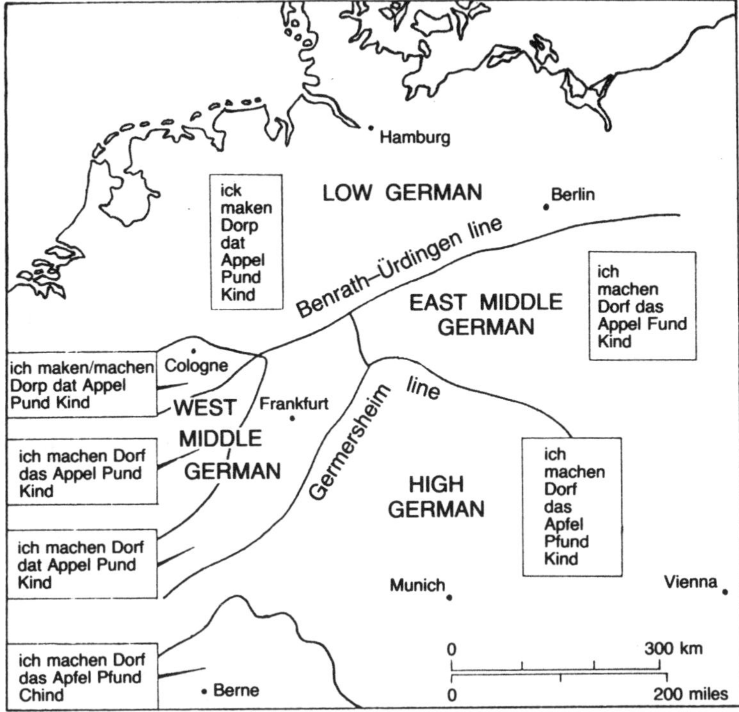

FIG 5.1 The operation of the High German sound shift: typical forms of common vocabulary items in traditional German dialects. Standard German forms: *ich* 'I'; *machen* 'make, do'; *Dorf* 'village'; *das* 'that, the'; *Apfel* 'apple'; *Pfund* 'pound'; *Kind* 'child'

standard variety, and processes such as the second Germanic sound shift are treated as faits accomplis.

I showed in Chapter 3 that sociolinguistic patterns reveal the uneven diffusion of standard languages through a social hierarchy. Some variables such as *h*-dropping and the loss of final *-t/d* examined in the last two chapters have considerable time-depth. Other variables studied today by sociolinguists, however, may be new ones. The amount of variation in a language at a particular time is a matter for investigation. The study of phonological variation in western industrialized societies has led to the development of methods for charting the spread of innovations. Variation in time and space such as is illustrated above has shown the complexity of dialect differentiation and the need to invoke explanations from internal as well as external factors.

Part of the explanation for the pattern of variation found in the Rhenish fan comes from cultural history. The Benrath line corresponds to the extent of influence of the city of Cologne from the thirteenth century, and the Urdingen line to its influence from the sixteenth century. The forms for *machen* were fixed at an earlier date than those for *ich*. The differences in the isoglosses can be accounted for by assuming that a sound change had taken place in southern Germany and spread northward. The extent of spread of this innovation was determined by both geographical and social factors. Among the latter was the social prestige of the urban speakers who used the new forms. Such areas of prestige form focal points which transmit innovations into the surrounding hinterland.

At the limits or peripheries of such centers of diffusion we find transition areas which typically show characteristics of two neighboring focal areas. Beyond these are relic areas which are removed from the effect of expanding isoglosses. Relic areas are generally found in places that are not so easily accessible. Prestige innovations and settlement patterns can often be traced by examining isoglosses and place names. Linguistic innovations often hop or leapfrog from one urban center to another bypassing the areas in between, as we will see later when we look at the regional distribution of postvocalic /r/ in the United States. Only later do they spread out to the rural hinterland surrounding major urban areas.

The Rhenish fan is an important isogloss not just in dialectology, but also for the questions it raises about change for historical linguistics more generally. In Table 5.1, which is a schematized diagram of the isogloss bundle, we see a step-like patterning of the isoglosses between north and south German in

Table 5.1 Isoglosses between Low and High German consonant shift /p t k/ → /(p) f s x/

Dialects	Lexical items					
	ich	machen	dorf	das	apfel	pfund
Low German						
1.	ik	maken	dorp	dat	appel	pund
2.	ich	maken	dorp	dat	appel	pund
3.	ich	machen	dorp	dat	appel	pund
Middle German						
4.	ich	machen	dorf	dat	appel	pund
5.	ich	machen	dorf	das	appel	pund
6.	ich	machen	dorf	das	apfel	pund
High German						
7.	ich	machen	dorf	das	apfel	pfund

geographical space. This model suggests that the new pronunciations gained in frequency while both shifted and unshifted forms coexisted. The numbers 1 to 7 can be thought of as different dialects. Stage 1 represents a dialect which has undergone no change and stage 7 shows the completed change. Dialects 2 to 6 show intermediate stages in the shift. For all practical purposes, if we examine the beginning and end stages, the net effect of the change is the same as if it had applied uniformly and simultaneously to all dialects.

This diagram gives us a picture of the transition phase and the line drawn through it indicates the trajectory of the change as it spreads from dialect to dialect and from one lexical item to another. In more recent theoretical discussions this pattern of change has been referred to as 'lexical diffusion'. On the basis of evidence from patterns such as these, a French dialectologist proposed that 'chaque mot a son histoire' [Each word has its own history].

More recent work on dialect variation has attempted to formalize this view of change which assumes that innovations spread in waves. Models have been proposed which predict that a change moves through the grammar (in the case of the Germanic sound shift, a rule which changes *p* to *f*, etc.), affecting one environment in one (iso)lect at a time. The term *lect* has been backformed from *dialect* as a more neutral term for a clustering of linguistic features. Many linguists now prefer the term *variety* or *lect* to avoid the sometimes pejorative connotations that the term 'dialect' has.

Table 5.2 shows a formal model called an 'implicational scale' for the sound

Table 5.2 Implicational scale of isoglosses between Low and High German consonant shift /p t k/ → /(p) f s x/

Dialects	Lexical items					
	ich	machen	dorf	das	apfel	pfund
Low German						
1.	–	–	–	–	–	–
2.	+	–	–	–	–	–
3.	+	+	–	–	–	–
Middle German						
4.	+	+	+	–	–	–
5.	+	+	+	+	–	–
6.	+	+	+	+	+	–
High German						
7.	+	+	+	+	+	+

shift in which lects and lexical items are implicationally ordered. Environments either have a rule (+) or they don't (–), while others are variable, i.e. in the process of transition from plus to minus, or vice versa. Since isolects are located in both space and time in such a model, they participate either earlier or later in an incipient rule change at any given point in the spatio-temporal continuum. It is possible to incorporate many lects into a polylectal or panlectal grammar, which would consist of all possible sets of rules for an arbitrarily limited area in space and time. Some linguists would also claim that such models are also psychologically real because speakers have polylectal competence rather than just competence in their own lect.

At this stage, we can usefully return to one of the sociolinguistic variables examined in Chapter 3 to look in more detail at the internal and external constraints on its operation, namely final *-t/d* deletion in *missed/grabbed*, *mist/hand*, etc. Although deletion of *-t/d* in consonant clusters is normal in casual, non-standard speech throughout most varieties of English, there are differences in the frequency of deletion depending on whether a word beginning with a vowel or a consonant follows (e.g. *missed train* v. *missed Alice*) or whether the final member of the cluster is the past tense morpheme (e.g. *missed* v. *mist*).

Variable constraints can be ordered in a hierarchy according to how great an influence they exert on deletion. In this example, the linguistic constraints follow the hierarchy:

1. Monomorphemic > Bimorphemic
2. C > V

This means that the phonetic environment promotes deletion more than the grammatical constraint: monomorphemic forms such as *mist* are more likely to show deletion than bimorphemic forms such as *missed*, where there is a morpheme boundary between *miss* and the final *-ed* signalling the past tense. Where a word beginning with a consonant follows word-final *-t/d*, as in *missed train*, deletion is most likely.

Explanations for this kind of internal linguistic variability have appealed to a variety of factors such as markedness and universals. A number of sociolinguists, for instance, have treated *-t/d* deletion as a slightly more specific version of a more general articulatory reduction rule because the loss of final consonants is a universal phonetic tendency operative in a wide range of languages. We saw in Chapter 3, for instance, that Swedish is affected by a similar process. Thus, speakers tend to simplify consonant clusters presumably because sequences of consonants are more marked (i.e. more difficult to produce from an articulatory point of view and therefore, more difficult to acquire and less frequently found in languages of the world) than a sequence of consonant followed by vowel. This constraint operates to maintain the preferred universal canonical syllable structure CVC.

Likewise, it has been assumed that a one-to-one relationship between form and meaning is the most natural one. Semantically relevant information tends to be retained in surface structure. Therefore, the final /t/ of *mist* is more likely to be deleted than the final /t/ of *missed* which carries meaning. A meaningful feature is more marked if it has no phonetic realization. If languages tend to block rules which would wipe out surface morphological distinctions, then we can predict that a phonological rule of deletion would tend not to operate across morpheme boundaries. In general terms, we could say that the grammatical constraint reflects a functional principle because deletion in this environment would result in syncretism between the present (except for third person singular forms) and past tense forms. Thus, at a larger level, the two constraints on *-t/d* deletion represent opposing forces and work to balance one another over the long term. Phonological change works against the demands of ideal morphology with optimal encoding being expressed by uniform encoding of one form/one function.

Using these insights, we can generate a markedness metric for the environments in which *-t/d* deletion occurs, as shown in Table 5.3. The constraint of a following consonant outranks that of a preceding morpheme boundary, so environment (*a*) is the most favourable to deletion because the unmarked values for both features [morpheme boundary] and [syllabic] co-occur; environment (*d*) is most resistant because here both features are marked.

Table 5.3 Markedness metric for *-t/d* deletion

Environments	Constraints	
	[morpheme boundary]	[syllabic]
(a) mist #C	u	u
(b) mist #V	u	m
(c) miss + ed #C	m	u
(d) miss +ed#V	m	m

Note: u = unmarked; m = marked.

The relationship between variation and change

One of the tenets of sociolinguistics is that synchronic variation of the type illustrated here and in the examples in Chapter 3 represents a stage in long-term change. We can also use this constraint hierarchy to predict the development through time of varieties, on the assumption that linguistic change proceeds in step-wise increments with rules generalizing as they spread through time and space, as suggested, for instance, in the wave model of diffusion shown in Tables 5.1 and 5.2. Initially, a rule may have a probability of application of zero in all environments, and then the probability of application increases environment by environment. This is shown in Table 5.4, where the onset of change is in Variety (*A*) at Time (*i*) in environment (*a*). We can generate the following continuum of varieties, in which the environments (*a*), (*b*), (*c*), (*d*) are temporally successive.

In assigning the heavier weight to the following consonant and the lighter one to the morpheme boundary, the model predicts that more deletions will occur in monomorphemic than bimorphemic clusters. The assumption here is that, all other things being equal, 'normal' linguistic change proceeds from heavier to lighter environments. Rules also tend to operate faster in heavier than in lighter environments. Thus, the oldest environment is the earliest and fastest. It becomes categorical earliest before the last environment begins to be variably operative. In other words, what is heavier has a greater effect on the

Table 5.4 Temporal development of varieties for the rule of *-t/d* deletion

Time	Variety	Environment			
		(*a*) mist #C	(*b*) mist #V	(*c*) miss + ed #C	(*d*) miss + ed #V
(i)	(*A*)	mis(t)	mist	missed	missed
(ii)	(*B*)	mis(t)	mis(t)	missed	missed
(iii)	(*C*)	mis(t)	mis(t)	miss(ed)	missed
(iv)	(*D*)	mis(t)	mis(t)	miss(ed)	miss(ed)
(v)	(*E*)	mis	mis(t)	miss(ed)	miss(ed)
(vi)	(*F*)	mis	mis	miss(ed)	miss(ed)
(vii)	(*G*)	mis	mis	miss	miss(ed)
(viii)	(*H*)	mis	mis	miss	miss

application of the rule. What is quantitatively less is slower and later. In Variety (*E*) deletion is categorical in the heaviest environment, while the others are variable. Variety (*H*), which is furthest in time and space from the point of origin, displays categorical deletion while Variety (*A*) is the least advanced. Here the rule applies variably only in the most favorable environment.

Environments are implicationally ordered so that a variety which shows categorical deletion in environment (*c*), for example, must also show categorical deletion in the lighter environments to the left, (*a*) and (*b*). This is shown in Variety (*E*).

Rules of course can become stagnant, die out, or be aborted at any point in their temporal development. They may also be stable over long periods of time, as is the case for *-t/d* deletion, for instance. There is no reason to believe that one day all final instances of *-t/d* will disappear because literacy acts as a break on change. Constraints on rules may also be reweighted as they develop in a particular direction or variety. Rules can also compete for the same territory and the same linguistic environment can host more than one change at the same time.

More generally speaking, the spread of linguistic change behaves much like the diffusion of other innovations, and even diseases. In fact, the models which biologists use to show how an epidemic spreads through a population are relevant to linguistic change. Fig. 5.2 shows an S-curve, so-called because it resembles a flattened S. We can imagine it as a model of either an epidemic or a change spreading through a population. At first, only a few persons are affected. Then the disease or change picks up momentum, and finally runs its course.

In addition, there are regular external or social factors affecting the realization of *-t/d*, as we saw in Chapter 3, including social class of the speaker, with higher-status speakers deleting less often than lower-status ones, etc. This variable is also sensitive to style, with more deletion in informal speech, and age, with younger speakers differing from older speakers with respect to the treat-

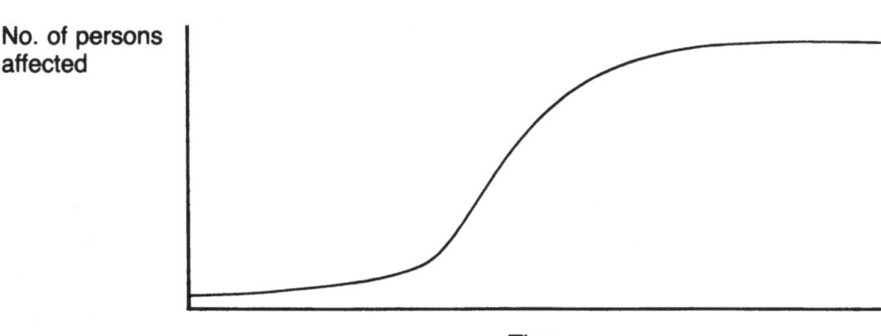

FIG 5.2 S-curve for language change

ment of verbs such as *keep*, where past tense is marked both by the final /t/ as well as by vowel change of the type found in strong verbs such as *come*. There are also differences relating to ethnicity and region, with African-Americans, for instance, deleting more frequently than whites. We also saw in Chapter 3 that Puerto Ricans who socialized more with African-Americans tended to behave like them linguistically and deleted more final -*t*/*d*s.

Using the present to explain the past and the past to explain the present

Armed with the knowledge of how variability is embedded in social and linguistic contexts in speech communities today, sociolinguists have tried to revitalize the study of historical change by incorporating within it an understanding of these sociolinguistic patterns. In other words, we can use the present to try to explain the past, and the past to explain the present. It is now clear that variability is a prerequisite for change. By extrapolating from the patterns of variation we find today, we can make some predictions about the direction change is moving in. For example, in later studies done by sociolinguists of the extent of influence of standard, i.e. High, German on the speech of Germans living in various parts of the country, we can see a dramatic advance of the standard /pf/ in *Pfund* etc. which is replacing the older /p/ forms among the younger generation of southern Rhinelanders. A study done of the speech of fifty men from the small town of Erp, once mainly an agricultural area but now a modernized satellite of Cologne, showed that the replacement of /v/ by standard /b/ in words such as *bleiben* 'to remain' is much more frequent in formal speech than in everyday casual conversation.

This downward diffusion of more standard speech from the formal to casual styles is what we would expect when standard and non-standard speech varieties are in contact. Changes may also enter the standard variety, and when this happens, it is usually from the bottom up, so to speak. They affect casual speech before more formal styles. This can be seen today in the impact which certain features of Cockney, i.e. working-class London speech, have had on RP.

Just as standard English once diffused out from the London merchant class, now vernacular London speech is spreading to other cities like Norwich, where many young people now say *bovver* and *togevver* instead of *bother* and *together*. Cockneys have used these forms for generations. There is evidence that the change from /th/ to /v/ is spreading by face-to-face contact rather than via the media since areas closer to London have adopted these features more quickly than areas further away, though the television program *East Enders* has made some features of Cockney accessible to millions.

Not even the royal family has been immune to this process of change. The British press has charged Prince Andrew with sounding like a Cockney, and Princess Anne has been accused of 'linguistic slumming'. A report in the *Daily Telegraph* in 1987 accused the Duchess of York of taking 'miwlk' rather than 'milk' in her tea and noted that the Princess of Wales believed she was married in a place called 'St. Paw's Cathedral'. The reporter uses these spellings to indicate that /l/ has been lost.

Increased glottalization has also been making headway among middle-class speakers, with the Princess of Wales heard noting, 'There's a loʔ of iʔ abouʔ'. Glottalization has now been reported from other parts of the English-speaking world such as New Zealand.

These patterns of change have led sociolinguists to distinguish between 'change from above' and 'change from below' to refer to the differing points of departure for the diffusion of linguistic innovations through the social hierarchy. Change from above is conscious change originating in more formal styles and in the upper end of the social hierarchy and change from below is below the level of conscious awareness originating in the lower end of the social hierarchy.

Despite popular belief that mass media are a major force in spreading change from above leading to the elimination of local dialects, their effects are clearly limited in ways that require further investigation. I began this chapter with one striking example of the influence of American pop culture in Scandinavia, and we frequently read or hear complaints and concerns about the Americanization of English. Yet in one study of adolescents in Oxfordshire, youngsters opted for British rather than American lexical variants when tested for items such as *chips* v. (*french*) *fries*, *jumper* v. *sweater*. Although such Americanisms are almost a feature of daily life in British advertising as well as in other parts of the world, they appear to have scarcely penetrated everyday use among the group where one might expect them to have the most prestige. The limited influence of popular media on actual speech behavior suggests that what is crucial is face-to-face social interaction rather than passive exposure. When moving from one country to another Americans and Britons may make great lexical accommodation, but not, it would seem, just through passive listening. People don't talk to their televisions (at least not when I wrote this, though 'interactive cable television' currently being experimented with on a limited basis may make my remark obsolete within a short time after this book is published)!

Although spontaneous innovations such as *nerd* occur all the time, introduced by acts of speaking on the part of individual speakers, many will not enter the language system at all and spread. Once they do enter the system, however, they follow predictable paths through social and linguistic structures. Through quantitative sociolinguistic work we now have considerable understanding of how linguistic change might proceed in a functional system by means of internal and external structuring of inherent variability which shows directional gradience through social groups, geographic space, and time. Research indicates that formal styles and high registers are more conservative, while informal speech draws on the latest innovations. Sometimes items lag behind in certain changes and remain in the speech of older people as stylistic variants. New variants often appear first in casual speech, while older ones remain in more emphatic formal styles. Formal styles may provide a locus for the introduction of prestige changes.

Gender too is critical. Chapters 2, 3, and 4 discussed studies with evidence both for women being in the vanguard of change to a more prestigious language or variety as well as their being laggard in their use of a vernacular language or non-standard variety. In the case of Oberwart, for instance, it was women who were ahead of men, in shifting from Hungarian to German. Similarly, in Harlem, New York African-American males are the chief exemplars of vernacular culture and speech which is a source of covert prestige. Women, particularly in the lower middle class, lead in the introduction of new standard forms of many of the phonological variables studied in the United States, the UK, and other industrialized societies.

In many other parts of the world, however, such as in Gapun village in Papua New Guinea, women are more genuine members of local indigenous cultures than men. In Bolivia this is also true, partly because women stay put while men move around, moving, for example, to their wives' villages when they marry. Women retain their Indianness in dress and language, by speaking Aymara, while men opt for Spanish. Similarly, in Peru, women are associated with the indigenous language, Quechua, rather than Spanish.

Early dialectologists held conflicting views about the conservatism or innovativeness of women. Many nineteenth- and twentieth-century dialectologists investigating European languages based their surveys almost entirely on the speech of men, some on the assumption that men better preserved the 'real' and 'purest' forms of the regional dialects they were interested in collecting. Most of the linguistic items whose geographical distribution was being mapped were associated with men's rather than women's lifestyles and roles, e.g. terms for farming implements.

Those who believed women were innovative never really gave any satisfactory explanations, although some did comment that women talked more than men! While it makes sense that those who use language the most stand a better chance of changing it, as I showed in Chapter 4, the talkative woman appears to be a stereotypical view of women not supported by empirical investigations.

Some have even blamed women for change, though the examples and explanations offered do not stand up to objective scrutiny. One historian claimed that women were responsible for the loss of tongue trilled /r/ in English and other languages. In his view tongue trilled /r/ is 'natural and justified when life is chiefly carried on out-of-doors, but indoor life prefers, on the whole, less noisy speech habits, and the more refined this domestic life is, the more all kinds of noises and even speech sounds will be toned down'. In a similar ad hoc explanation, French women were blamed for the loss of /r/ in the word for 'chair' since it was a domestic object which belonged more naturally to the speech of women. Thus, whether she stays at home and keeps quiet or goes out into the work-a-day world, 'Mrs Interior' runs the risk of being blamed for the degeneration of language!

In a similar fashion, some have blamed female speakers of minority languages such as Scottish Gaelic, Welsh, Saami, and Breton (to name only a few) for 'killing' these languages by not speaking them to their children. One reason why such languages were not transmitted to children is that they became symbolic of a despised female identity and thus were tainted with the stigma of conquest by more powerful peoples and their languages. Thus, some rural Breton-speaking women asked the parish priest not to deliver his sermons in Breton. His response was, 'It is almost as if Breton smells of cow-shit to them. They think they are ladies.' Indeed, one woman spoke French to her two teenage daughters, Breton to the cows, hens, and sows, but French to the animals' young offspring, an apparently odd choice on first glance, but quite intelligible upon further reflection of the symbolic value of French and Breton.

Faced with seemingly contradictory findings and much ad hoc speculation about the role of women in language change, investigators of language shift have moved on from simplistic correlations between language use and sex to focus on the symbolic and ideological dimensions of language. This allows us to understand how a vernacular language or non-standard speech variety may become linked to a stigmatized ethnic identity so that a subordinate group may abandon their language in favor of the dominant one, invested with greater symbolic capital. While most of this discussion has expressed the symbolic value of dominant languages and prestige varieties in terms of their supposed economic value on a linguistic market-place, recent work has paid attention to ideologies of femininity and masculinity.

In many western societies, an idealized femininity is often identified with refinement, and refinement in turn with the dominant language. Those aspiring to be ladies had to escape both literally and figuratively from their status as rural peasants by leaving the land and their language behind. The title-page of James Howell's multilingual dictionary of 1659 depicts the Welsh language as a scared, wild woodland warrior maiden in comparison with richly clad court ladies representing English and French. Modern European languages such as French and English became symbols of modernity, in particular of the newly emergent European nation-states, at the same time as they were associated with urbanity, finery, and higher social status. In the previous chapter I showed how education was an important factor in this transformation for girls wishing to be young ladies in the Victorian era.

Choice of language is part of a speaker's presentation of self. Thus, in Oberwart, the newly available status of worker associated with German became available to a community previously monolingual in Hungarian. Women's choice of German as well as German-speaking marriage partners is an expression of their preference for the newer social identity by comparison with a more traditional one associated with Hungarian, which, in turn, is linked with peasant status and male-dominated subsistence agriculture. The way in which gender gets mapped onto language choice is not straightforward but mediated through other identities and ideologies. This is simply to admit that as variables both gender and language comprise rather complex social practices and performances. Identity too is neither static nor homogeneous, but shifting and heterogeneous. Different roles and identities require different linguistic performances, and thus identities get constructed and reconstructed along linguistic lines in conformity with changing conceptions of masculinity and femininity over time.

The role played by women or men *per se* in language shift and change seems therefore to depend very much on the community concerned. In research on Norwegian immigrants in the United States it turned out to be men who led the community in the acquisition of English, while women lagged behind at first, but seemed to catch up by the second generation. In a study done in a formerly Saami-speaking area of northern Norway called Furuflaten (about 75 miles from the city of Tromsø), women appear innovative in some respects, though conservative in others. This part of Norway was originally Saami-speaking up until the turn of the last century, even though there were some Finnish immigrants. According to a survey done in 1860 at least one person in the sixteen families living in the village at that time was trilingual in Finnish, Saami, and Norwegian, although the first language of all the households was Saami. Most of the bi- and trilinguals were probably males, while women and children were monolingual in Saami.

Today, however, all the village children are monolingual in Norwegian, although the older generations are still bi- or trilingual. Knowledge of Finnish is declining, but most middle-aged people have passive knowledge of Saami. The reason for the men's greater bilingualism in earlier days was connected with the division of labor. The main sources of income were fishing and farming and most adult men went away to the fisheries in Lofoten and Finnmark twice a year. Although the mothers had no such contacts outside the home and therefore did not need Norwegian, they tried to bring their children up as Norwegian speakers. All education was in Norwegian and children who were already Norwegianized when they entered stood to gain more from their schooling. Nevertheless, at the same time as the women were innovative, they were conservative in other ways. The men have fewer substratum features in their Norwegian than do women. Substratum features are characteristics of Saami carried over into Norwegian, such as the lack of definite articles in the variety of Norwegian spoken by these Saami. This is due to the absence of articles in Saami, as in *det er lang historie* instead of the standard Norwegian *det er en/ei lang historie* 'It is a long story'. Substratum features such as these are widely recognized and stigmatized stereotypes of the Norwegian spoken by Saamis, yet they occur more in the speech of women than that of men.

Thus, while women have led in the introduction of the dominant, more prestigious language, Norwegian, they speak a more localized and stigmatized variety of it than men. One reason for this was probably simply time. Saami women went from monolingualism in Saami to monolingualism in Norwegian in a very short period of time without much of a period of transitional bilingualism, while for men, the shift was not as rapid or dramatic. It would appear then that neither women nor men can be described as innovative or conservative *per se* except relative to a particular change in a given community. We might interpret the findings of urban sociolinguistics in a different light by assuming that middle-class women are simply being conservative in their adherence to the standard, while lower-class women's aspirations towards the standard would be innovative.

A study of Saami language shift in Finland revealed that some women initially were hostile to the Finnish language and did not want to learn it. By resisting the encroachment of Finnish into their homes, they sought to protect themselves from the invading culture around them. Traditionally, Saami women had higher status in their own community than did the Finnish women in the surrounding area. Both sexes took care of the children, did handicrafts, and took part in reindeer herding chores. Even though women did not travel as much as men, they were still much more mobile than Finnish women as well as economically more independent. Saami women had their own brands to mark their own reindeer, the power to decide how their reindeer were to be cared for, as well as the right to divide their own estate at death. Thus, one cannot conclude, as in the case of peasant women in Austria who were leading the shift from Hungarian to German, that the Saami women shifted to Finnish more rapidly than men to escape from their low status. When women's status is high in their own culture, there is no reason for them to reject their own language.

Indeed, the same language can be a symbol of both oppression and liberation depending on the beliefs of those who use it. At the same time as rural Breton women abandon their language in favor of French, a number of young women involved in the Breton militant movement have gone back to the countryside in search of Breton grassroots authenticity, and have learned Breton as an act of liberation from French oppression. While the militants reject French finery, the peasant women, now their neighbors, look to femininity, the towns, and French. Thus, as far as the peasant women are concerned, there is a paradox in the fact that 'First they [i.e. the French] wanted us to speak French, now they want us to speak Breton.'

In Ireland too, the middle class moved away from Irish in order to secure their own socio-economic mobility when the masses spoke nothing else but Irish. With their Anglicized middle-class status firmly secured, they can now afford the luxury of returning to the language precisely as the masses drop it. The ideological fault line between the newly bilingual urban middle classes and the rural population is further strengthened when the former send their children to the west coast for exposure to native Irish. There they see that Irish is the language of poor struggling farmers and fisherfolk and conclude that the people who speak Irish are not their sort of people.

We must always look to the symbolic value of the languages or varieties in use, as I will show when considering some changes in forms of address a bit later in this chapter. I will also illustrate how some of the language forms resulting from feminist activism have also taken on different meanings in the context of opposing value systems, but first we must look at the effects of another external variable on language change—namely, age.

Change in real v. apparent time

Age, of course, makes a difference too. In a study done of the Gullah Creole spoken in parts of the south-eastern United States, older women were the heaviest users of Gullah because they worked in domestic and agricultural positions. Older men worked mostly in construction. Younger people of both sexes had more access to white-collar jobs and service positions which brought them into contact with standard English. Younger women were ahead of the younger men in their adoption of a more standard form of English.

Similarly, a study of Tunisian women in Morocco showed that older women categorically use diphthongs /aw/ and /aj/, while middle-aged women alternate between diphthongs and monophthongs. Younger women use the monophthongs characteristic of male speech. We can see the variation among the middle-aged women as a 'phonological identity crisis' reflecting their identities as local, traditional Tunisian women and modern, educated women. Often these conflicting identities are encoded in two distinct languages, and code-switching functions much like style-shifting. Indeed, in Tunis the situation is complicated by the presence of French and Arabic, as noted in Chapter 2.

A similar case can be found in women's speech in Dakar, Senegal, which shows both innovatory and conservative tendencies. The preservation and use of the traditional language, Wolof, is linked with women, but at the same time there is a small group of young women known as 'les disquettes' (disco girls) who dress in western-style clothing and refuse to speak Wolof under any circumstances, preferring French instead.

While some patterns of 'age-grading' (i.e. variation in relation to age) may reflect a passing fad such as the Swedish teenagers' use of *nörd*, or simply be repeated anew in each generation, other cases may represent change in progress. This can only be determined by comparing the usage of speech communities at two points in time. Only then can we tell if contemporary variation, or what we might call 'change in apparent time', is a stage in long-term change, or 'change in real time'. One of the first demonstrations of age-grading in the transmission of change is found in a study done in the Swiss village of Charmey in 1905. The middle-aged generation of speakers fluctuated with respect to the use of both old and new norms as exemplified in the speech of the older and younger generations respectively. Another investigation some twenty-five years later demonstrated that the variant used by the younger generation had established itself as the new norm. Both studies showed the importance of variation and age-grading as a mechanism of change.

The social dimensions of linguistic change were explored in more detail on Martha's Vineyard, a small island community off the coast of Massachusetts, where a group of fishermen were introducing increasingly centralized vowels in words such as *night* and *house*. Such variants had not been recorded by earlier dialect geographers and were new to the community. There was a strong correlation between the degree of centralization and the extent to which speakers identified with life on the island and wanted to remain.

We can now come back to examine the diffusion of postvocalic /r/ in the United States and Britain in a historical and geographical perspective. The availability of the dialect atlases and sociolinguistic research on both sides of the Atlantic allows us to make some detailed comparisons of dialect patterns in the two countries. In general, American isoglosses rarely terminate abruptly, which indicates a basic difference between the structure of dialect differentiation in the two countries. The American population has always been more mobile both socially and geographically so that the conditions for the development and maintenance of local dialects were never met to the same extent in the United States as they were in Europe. We have already seen this in Chapter

3, where an examination of some phonological variables showed more finely graded patterns of social stratification in the United States than in Britain.

Nevertheless, the findings of American dialectology dispelled the myth that there was a general American speech. Instead, there were a number of speech areas, each of which was divided into a number of smaller sub-areas. Each major region constituted a unity and had its own regional standard of pronunciation. Because the American colonies lacked a single center of linguistic prestige, the influence of major US cities has been much more regionally limited. Even though the major port cities of Boston, New York, Philadelphia, and Charleston were important points of contact with Britain and centers of diffusion for their respective hinterlands, none was London's equal with respect to the development of standard English.

In Britain, however, the most local dialects were associated with the groups at the lower end of the social hierarchy, while those at the top spoke RP, which showed no trace of regionalisms. In the eastern United States three major dialects were identified: North (including New England and the Hudson Valley); Midland (Pennsylvania and the Alleghenies); and South (Chesapeake Bay, Virginia Piedmont, and the Carolinas), as seen in Fig. 5.3. Each major area is enclosed by a large number of isoglosses representing differences in lexis, grammar, and phonology.

It is also possible to trace the transference of patterns from Britain to the United States. The prevailing opinion was that American English was essentially Southern Standard English of the seventeenth and eighteenth centuries as modified locally. Research, however, demonstrated that most of the dialect differences in the United States had their basis partly in regional varieties of British English which earlier settlers brought with them. In England, for instance, the words *brook*, *burn*, and *beck* show broad regional distribution. *Brook* is dominant throughout the Midlands and into the south; *beck* is found in the area of former Danish settlement, and *burn* (from Scots) extends from Scotland into the border counties of northern England. The term *brook* was transported across the ocean. Although it had strong regional ties in England, it was the form accepted as standard. Its rival regional variants were left behind and two new regional forms developed in the United States, *run* (found in the Midland dialect) and *branch* (Southern). The form *brook* is Northern. Thus, an item showing a broad regional pattern in England became narrowly local in the United States.

There is linguistic evidence for a historical connection between American speech of the north and west and that of northern England, and to some extent the south and the pronunciation of southern England. These linguistic similarities are well supported by the history of American colonization, patterns of westward movement, and later immigration. This is illustrated in the

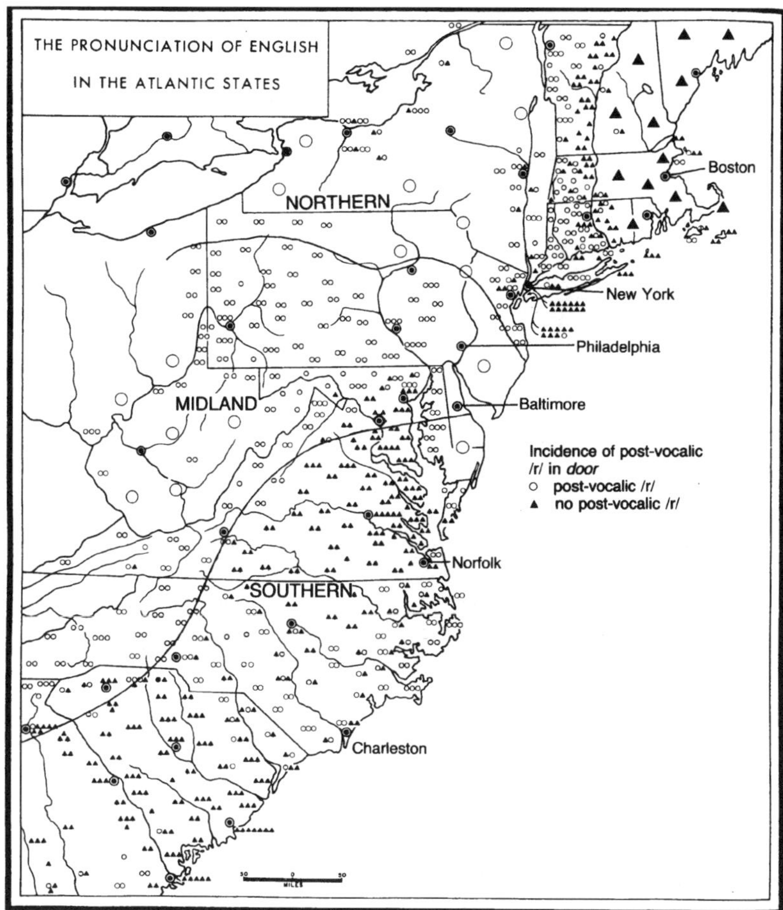

FIG 5.3 Map of the eastern United States showing speech areas and incidence of postvocalic /r/

distribution for postvocalic /r/, as in *cart*, *barn*, etc. in Fig. 5.4. In Britain the distribution of postvocalic /r/ based on dialect research shows that non-rhotic dialects, i.e. those without /r/, were the result of a historical innovation which began somewhere in the east or center of England before spreading northwards.

Before Irish immigration to the United States, the population of eastern New England came from the south-eastern counties of England, where varieties closest to RP are spoken. RP lacks postvocalic /r/. Western New England, on the other hand, had a large number of Scots-Irish immigrants, whose dialects had postvocalic /r/. The Virginia tidewater region and the coastal south were also settled largely by the Scots-Irish. Thus, non-rhotic speech was typical of coastal areas and rhotic speech of inland areas.

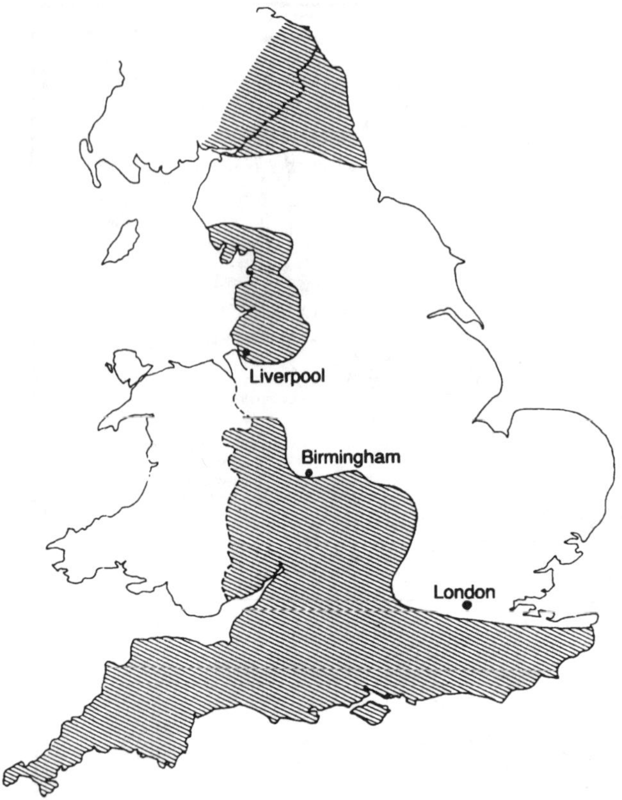

FIG 5.4 Areas (*shaded*) of England where /r/ may still occur in the speech of older, rural, working-class speakers

Fig. 5.3 shows clusters of non-rhotic speech around the major ports of Boston, New York, and Charleston. This was true not only for reasons having to do with settlement patterns, but for cultural reasons too. The coastal areas which had non-rhotic speech kept it because the elite classes there were in touch with English prestige patterns of speaking. The population of the mid-Atlantic states was mixed. Philadelphia was an exception to the port pattern of non-rhotic speech due to Quaker settlement. The Quakers attracted immigrants from all parts of Britain and the rest of Europe. They maintained less trade with Britain and sent fewer children back to English universities. The southern planters and merchants and the New England aristocracy, however, often had their children educated in England or imported English tutors. As long as these networks of communication were intact, they ensured that prestige innovations would cross the Atlantic, enter these port cities, and diffuse outwards from there geographically, and downwards through the social hierarchy.

Since the Second World War, however, rhotic speech has become more prestigious in the United States. It is this increased prestige which was reflected in the sociolinguistic study of New York City, discussed in Chapter 3, which revealed that the middle class used more /r/s than the working class (see Table 3.1). This suggests a change from above. However, in England, the mechanism for change may have come originally from below.

At the time when postvocalic /r/ was lost in many varieties of English, discrimination by accent became an important issue. Some associated the loss of /r/ with the working-class Cockney speech of London. Henry Alford, for instance, wrote in 1864 that the loss of /r/ was a worse fault than the misuse of the aspirate /h/. He quoted extensively from a letter professedly from a correspondent in the House of Commons to the effect that: 'the honourable members may talk of "lawrr" of the land, scawn the "idear" with perfect impunity.' Although Alford denounces this as 'enough to make the hair of anyone but a well seasoned Cockney stand on end', it is evident from this and other examples that the vocalization of /r/, /h/ dropping, and the phenomenon of intrusive /r/ were widespread in the best society in nineteenth-century England. These features may originally have made their way into the language via the lower classes and would be examples of 'change from below'. As noted in Chapter 3, it was not the highest-ranking classes who first adopted what one historian of English called the 'new-fangled' English, i.e. the newly codified standard that was beginning to emerge. It was instead the nouveaux riches who eagerly sought the refinements the grammarians had to offer as signs of their emergent status as educated persons. The impetus for standardization thus diffused both upwards and downwards in the social hierarchy from this new middle class.

At the moment sociolinguistic patterns are rough guidelines based on generalizations from the studies available. Part of the problem in making extrapolations from these patterns to build a theory is that the relationship between language and social structure may vary considerably, both synchronically and diachronically.

Language change and social ideology

I showed in Chapter 4 that titles and other forms of address are important, sensitive (and often also obligatory) indicators of status. Due to the social significance of personal reference, pronouns, titles, and other forms of address are particularly susceptible to modification in response to social and ideological change. Such changes may provide important clues to the social class hierarchy and the attachment of social values to linguistic forms. We saw in Chapter 4 how women have sought to engineer change in the way that society perceives them by introducing new terms of address such as *Ms*.

Some of the most important changes affecting English and other European languages since the 1970s have arisen from changes in society's attitudes towards women prompted by political activism. In many countries the use of non-sexist language is now legally mandated in certain quarters such as in job advertisements, government publications, and media.

The *New York Times*, for example, stopped using titles like *Mrs* and *Miss* with the names of women. At first, it resisted the adoption of the new title *Ms*, but eventually the editor acknowledged that the *Times* believed it was now part of the language. The London *Times*, however, still uses androcentric forms such as *spokesman* and the titles *Mrs* and *Miss*, unless a woman has asked to be referred to as *Ms*. The *Los Angeles Times* has adopted guidelines suggesting alternatives to language that may be offensive to ethnic, racial, and sexual minorities. Such differences in policy are signals of the social and political outlook of editors, who play important roles as gatekeepers in determining which forms they will adopt and thereby help sanction and spread.

At the moment, however, usage is still in flux and where choices exist, they are symbolic of different beliefs and political positions. Compare *Ms Johnson is the chair(person)* with *Miss Johnson is the chairman*. While a narrow linguistic analysis would say they mean the same thing and refer to the same person who happens to hold a particular position, choosing one over the other reveals approval or disapproval of, for example, feminism, language reform, political conservatism or liberalism. There is no way to maintain neutrality now. The existence of an alternative forces a re-evaluation of the old one. With several alternatives available, a woman can sometimes be referred to on the same occasion as *Madame Chairman*, *chairperson*, and *chairwoman*, as I heard one male conference moderator do all in the space of a few minutes without evidently being aware of it.

As another example of the effect of ideology on language change we can look at some of the European languages other than English which have two forms for the pronoun meaning 'you'. One of the pronouns is reserved for use with persons higher than the speaker in social status or persons with whom the speaker does not have a close personal relationship. In many of these languages, such as French and Swedish, the polite form is actually a plural form, while the intimate form is the singular (cf. French *tu/vous*). In others such as German, the deferential form is the same as the third person plural, *Sie*. Such systems of pronominal address have been called T/V systems, following the fact that in Latin and French, the familiar forms begin with the letter T, and the polite forms with V. In fact, the French system served as a model for other languages like Russian. While such systems of address are less complex than the speech levels of Javanese, they are still more complex than those of English, which uses only 'you'. Historically, English also had such a distinction between *thou* and *you*, but it has since been lost.

Much can be learned, however, about how the English system worked in the seventeenth century by examining the usage of the Quakers, who deliberately flouted the conventions of polite society for religious reasons. They refused to use honorific titles and deferential forms of address such as *your excellency*, *my lord*, because they were not literally true. To greet someone as *your humble servant* when you were not was thought to be hypocrisy. Moreover, it violated Quaker ideas about the vanity and worldliness of such titles, for they believed that Christ respected no man's person. The Quakers also rejected the use of *you* as a polite form of address, and preferred *thou*, which to them signalled intimacy and equality. By refusing to use *you* because they took it as a deferential form of address, the Quakers provoked hostility from others who regarded their behavior as a sign of contempt. The repercussions of such deviant usage were severe for some Quakers such as Richard Davis, who reported that when he addressed the lady of the house in which he worked as *thou*, 'she took a stick and gave me such a blow upon my bare head, that made it swell and sore for a considerable time. She was so disturbed by it, that she swore she would kill me.'

Although the change to the use of a socially unmarked *you* is now complete, and *thou* is reserved only for some religious contexts, changes are taking place right now in other languages such as Swedish, where the solidary form, *du*, has over the past few decades come to be more widely used across a broader social spectrum than previously. One social historian points to this phenomenon as an index of social change in line with the fact that the Social Democratic Party which dominated the Swedish political scene for nearly six decades of the twentieth century stressed egalitarian relations in its programs for social, educational, and economic reform. When systems undergo change, the rules for usage may be somewhat ambiguous and variable. The Swedish address system underwent rapid change in the 1960s and 1970s, so that in 1965 police officers in patrol cars addressed each other indirectly with titles and last names. Today they all use *du*. While there were ambiguities going back a hundred years, people seemed to be even more sensitive in the 1970s since it was not clear what the new norms were. In fact, at that time some Swedes reported that their choice of address on some occasions was governed by whether they felt irritable or cheerful. Of course, linguistic and social systems do not necessarily change in synchrony with one another. Sweden is still a highly stratified society, and some of the problems in deciding what forms to use may derive from attempts to reconcile conflicts between this stratification and the ideology of social democracy. In 1991 with the election of a more conservative government, there is now an ideological shift in the opposite direction.

Historically, Old Swedish had only one pronoun of address, the singular *du* 'you'. In the 1600s the plural pronoun *I* came to be used in address to a single person under the influence of the Byzantine court. This pronoun is the source of modern Swedish *ni* when it took on the plural suffix of the preceding verb-form, e.g. *haven I* 'do you have?' The peasantry never adopted this new polite form which spread among the elite class, but stuck to the use of *du* as a form of solidary address among mutual acquaintances. To superiors, they used occupational titles such as *Herr Tågbefälhavaren* 'Mr Train Commander'. This peasant use of *du* among the working class has survived today and become a hallmark of membership in the Social Democrat Party. In the 1970s many Swedes said they would address the Prime Minister as *du* because he was a fellow Social Democrat. The increased use of solidary *du* is an example of change from below.

From the middle of the 1800s, well in advance of social democracy, there was pressure to regularize *ni* as a form of address. Again in the 1920s and 1930s, in particular, reformers attempted to gain wider acceptance for *ni*. Many people felt that the system of titles was cumbersome. Some schools and hospitals posted signs which said 'Here we say *ni*'. The reluctance to use *ni* in cases where *du* is not considered appropriate results in indirect address, so, for instance, it is possible for a salesperson to address a young female stranger by asking *Vad vill fröken ha?* 'What does the woman want?' There are other formulas which avoid address forms and titles altogether such as *vad får det vara* 'what will it be?' In 1944 a Gallup poll showed considerable variation in the forms people said they would use with a stranger: 37 per cent said they would say *ni*; 24 per cent titles such as *frun, herrn, fröken*; 17 per cent *du*; and 15 per cent *min dam, min herre, damen*. Of course, factors such as age and perceived social status of the addressee relative to the speaker were not investigated in this opinion poll, so it is hard to tell precisely what the survey means, except that people thought both *ni* and *du* as well as titles were apparently in use at this time.

The *ni* reforms were largely ineffectual. In the 1960s a number of public institutions such as the universities, hospitals, businesses, and factories in the private sector instituted a reciprocal use of *du*. Some organizations such as the Red Cross also institutionalized the use of *du* among its members, in spite of opposition to it, and *du* continued to gain ground over *ni* for most of the twentieth century. Some examples of this transition can be seen across the generations of a family, where it is not unusual to find parents reporting that their children had not addressed them as *du*, but their grandchildren now do. Most children in the 1960s and 1970s have grown up with the use of *du* as the most common form of address. While *du* made great strides in the post-war period, to the extent that some predicted the disappearance of *ni* by the turn of the twenty-first century, in fact, *ni* seems to be making a comeback in the 1980s and 1990s among the younger generation.

In order to understand these changes, we have to look at the social significance which *du* and *ni* have for different groups. *Du* conveys both solidarity as well as intimacy, while *ni* may signal condescension or respect. Nowadays, in its intimate functions *du* normally occurs with the use of first name, kin title, or no name. Occasionally, it occurs with a title, but this is felt as odd. Etiquette books say that the choice between polite *ni* and intimate *du* is governed by sex, age, and social rank, so that, for instance, a woman should be the first to suggest a shift to *du* to a man, those older suggest a shift to younger people.

It is not always recognized that there are two distinct uses of *du* since they are divided along class lines. One graduate student, for instance, told me that while she would always address a much older female professor in her department with *du*, she would never address her by her first name. This use of *du* is solidary, indicating that there is no social distance between speaker and addressee, but it is not intimate. One maintains personal though not social distance. Intimacy is indicated by the use of first name plus *du*, and people who are on *du* terms with one another in a solidary but not intimate relationship will avoid each other's first names.

The clash between the two different understandings of *du* can be illustrated in this anecdote about the usage between Mr and Mrs N, a middle-class couple (formerly of working-class origin), and Mr and Mrs B, members of the Stockholm upper class. Mr N is the caretaker of Mr B's farm and both are roughly the same age. Because of his higher social rank, it is appropriate for Mr B to suggest the reciprocal use of *du* to Mr N. So they are now on *du* terms. However, as far as Mr B's norms of politeness are concerned, it is always up to a woman to propose to a man that they put away titles and use *du*. Mrs N, however, operates with a different convention which dictates that a superior must initiate a switch to *du*. So she addresses Mr B as *Direktör B* 'director', which he dislikes intensely. Mrs B for her part knows that Mr and Mrs N would prefer to use *du* with her and her husband. Here there is no clash between rank and gender since by either criterion she should be the one to suggest a switch to *du*, but she refuses to. Mrs B does not realize that to Mrs N the choice of *du* means simply solidarity and not intimacy, since Mrs B always reserves the use of *du* to her intimates. Mrs N, however, is likely to perceive Mrs B as stuck-up and distancing herself for reasons to do with class. The differences between the Bs and the Ns reflect a clash between change from above and change from below.

When it isn't apparent what social class a person comes from, or what age they are, many speakers find themselves during this period of transition in situations where they do not know what to do because as one man said, 'You don't want to use titles if they are workers and one doesn't dare use *du* in case they aren't.' One result of the conflict in norms in this changing system was that some people developed strategies for suggesting a switch to *du* such as a younger person who says to an older, 'I wouldn't dare suggest *du* because you're older.' This is a hint to the older person to initiate the shift. Although members of the upper class are adopting the use of solidary *du*, sometimes their use of *du* is not returned by the working class who perceive it as condescending. People seem to operate on the assumption that they should wait for others to address them and follow their lead.

The institutional use of *du* has caused problems for businesses with contacts elsewhere in Europe since it is not clear how to translate this solidary but not intimate *du* into other European languages such as French and German. Applying her own norms of usage, for example, a Swedish secretary might address the president of a Danish branch office as *du*, when he might not be on *du* terms with his secretary whom he has known for thirty years. Visiting German businessmen who would be on V (*Sie*) terms with one another find themselves forced into a situation where they have to use T (*Du*) forms to their Swedish colleagues and then it becomes awkward to remain on *Sie* terms with each other, while conversing with a complete stranger using *Du*. Of course, the use of English avoids these problems, and is often preferred in international business. Finally, a Swedish friend, who is a native speaker of Dutch, told me of an occasion when he acted as a court interpreter. Dutch has a T/V distinction with *je* being the familiar and *U* the formal form. He interpreted the unmarked Swedish *du* as *U*, and *ni* as *je*.

Just at the time when *du* seemed to have won the day, however, *ni* is apparently returning. A Swedish linguist who studied this in the mid-1980s noted that she found herself more and more often referred to as *ni* by strangers who were the same age and younger. Some people are unhappy about this new '*ni* trend' and have written to the newspapers to complain that it must be stopped because *ni* is a sign of class barriers in a society which is supposed to be democratic and founded on equality. Others, however, have never been happy with the *du* reforms. As one woman noted in her letter to the newspaper, if she went into a shop or office and people addressed her as *du*, she would leave!

The study done in the mid-1980s with high school students born in the 1960s who would have grown up with the generalized solidary use of *du* found that the majority of them reported they would use *ni* with a person who was older and/or in a position of authority. Apparently these young people think it is less risky to use *ni* with strangers because more people are likely to take offense at being addressed as *du* than *ni*. However, that impression may not actually be correct since some older people do not like being called *ni*. Because the younger generation were not familiar with the older system, they do not attach some of the negative connotations to *ni* that older speakers do. For younger speakers, it simply marks a politeness boundary between strangers, especially when there is an age difference between them.

In other European languages there appear to be similar competing understandings of the semantics of the familiar and the polite forms such as in German. For some Germans, *Du* is the unmarked pronoun of solidarity, while for others it signals intimacy. *Sie* indicates social distance and formality. Before the late 1960s German students and university professors used *Sie* to one another and among themselves, but around the late 1960s the students adopted *Du* among themselves. Now that there is a swing back to political conservatism, norms may change again. During periods of change, people are uncertain about their usage and ambiguities may arise.

Norms for the use of T/V forms may be undergoing change in France too. The problem is well illustrated in the cartoon in Fig. 5.5, where a man addresses a woman as *vous*, but uses the verb form appropriate for the *tu* pronoun. The article accompanying the cartoon is entitled 'Monsieur, où est ton dossier?' 'Sir, where is your dossier?', which illustrates a conflict between the use of the title *Monsieur*, and the familiar pronoun *ton*. A recent study done at a French business revealed that gender, age, social hierarchy, and proximity determined choice of *tu* or *vous*. Among themselves, women at the office never used a colleague's last name without preceding it with the title *Madame*. When they used first names, they also used the familiar pronoun *tu*. Men, however, used the familiar form with their male colleagues' last names, even though some felt uncomfortable

FIG 5.5 'Vous as un joli vouvou'

about it because the last name seemed too formal to be associated with the familiar pronoun.

When a new person comes into the office, how does he or she fit into the established system? One woman said she just called everyone *vous* as a sign of respect. A former military man who had joined the firm said he never used the term *monsieur* because that was not done in the army. There is a transitory period while everyone adjusts to a new environment and the new employee tries to situate himself or herself into the existing social context of the office. It is during this time that apparent oddities such as 'Monsieur, où est ton dossier' are likely to arise. However, there is apparently a lot of leeway in the system, which is negotiated on the spot, since once colleagues have used the T form to one another, they may still on some occasions revert to V. One man said that depending on whether he called his boss *Frémont* or *Monsieur Frémont* on the phone, the boss replied with T or V. In other cases, the entrance of a stranger into a context where others have established a T relationship may lead to a choice of V, such as when a boss addresses his secretary in front of a stranger by saying *Mireille, voulez-vous me passer le dossier*? 'Mireille, would you pass me the file?' Or, to take another example, if the boss and one of his workers play sport at the weekend, they will call each other *tu*, but revert back to *vous* at the office.

These examples are reminiscent of my discussion of code choice in Chapter 2, where speakers such as the brother and sister in the shop in western Kenya use code choice to define the situation in terms favorable to their own respective roles as storekeeper and customer. Use of a T form can be a big put-down if one expects to be addressed with V. Conversely, the use of the polite form can also be seen as putting one in one's place if it is not expected, as in Sweden, when after the Christmas holidays in the mid-1970s, sales clerks were heard addressing the hordes of customers returning unwanted gifts as *ni*, apparently because they were overworked and irritable. Upper-class customers would probably have considered this polite, but middle- and working-class people would perceive it as rude. Over time, however, such choices, whether consciously made or not, can lead to long-term change.

Similar changes have taken place in non-western languages too in response to social and political change. Since the Islamic Revolution of 1979 Persian forms of address have undergone change which reflects the shift from power to solidarity. Asymmetrical forms which reflected the complex social structure of pre-revolutionary Iran have declined and now plain speech and forms of address marking solidarity have become more popular. The terms 'brother' and 'sister' emerged as solitary forms of address after the Revolution just as in the former Soviet Union and China 'comrade' enjoyed widespread use.

Another example of change in an address system motivated by changing societal values has been taking place in Nahuatl, spoken in parts of Mexico.

Nahuatl has become a language of solidarity in the face of the threat posed by Spanish, which has been replacing Nahuatl for some time. Nahuatl once had an extensive system of honorifics, which affected not only the choice of pronouns, but also the forms of verbs, nouns, and pronouns. In traditional Nahuatl there were four levels, as illustrated in the different ways speakers would say 'give me' (*maca* is the verb 'to give'). Level I is the lowest and would be used for addressing intimates or subordinates, Level II for strangers and kinsmen, Level III for very old or distinguished people, and Level IV is like Level III, except that it refers to the person addressed in the third person.

Level I: *teh tinehmacha* 'you give me'
Level II: *tehhuatzin tinechonmacha* 'you give me'
Level III: *momahuizotzin tinechonmomaquilia* 'your reverence gives me'
Level IV: *imahuizotzin nechonmomaquilitzinoa* 'his reverence gives me'

This system has now become narrowed and is being lost in reference to people, although it is still used in direct address, probably due to fear of giving offense to people in face-to-face interaction. When people are referred to who are not there, it is less likely that the person referred to without honorifics will hear of it. The development of ethnic self-consciousness and egalitarianism has led to this narrowing of honorific usage. Sentiments of group solidarity expressed towards Nahuatl have also resulted in the stigmatization of Spanish loanwords. The highest rate of Hispanisms is found in the speech of younger men who are not committed to community life.

The meaning of identity and ethnicity can change according to context, especially in the face of threat from outside. During the Second World War, for instance, people who would have addressed each other asymmetrically in Sweden adopted the egalitarian *du*. In recent years in Britain we can see the emergence of a more general Asian or even black ethnicity which includes both Asians and blacks. In the eyes of most Britons, south Asians function as a single 'ethnic' or 'racial' category, even though they are of very different linguistic, cultural, and religious origins. Thus, the local shop run by a Bengali family might be called by white Britons the 'Pakistani', 'Indian', or 'Asian' shop, regardless of the precise national, religious, and ethnic affiliation of its owners. Now, however, the alien environment of Britain seems to be redefining previous outsiders as 'fellow Asians' and even 'fellow blacks' due to the similarity in their present circumstances as minority groups in Britain.

The *Sunday Times* (26 June 1988) carried an article entitled 'Black? Not us, protest Asians'. It described the negative reaction of some community leaders to the annual report of the Commission for Racial Equality in which Asians were classified as 'Blacks'. A new group called the Asian People's National Association has been founded to fight for independent recognition. The Deputy

Chairman of the CRE, a Gujarati from India, estimated that about 70 per cent of Asians resented the term 'black' applied to them, while about 10 per cent identified themselves as 'black'. He noted that those who accepted the term 'black' did so initially because they believed they shared a common predicament with Afro-Caribbeans. Some influential leaders in the Afro-Caribbean community are not pleased with the possibility that membership in the 'Black' community may be redefined in this way. The issue has apparently divided some Asian families too. The article noted the case of one restaurant owner and his 27-year-old daughter, who is a London barrister. The father was adamant he was not black, while the daughter said, 'Black is not derogatory. I consider myself to be black. So do most young Asians.' The relative discreteness of languages/varieties as well as the salience and prestige of them as markers of distinct ethnic identities will affect people's ideas of what to call the language they speak as well as what to call themselves. These perceptions may change over time in response to social pressures of various kinds. The choices people make serve to align their allegiances with one group or another to whom they attribute some similarity.

The importance of network as a factor in change was highlighted by some of the studies I talked about in Chapters 2 and 3. A study done in a Detroit suburban high school of two teenage peer groups called Jocks and Burnouts shows how the development of adolescent social structure provides a major impetus for phonological change. The Jocks are largely of middle-class background and involved in school activities, while the Burnouts are mainly from blue-collar families and some are involved in drugs and other dangerous activities not sanctioned by the school. The Burnouts' contacts with peers from closer to the inner city brings them into closer touch with changes going on in the city, and they regard use of urban speechways as symbolic of their knowledge and endorsement of urban lifestyles. Many have friends in Detroit, go to parties there, and regard the city as a desirable place to 'hang out'. When they leave school, most will seek employment locally and life after high school will involve a continuation of some of the same friendships. They are ahead of the Jocks in certain sound changes already observed to be under way in the adult population. The Jocks, on the other hand, socialize in peer networks drawn from the more localized suburban area and have less contact with urban culture. However, the Jocks are also more upwardly mobile. When they leave school, most will go on to college outside their community.

We have seen in this chapter how language is essentially a human cultural product situated in an ever-changing historical context. The concepts of social as well as geographical space are vital to understanding the diffusion of change. Different types of social structures may give rise to different kinds of changes. The most innovative varieties are more likely to be spoken by those with weak network ties, while those with dense, multiplex networks tend to conserve local varieties. Geographically speaking, central areas are innovative, while peripheral areas are conservative. Cities represent, of course, high contact areas, where chances are significantly greater for interactions with strangers than in small rural villages.

Not coincidentally, it is in rural and working-class communities, where the most local forms of speech are still most strongly preserved today, in those parts of society furthest removed from literate traditions. Residents of areas of cities which have long been typically working class are better able to preserve the strongest form of urban dialect.

It is interesting to compare in this respect the course of linguistic change in English and Icelandic. While English has changed dramatically over the course of the last seven centuries, not so Icelandic. The conservatism of Icelandic is explained only partly by geographic isolation. Possibly more important is the nature of Iceland's social structure, which is based on strong kin and friendship networks. Britain, by contrast, has a very different socio-political and settlement history. The course of the history of English was drastically interrupted twice, first by Danish settlers arriving in the ninth and tenth centuries, and secondly, by the Anglo-Norman conquest in the eleventh. London had already begun to emerge as a center of commerce in the thirteenth and fourteenth centuries, when urbanization in Iceland was almost totally absent.

Migration to urban centers has resulted in a levelling of the dialect differences among the different groups of incomers. Small communities such as the villages of north-west New Britain we looked at in Chapter 1 are in a better position to maintain linguistically complex and distinct structures through regular in-group interaction. We saw that the Siassi languages functioned widely as lingua francas in the area, while Anêm and Amara were of no value since they could not be used dual-lingually with any other language. A language which is not used across group boundaries as a second language can afford to maintain complexity and irregularity, while a lingua franca must be more easily learnable if it is to function efficiently. Thus, it is the Siassi group languages which are the simplest. In the next chapter I will look at what happens in situations of high contact where special kinds of languages called pidgins and creoles are formed.

Annotated bibliography

An overview of German sociolinguistics can be found in Stephen Barbour and Patrick Stevenson's book (1990); see also the articles by W. Hefner and P. Sture Ureland (1980) and Mattheier (1980).

One formulation of the idea that semantically relevant information tends to be preserved in surface structure can be found in Kiparsky's (1972) Distinctiveness Condition. The report about the royal family engaging in 'linguistic slumming' was written by Martyn Harris (1987); further details can be found in Rosewarne's (1994) article. Janet Holmes's (1995) article documents glottalization in New Zealand.

Uriel Weinreich et al.'s article (1968) explains how traditional historical linguistics can be rethought in a sociolinguistic framework. James Milroy's (1991) book offers a sociolinguistic perspective on the history of English; see also James and Lesley Milroy's (1985 *b*) article. William Labov's (1994) book provides a synthesis of what is known about the internal constraints on variation and change. The notion of lexical diffusion is discussed in Matthew Chen and William Wang's article (1975). C.-J. Bailey's book (1973) attempts to explain implicational patterning of variability. Suzanne Romaine's (1984 *b*) article traces the history of the *-t/d* variable. J. K. Chambers (1992) did the study of American influence on the speech of Oxfordshire adolescents.

Articles by Penelope Eckert (1989) and William Labov (1990) investigate the role of women in linguistic change. For some studies of the retention of indigenous languages by women in Latin American, see Spedding (1994) on the use of Aymara in Bolivia, Harvey (1994) on the use of Quechua in Peru, and Hill (1987) on Nahuatl in Mexico. The studies of women in Tunisia and Senegal were done by Chedia Trabelsi (1991) and Leigh Swigart (1992), respectively. William Labov's (1972 *b*) article illustrates some of the forms of African-American vernacular English used by Harlem adolescents. Maryon McDonald's (1994: 91, 102, 103) article is the source of the quotations relating to Breton. Otto Jespersen (1922: 214) is the source of the claim that women were responsible for changes concerning /r/. The study of Norwegian in the United States can be found in Einar Haugen's book (1953), and the one on Saami/Norwegian bilingualism in northern Norway in Tove Bull's article (1991). Marjut Aikio (1992) is the author of the study of Saami in Finland.

The Martha's Vineyard study was done by William Labov (1963). The Gullah research can be found in Patricia Nichols's article (1983). The Quaker study is described in Richard Bauman's book (1983). Information on Swedish pronominal usage can be found in Christina Bratt Paulston's article (1976) and Eva Mårtennsson's article (1986). The study of pronominal usage in the French firm was done by Denis Guigo (1991). The study of Nahuatl was done by Jane H. and Kenneth C. Hill (1980). The study of adolescents in Detroit is described in Penelope Eckert's book (1989). For information on changes in Persian, see Mohammad H. Keshavarz's article (1988).

Chapter 6

Pidgin and Creole Languages

IN his speech to the English-speaking Union Conference in Ottawa, the Duke of Edinburgh made reference to one of the best known pidgin and creole languages in observing that he was 'referred to in that splendid language as "Fella belong Mrs. Queen"'. Although the Duke was right to consider Tok Pisin ('talk pidgin') spoken in Papua New Guinea as a language rather than a dialect of English, he was wrong about his designation. He would be called 'man bilong kwin'. Contrary to what many Europeans think about Tok Pisin, *fella* cannot be used in this way at all to mean 'man' or 'husband', so the Duke's statement is ungrammatical. *Fella* can be used only as a suffix in Tok Pisin and has a number of grammatical functions, e.g. to mark adjectives and numerals, as in *tupela blakpela pik* 'two black pigs', and to mark the second person plural form of 'you', as in *yupela i no ken go* 'you (plural) cannot go'.

Although there is no agreement on how to define pidgins and creoles in precise linguistic terms or where they came from, all linguists recognize that there is such a group of languages. Their distinctiveness lies not so much in terms of a common historical origin, but in shared circumstances of socio-historical development and use. This is one reason why sociolinguists have been very interested in them; another reason is that they are highly variable and present many challenges to the models of variation examined in Chapter 3. Because pidgins and creoles are the outcome of diverse processes and influences in situations of language contact where speakers of different languages have to work out a common means of communication, variation may have a number of different sources such as mixing, first and second language acquisition, and universals.

At present, there is no way of deciding whether a language constitutes a pidgin or creole unless reference is made to three criteria: linguistic, social, and historical. A pidgin is a contact variety restricted in form and function and native to no one, which is formed by members of at least two (and usually more) groups of different linguistic backgrounds. Structurally speaking, pidgins are simplified languages characterized by a minimal lexicon, little or no

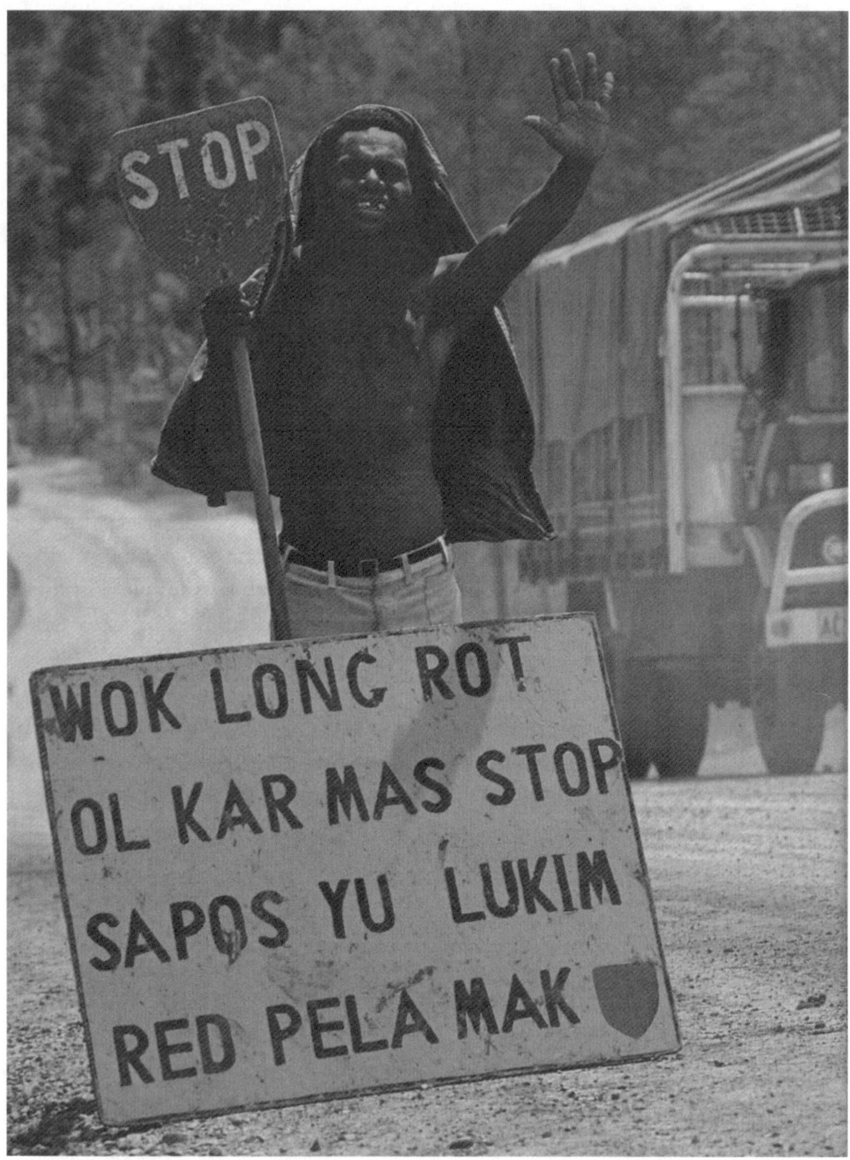

FIG 6.1 Sign in Tok Pisin in Papua New Guinea warning all cars to stop if they see the red stop sign

morphology, and limited syntax. A creole is a nativized pidgin, expanded in form and function to meet the communicative needs of a community of native speakers. In this chapter I will say something about the distribution, origins, structure, and use of pidgins and creoles in society.

Distribution

Pidgin and creole languages are spoken mainly in Third World countries. Their role there is intimately connected with a variety of political and social questions. The exact number of languages is difficult to establish because it depends on how we define the terms 'pidgin' and 'creole'. There are probably more than 100 pidgin and creole languages in daily use around the world, and more speakers of these languages than there are of Swedish. Today in Melanesia, for instance, varieties of pidgin/creole English have become the most widely known languages of highly multilingual populations. In fact, Tok Pisin is the largest language in the south Pacific today with as many as 2 million speakers. In addition, over a quarter of a million Melanesians in Vanuatu and Solomon Islands speak related varieties.

Most of the pidgins and creoles linguists have studied in detail are based on European languages, in particular, Spanish, Portuguese, French, English, and Dutch. However, those based on English are more numerous than those based on any other language, attesting to Britain's three and a half centuries of imperialism which spread not just varieties of standard and regional English but also more pidgins and creoles than any other language. The next largest group is based on French, and a much smaller number based on non-European languages, such as Sango spoken in the Central African Republic.

The standard view that pidgins and creoles are mixed languages with the vocabulary of the superstrate (also called the lexifier or base language) and the grammar of the substrate has been the traditional basis for classifying these languages according to their lexical base. Thus, when scholars speak of English-based creoles, they are referring to all those creoles which have taken most of their vocabulary from English, such as Tok Pisin. Terms such as 'English-lexicon or lexifier pidgin/creole' are also used. Thus, in the case of Tok Pisin, English is the superstrate and the indigenous languages of Papua New Guinea are the substrate. In the case of Haitian Creole French, French is the superstrate, and West African languages are the substrate, because the creole emerged among a linguistically mixed population of slaves brought to Haiti from West Africa.

Although scholars have often treated English-based pidgins/creoles as

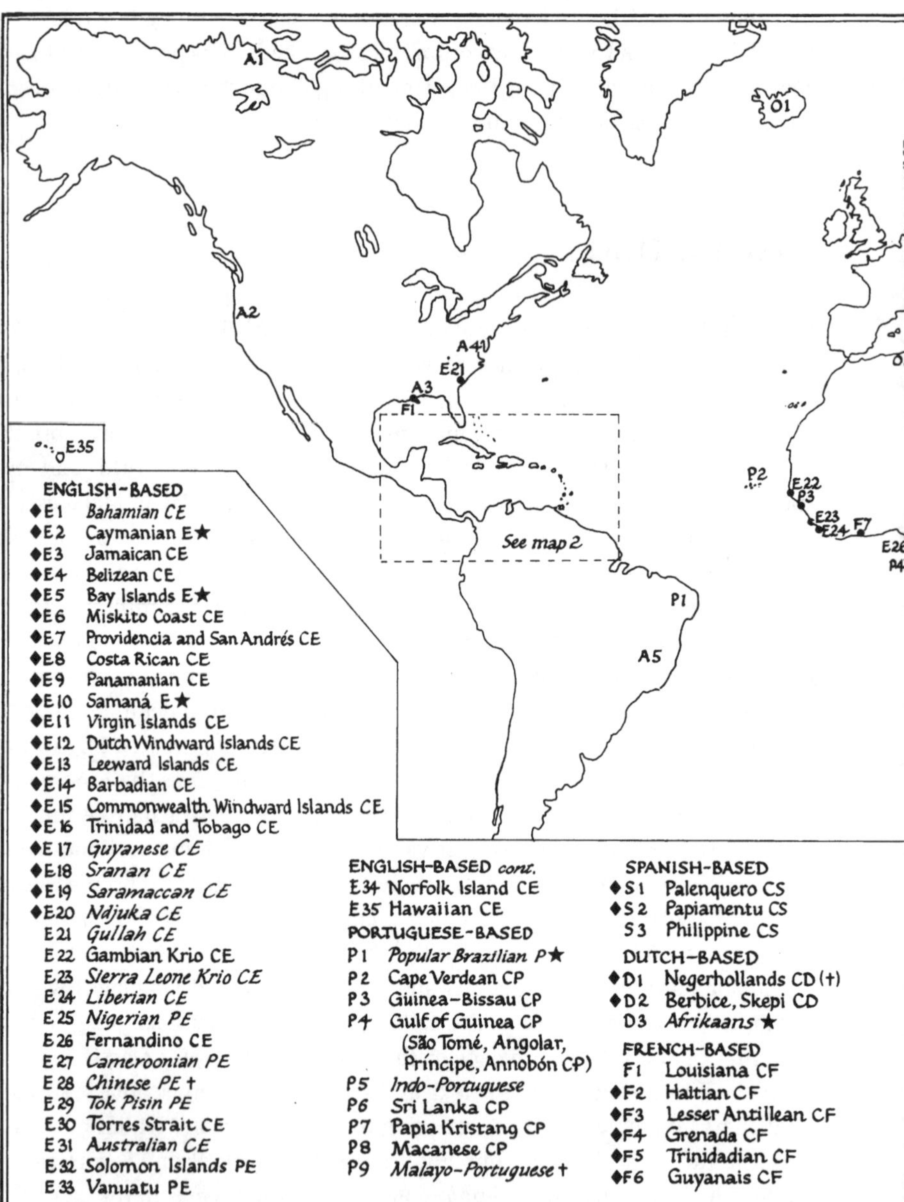

A1
O1
A2
A4
E21
A3
F1
E35
See map 2
P2
E22
P3
E23
E24
F7
E26
P4
D3
P1
A5
ENGLISH-BASED
♦E1 Bahamian CE
♦E2 Caymanian E★
♦E3 Jamaican CE
♦E4 Belizean CE
♦E5 Bay Islands E★
♦E6 Miskito Coast CE
♦E7 Providencia and San Andrés CE
♦E8 Costa Rican CE
♦E9 Panamanian CE
♦E10 Samaná E★
♦E11 Virgin Islands CE
♦E12 Dutch Windward Islands CE
♦E13 Leeward Islands CE
♦E14 Barbadian CE
♦E15 Commonwealth Windward Islands CE
♦E16 Trinidad and Tobago CE
♦E17 Guyanese CE
♦E18 Sranan CE
♦E19 Saramaccan CE
♦E20 Ndjuka CE
E21 Gullah CE
E22 Gambian Krio CE
E23 Sierra Leone Krio CE
E24 Liberian CE
E25 Nigerian PE
E26 Fernandino CE
E27 Cameroonian PE
E28 Chinese PE †
E29 Tok Pisin PE
E30 Torres Strait CE
E31 Australian CE
E32 Solomon Islands PE
E33 Vanuatu PE
ENGLISH-BASED cont.
E34 Norfolk Island CE
E35 Hawaiian CE
PORTUGUESE-BASED
P1 Popular Brazilian P★
P2 Cape Verdean CP
P3 Guinea-Bissau CP
P4 Gulf of Guinea CP
(São Tomé, Angolar, Príncipe, Annobón CP)
P5 Indo-Portuguese
P6 Sri Lanka CP
P7 Papia Kristang CP
P8 Macanese CP
P9 Malayo-Portuguese †
SPANISH-BASED
♦S1 Palenquero CS
♦S2 Papiamentu CS
S3 Philippine CS
DUTCH-BASED
♦D1 Negerhollands CD (†)
♦D2 Berbice, Skepi CD
D3 Afrikaans ★
FRENCH-BASED
F1 Louisiana CF
♦F2 Haitian CF
♦F3 Lesser Antillean CF
♦F4 Grenada CF
♦F5 Trinidadian CF
♦F6 Guyanais CF

FIG 6.2 Map showing some of the world's pidgins and creoles

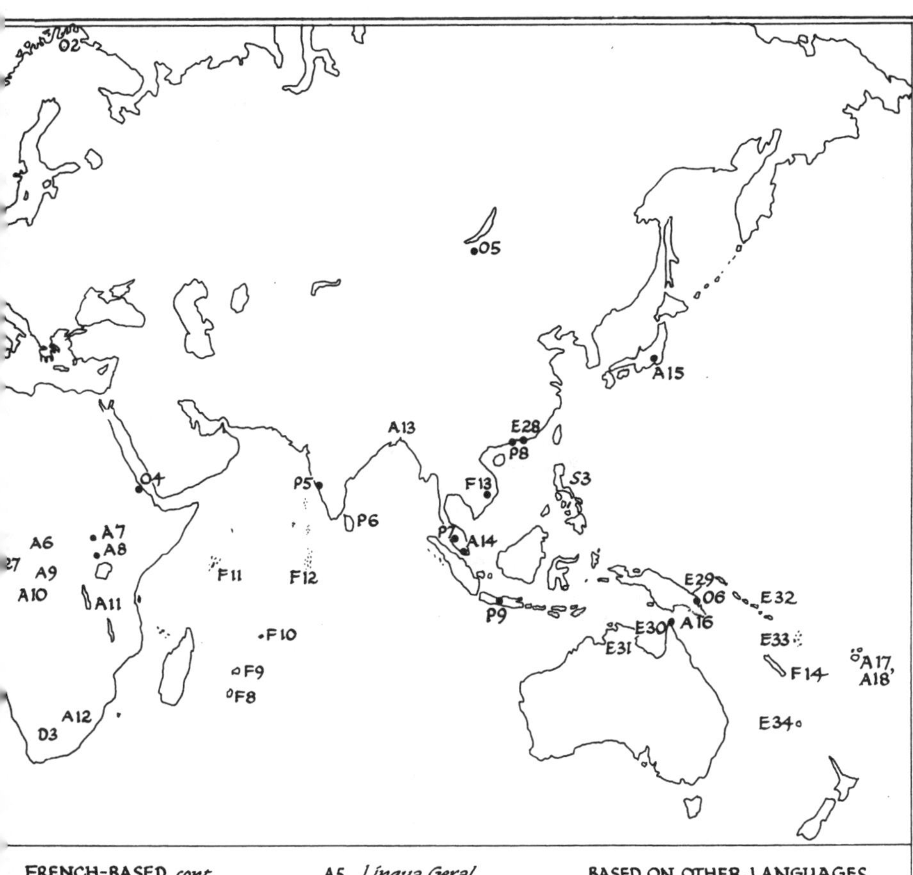

FRENCH-BASED *cont.*
F7 West African PF
F8 Réunionnais ★
F9 Mauritian CF
F10 Rodrigues CF
F11 Seychellois CF
F12 Diego Garcia CF (Chagos Arch.)
F13 Vietnamese PF †
F14 New Caledonian PF †

AFRICAN-, ASIAN-, AUSTRONESIAN- AND AMERINDIAN-BASED
A1 *Eskimo Trade Jargon* †
A2 *Chinook Jargon* †
A3 *Mobilian Jargon* (†)
A4 *Delaware Jargon* †
A5 *Lingua Geral*
A6 *Sango P/C*
A7 Juba Pidgin Arabic
A8 Nubi Creole Arabic
A9 *Lingala*
A10 *Kituba*
A11 *Swahili P/C*
A12 *Fanakalo*
A13 Naga Pidgin
A14 Baba Malay
A15 Pidgin Japanese †
A16 Hiri Motu
A17 Pidgin Fijian
A18 Pidgin Hindustani

BASED ON OTHER LANGUAGES
O1 Pidgin Basque †
O2 *Russenorsk* †
O3 *Lingua Franca* †
O4 Eritrean Pidgin Italian
O5 Chinese Pidgin Russian †
O6 Unserdeutsch

† Extinct
★ Semi-creole
Italics Spoken over a wider area
♦ Shown on map 2

FIG 6.3 Map showing the Caribbean creoles

ATLANTIC

OCEAN

VIRGIN ISLANDS
E11, D1
Anguila
St.Martin
E10
DOMINICAN REP.
F2
E12
Antigua
Saba
E13
Montserrat
PUERTO RICO
St.Kitts
Nevis
Guadeloupe
LEEWARD ISLANDS
Dominica
F3
Martinique
SEA
WINDWARD ISLANDS
St.Lucia
St.Vincent
Barbados
E14
E15
F4
Grenada
Aruba
S2
Bonaire
Curaçao
Tobago
Trinidad
E16, F5
VENEZUELA
E17
D2
GUYANA
E18
F6
FRENCH GUIANA
E19
E20
SURINAME
A

0 500 1000 km
0 500 miles

† Extinct
★ Semi-creole
Italics Spoken over a wider area

dialects of English and French pidgins/creoles as Romance languages, etc., most now recognize that creoles are languages in their own right with an independent structure. They are not parasitic systems or corrupted versions of the languages to which they are most closely related at the lexical level. The example of *-pela* in Tok Pisin shows how what was originally an English word with no grammatical function has been pressed into service in a very un-English way to mark grammatical distinctions in Tok Pisin.

It is customary practice to label pidgins and creoles with a formula which includes their location and their principal lexifier language, e.g. Chinese Pidgin English, Berbice Creole Dutch, Rabaul Creole German. Since some pidgins and creoles may change their lexical affiliation through a process known as relexification, such as Berbice Dutch did when Dutch was superseded by English as the superstrate language, these labels are not entirely satisfactory. Other creoles such as Tok Pisin and Sranan, an English-based variety spoken in Suriname, have been affected by this kind of change too. However, no one has suggested replacing the name Berbice Creole Dutch with Berbice Creole English. These labels are unsatisfactory for other reasons too. One is that they imply a separation between lexicon and syntax and give more weight to the lexicon in deciding relationships among languages. Another difficulty is that the first term in such labels may be ambiguous as to whether it specifies a language, a group of speakers, or a geographical location. Thus, in the name Hawaiian Creole English the adjective Hawaiian is ambiguous because it could refer to the geographical location of Hawai'i, to people of Hawaiian descent, or to the Hawaiian language.

Moreover, linguists' names for pidgins and creoles are not always widely used by the speakers of the languages themselves. Thus, Tok Pisin has sometimes been referred to by linguists as Neomelanesian or New Guinea Pidgin English, while its speakers call it Tok Pisin, or simply pidgin. Similarly, speakers of Torres Strait Creole English call their language Broken (i.e. broken English), while speakers of Australian Creole English call their language Kriol and Hawai'i Creole English speakers call their variety 'Pidgin', etc. Sranan is sometimes also called Sranan Tongo 'Suriname tongue' or Taki-Taki 'talktalk'.

Creolists recognize two major groups of languages, the Atlantic and the Pacific, according to historical, geographic, and linguistic factors. The Atlantic group was established primarily during the seventeenth and eighteenth centuries in the Caribbean and West Africa, while the Pacific group originated primarily in the nineteenth. The Atlantic creoles were largely products of the slave trade in West Africa which dispersed large numbers of West Africans to the Caribbean. Varieties of Caribbean creoles have also been transplanted to the United Kingdom by West Indian immigrants, as well as to the USA and Canada. The languages of the Atlantic share a West African common substrate and display many common features, some of which we will examine later in this chapter.

In the Pacific different languages formed the substratum and socio-cultural conditions were somewhat different from those in the Atlantic. Although the plantation setting was crucial for the emergence of pidgins in both areas, in the Pacific laborers were recruited and indentured rather than slaves. Apart from Hawai'i, a history of more gradual creolization has distinguished the Pacific from the Atlantic (particularly Caribbean) creoles, whose transition has been more abrupt. Although this traditional grouping is geographically convenient, it may obscure a far more complex picture of interrelationships. It also does not take into account, for instance, that there was probably some interaction between Atlantic and Pacific, and that judgements about the degree to which creolization was abrupt depend on historical evidence which may not be available. The sharing of many of the features in the Atlantic and Pacific pidgins and creoles has led some creolists to argue for the diffusion of a nautical pidgin from the Atlantic to the Pacific. Sailors probably played an important role in spreading linguistic features across vast areas and this may explain why there is some lexical sharing among distant pidgins such as Hawai'i Pidgin English, Chinook Jargon, a contact language used for trade in the Pacific north-west, and Eskimo Jargon.

Words from European languages such as *savvy* (⟨Portuguese/Spanish *sabir/saber* 'to know') and *picanniny* 'child', 'baby' (⟨ Portuguese/Spanish *pequeño* or *pequeniño* 'small') were probably diffused by sailors from the Atlantic to the Pacific, where these and a few other words of European origin are attested early and still current in pidgins and creoles spoken today, such as Jamaican Creole, Tok Pisin, and many others. Indeed, *savvy* is one of the notably few items to have entered standard English from pidgin English (to be more precise—probably Chinese Pidgin English, which developed around the port of Canton in 1700).

Meanwhile, other words from indigenous languages such as *kanaka* (⟨Hawaiian 'human being', 'person', 'man'), for instance, occur in both English- and French-based pidgins and creoles throughout the Pacific, although its meaning and, in particular, connotations vary somewhat from language to language. In Tok Pisin, for instance, it was originally a term used by Europeans to refer to the indigenous population, often pejoratively, and it has these negative overtones in Tok Pisin today. To refer to someone as a 'kanaka', especially a 'bus kanaka' (bush kanaka) is insulting because it implies they are backward and unsophisticated. In the French overseas territory of New Caledonia, however, the term is used as a symbol of Melanesian unity and pride in the face of the continuing French colonial administration. In 1984 Melanesian activists declared an independent state to which they gave the name Kanaky, but independence has yet to be recognized by France. In Hawai'i, the term has also been reclaimed by native Hawaiians who call themselves *kanaka maoli* 'indigenous people'.

The word *kanaka* is also found in non-European based varieties such as Chinook Jargon, a trading language used along the Pacific north-west coast, where it and other items spread after the development of the fur trade along the north-west coast of North America in the late eighteenth century. Similarly, Eskimo Jargon has *kaukau* 'food', itself a loanword in Hawaiian, introduced from Chinese Pidgin English *chowchow*. The term *kaukau* is still used in Hawai'i Creole English to mean 'food' or 'eat', although most of the younger generation use the term *grind* in the sense of 'eat', and *grinds* in the sense of 'food'.

Recent work on the history of the Pacific languages places a great deal of emphasis on indigenous people, particularly pacific islanders such as Hawaiians, who served on whaling ships alongside Europeans, in the spread and stabilization of pidgin English in the Pacific. During the nineteenth century contacts across the north Pacific became routine. The Hawaiian islands became a frequent port of call and a wintering place for ships. Even by the late 1780s, however, well before the whaling trade began in earnest in 1820, some Hawaiians had been to Canton and Vancouver Island. On the North American west coast, they served as trappers and canoeists. By the 1820s groups of Hawaiians could be found in New England ports such as Nantucket and along the coast of California. These Hawaiians overseas were part of a much larger group of as many as 3,000 Hawaiians who served on foreign vessels, many never to return to Hawai'i. By the 1840s, over 1,000 Hawaiians left the islands each year for employment and as many as third of the crew on most Pacific whalers were Hawaiians; by the 1860s, that portion climbed to half.

Richard Henry Dana, Jr., a young New England gentleman, who wrote a detailed account of his experiences as a common seaman in the years 1834–5, described one such temporary expatriate community of Hawaiians at San Diego, who had set up a makeshift residence in a bread oven left behind by the crew of a Russian ship. The oven became known as the *Kanaka Hotel*. Hawaiians also served as missionaries in other parts of the Pacific such as the Marquesas.

There is still some dispute over the status of the varieties spoken on Pitcairn and Norfolk Islands spoken by descendants of the nine English-speaking sailors who mutinied on HMS *Bounty* in 1789 and their nineteen Polynesian companions. Before 1790 Pitcairn Island was uninhabited, but the arrival of twenty-eight people marked the beginning of a community which existed in isolation for thirty-three years.

Because the mutineers were outnumbered by two to one, the numerical odds were that Pitcairn would become predominantly Polynesian in language and culture, particularly given the fact that all the women were Polynesian (most of them from Tahiti), and would have been the primary caregivers to the children.

Moreover, nearly 90 per cent of the founding male population was murdered by 1800, leaving only John Adams, a Cockney speaker, 33 years old, who remained with nine surviving women and the twenty-three children born on the island. Yet the language of power was clearly English. Their first contact with the outside world occurred sixteen years after settlement in 1808 when Captain Folger of the *Topaz* from Boston was greeted in a language recognizable as English by Friday October Christian and was asked whether he knew Captain Bligh.

The first separation in a community that had lived together as a family for sixty years occurred when many were resettled on Norfolk Island after 1856. Although there have been a few studies of Pitcairn-Norfolk speech, no consensus on its classification has emerged. It has a clearly identifiable English-based lexicon and shares many features with English-based and other creoles, though it also shows some 'exceptional' features. For example, the presence of consonant clusters, which are not found in Tahitian, is hard to explain because most pidgins and creoles tend to have a simple syllable structure consisting of a consonant and a vowel (see below). From one description it appears that Pitcairn-Norfolk displays quite a large number of the characteristics typical of creoles more generally. However, it does not show any distinctly Pacific characteristics. This is of course not surprising since it has no direct historical link with earlier varieties of Pacific Pidgin English and developed in isolation from them.

Origins and structure

The example of Pitcairn-Norfolk creole illustrates how the question of pidgin/creole origins cannot easily be discussed separately from an account of their structural characteristics. Creolists have proposed a variety of theories to explain why the structures of pidgins and creoles show more similarities to one another, regardless of their base language, than they do to their lexifier or base language. It is in the area of syntax that the boldest claims have been made for the distinctiveness of creoles. In fact, some time ago, scholars noted in connection with Jamaican Creole that the most striking differences between the deepest varieties of creole and those closest to English lay not so much in phonology and vocabulary as in grammar. Although the reason offered by many was that creole grammar had African origins, the conclusion was that basilectal (i.e. the deepest) Jamaican Creole could not be regarded simply as a dialect of English, but was instead a new and different language.

Many linguists now find the concept of a common 'creole syntax' uncontroversial, even though there might be disagreements about exactly which features are included and why such similarities exist. Do pidgins and creoles share so many common characteristics because they had a common historical ancestor, or did they arise independently but develop in parallel ways because they used common linguistic material and were formed in similar socio-historical circumstances? Was syntax diffused in a way similar to some of the words like *savvy*? Or do the common elements perhaps reflect biological and cognitive constraints on what constitutes a minimal human language?

Traditional approaches to historical change have relied on the family tree model, which is based on the assumption that over time languages gradually diverge from a common ancestor. This model has been widely applied to explain the historical origins of pidgin and creole languages and has been referred to as the 'monogenetic hypothesis', i.e. that pidgins and creoles are to be derived from a single common ancestor. Many espoused the view that all the European-based pidgins and creoles were originally descended from a fifteenth-century Portuguese pidgin first used along the African coast and later carried to India and the Far East. This pidgin may have been a relic of Sabir, the medieval lingua franca believed to have been the language of the Crusaders and a common Mediterranean trading language.

While a common Portuguese origin would account well for certain lexical similarities such as the case of *picanniny* and *savvy* found across the Atlantic and Pacific pidgins and creoles, we can see that diffusion is probably a more likely explanation. In addition, we would have to invoke the notion of 'relexification' to account for the many other differences which exist between the pidgins and creoles with different bases. The monogenetic theory would also have nothing to say about the origins of non-European-based pidgins and creoles.

Most linguists reject such a strict monogenetic view because pidgins and creoles are typically formed through a convergence of linguistic structures from more than one genetic stock. It was the Romance linguist Schuchardt (1842–1927), often called the father of creole studies, who used data from pidgin and creole languages to argue against prevailing nineteenth-century views on the regularity of sound change.

Syntax

Although it is possible to trace the origins of some vocabulary items such as *kanaka* or *savvy* to the movements of people, the existence of common features of syntax is not so easily explained by diffusion. For example, how do we explain the fact that a number of creoles use the same word to mark the grammatical functions of both possession ('have') and existence ('there is/are')? In most English-based creoles a form of the word *get* serves this function. Compare, for example, how one would say 'There is (existence) a woman who has (possession) a daughter'.

Guyanese Creole: *get wan uman we get gyal pikni*
Hawai'i Creole English: *get wan wahine* [< Hawaiian 'woman'] *shi get wan data*
Tok Pisin: *i gat wanpela meri i gat wanpela pikinini meri*

Here the problem is how to account for the existence of the same grammatical pattern when different substrate languages are involved. Moreover, although these three languages have a common superstrate, they have not borrowed this grammatical pattern from English. In addition, French- and Portuguese-based creoles show a similar construction, not found in their respective superstrates. Compare Malaccan Creole Portuguese, where forms of the verb *tem* 'to have' are used for both possession and existence: *irmang machu teng na rua* [brother have in street] 'my brother is in the street' and *yo teng irmang machu* [I have brother] 'I have a brother'.

Proponents of substratum explanations for the origins of pidgins and creoles claim that models for many of the structures common to these languages can be found in the substratum, particularly the languages of West Africa which have had a great influence on the Atlantic creoles. Serialization, for instance, has been attributed to substratum from the African languages, particularly the Kwa group. Serial verb constructions are chains of two or more verbs which have the same subject, e.g. *im tek im fut kik me* (Jamaican Creole) [he take foot kick me] 'He kicked me'. In creoles they are used for marking functions such as direction and instrumental, which in other languages may be marked either by inflectional case or prepositions, as in these examples: *a waka go a wosu* (Sranan) [he walk go to house] 'he walked home' (direction), and *a teke nefi koti a meti* (Ndjuka) [he take knife cut meat] 'he cut the meat with a knife' (instrumental).

This is an instance where syntax makes up for losses in other areas such as morphology. In many cases the verbs involved in serialization can be translated into English with a single verb, and the first verb in the series is often *come*, *go*, *take*, etc. The length of such constructions is apparently not constrained in some languages and thus in Nigerian Pidgin English three or more verbs may be concatenated together across a multiple clause structure as in this example: *Dem come take night carry di wife, go give di man* [they come take night carry the wife go give the man] 'they came at night, got the wife, and gave her to her husband'.

Parallels with African languages can be seen in examples such as *akoroma no kyeree akoko no wee* (Twi) and *di haak kets di tskikin iit it* (Jamaican Creole) [the hawk caught the chicken ate] 'the hawk caught the chicken and ate it'. Compare also *Kòkú sò àsón wá àxì* (Fon) and *Jan pran krab ale nan mache* (Haitian

Creole French) [Koku/John take crab go to market] 'Koku/John brought a crab to market'.

Similarly, in the Pacific, it has been suggested that there may be Austronesian substratum influence in the serial constructions found in Tok Pisin. Compare, for instance, *boro di-rau-mate-i* (Manam) [pig they hit die it] and *ol i kilim indai pik* (Tok Pisin) [they hit die pig] 'they killed the pig'. However, serialization has a much more limited occurrence in the Pacific creoles and is arguably of a different character.

A clearer case in point of substratum influence is the inclusive/exclusive distinction in the Tok Pisin first person plural and dual pronouns, e.g. *yumi* 'we (inclusive of speaker and hearer)' v. *mipela* 'we (exclusive of the hearer)'. Thus, the English utterance 'we are going to town' can be translated into Tok Pisin either as *mipela go long taun*, which means that the speaker and someone else excluding the hearer are going to town, or as *yumi go long taun*, which means that the speaker and hearer are included.

Yet another kind of explanation may be required for other widely shared features of the Atlantic and Pacific languages such as the zero copula, i.e. lack of forms of the verb 'to be', as in: *me mickonaree* 'Yes, I am a missionary', or preverbal negation. Compare *Hongri man no de set dan won ples* (Kru Pidgin English) 'A hungry man doesn't sit down in one place' and *Melabat no kaan go garram yumob* (Australian Kriol) 'We can't go with you'.

Here we need to appeal to universal pressures of a functional type which exist in any communicative situation where speakers do not share each other's language. There will be pressure towards simplification, greater reliance on context, slower rate of speaking, etc. The language used to foreigners or 'foreigner talk', i.e. 'me Tarzan, you Jane', 'I no speak English', is a good example of these strategies. Some of these same features can be found in the speech addressed to young children, or 'baby talk', e.g. *Daddy go byebye*. In situations where the communicative partners are not social equals, the access of the subordinate group to the language of the dominant group may be only partial. Therefore, imperfect learning may lead to the emergence of a reduced version of the upper group's language.

A more far-reaching type of universalist explanation is based on an alleged innate 'bioprogram', which contains a blueprint for the features the creole must have. The bioprogram hypothesis links the emergence of creoles with first language acquisition as well as with the evolution of language in the human species more generally. It claims that the features which children learn early and effortlessly are among those prominent in creole languages. The existence of a bioprogram is argued for by appeal to the alleged lack of adequate input which children receive in a pidgin-speaking community. Under such circumstances children fall back on the bioprogram to produce rules for which they have not had models in the input from the older generation. This theory has provoked a great deal of controversy, particularly since its claims cannot be tested directly. No children are currently acquiring a creole language under the relevant circumstances required to validate the operation of the bioprogram.

The bioprogram has been offered as an explanation for one of the most commonly discussed features of creole syntax, namely the system of verbal markers. As early as the nineteenth century scholars commented on markers of tense, mood, and aspect which were shared across creoles with different lexical bases. Although these markers are usually clearly derived from words in the superstrate, they share some striking similarities which are not easily explained by appealing to substrate or superstrate influence.

The first of these is that the simple form of the verb without any markers refers to whatever time is in focus. In this example, a speaker of Nicaraguan Miskito Coast Creole English is explaining how each jungle spirit guides the animals under his protection to hide them from hunters. *Him a di uona. Him tek dem an put dem an dis wie . . . die kom an him liiv dem all hiia an guo de.* 'He is their owner. He takes them and puts them on the right path . . . they come and he leaves them all in that place and goes off.' All the verbs refer to a permanent state of affairs. In this next one, however, unmarked verb forms refer to the past: *Wi liiv from der an kom doun hiir fo stodi* 'We left there and come down here so I could study'.

The second similarity is that each creole language tends to have three markers: one to mark anterior tense (simple past for states and past before past for actions), one to mark irrealis mood (future, hypothetical, and conditional), and one to mark non-punctual aspect (progressive and habitual). In the case of Hawai'i Creole English, for instance, the markers are *bin* (anterior), *go* (irrealis), and *ste* (punctual), as in these examples: *a bin go si Toni abaut go spansa da kidz, ae, da baesketbawl tim, da wan ai ste koch fo* 'I went to see Tony about sponsoring the kids, eh, the basketball team, the one I am coaching'; and *Bambai til tumoro he go teli telifon* 'Later, by tomorrow, he'll call'.

The third shared feature is that where there is more than one particle accompanying a verb, the particles always have a fixed order before the verb: tense-mood-aspect. Although all combinations are not found in all creoles, examples of this pattern can be seen in conservative creoles such as Saramaccan and Sranan, as in this example from Sranan, *me ben sa e go* 'I would have been going', and this one from Jamaican Creole *mi en a go sing* 'I was going to be singing'.

The best examples of the full three-term system of tense-mood-aspect marking tend to be found in the Atlantic rather than the Pacific, although there has been significant development in Tok Pisin, for instance, in recent decades. As recently as the late 1960s and early 1970s there appears to have been a constraint in Tok Pisin against having two particles in preverbal position. This has since been clearly abandoned by some speakers, as is evident in these examples, where combinations of various particles occur: *ok. yu ken bai kisim* 'OK, you can take it', and *yumi mas bai helpim* 'We (inc.) will have to help'. The reasons for these differences between the Atlantic and Pacific creoles are not yet clear, but they may have to do with time-depth since the Pacific creoles are all relatively younger. The contribution of decreolization, motivated by increased influence of the superstrate, to the development of tense-mood-aspect systems is also unclear. In Hawai'i, for example, the form *bin* has subsequently been replaced by either *wen* (⟨English went) or *had*, e.g. *ai wen/had play* 'I played'. Although the creole form *had play* looks similar to standard English *had played*, in Hawai'i Creole English it is equivalent to the simple past.

Although most creoles have preverbal particles rather than inflections, Berbice Dutch is unique among the deeper creoles of the Caribbean in its use of a mixture of preverbal particles and suffixes in its tense-mood-aspect system. The suffixes come from Dutch. Thus, while some creole features may be clearly attributable to substrate or superstrate influence, and others require a universalist explanation, other features may reflect a convergence of forces.

Morphology

The overall simplicity and regularity found in pidgins and creoles is a general design feature, which reflects the function of these languages as lingua francas. In fact, there is relatively little to be said about morphology in pidgins and creoles since lack of it is one of the defining characteristics of the pidginization process. The absence of highly developed inflectional morphology was generally equated with lack of grammar and thought to reflect the primitiveness of both the language and its speakers. Pidginization can entail loss of all bound morphology, many free grammatical morphemes, and even a large part of the vocabulary.

For example, we can compare Yimas, a language spoken in the Sepik region of Papua New Guinea, with Pidgin Yimas, a variety used for inter-tribal trade. Yimas proper is a highly complex language morphologically while Pidgin Yimas is vastly simplified. While Yimas proper makes seven tense distinctions, Yimas Pidgin only makes two. Yimas proper distinguishes four numbers in its pronominal paradigm (singular, dual, paucal, and plural) while Yimas Pidgin has only three. This economy appears to represent convergence towards Arafundi (the language spoken by the main trading partners of the Yimas), which has only three.

Most of the grammatical features commonly found in European languages are usually lost, e.g. gender and case. Loss of gender, which in European languages only vaguely corresponds with the semantic concept of sex, will not involve a conceptual loss, but it will result in a substantial simplification. Lexicalization of gender (expression of gender by lexical means) results in irregularity, as can be seen in the English sets like *sow/boar*, *cow/bull*, *mare/stallion* as compared to Tok Pisin *pik meri/pik man*, *bulmakau meri/bulmakau man*, *hos meri/hos man* (where *meri* means 'woman' and *man* means 'man'). Compare also Jamaican Creole *man hag/uman hag* 'boar/sow'.

In Rabaul Creole German there is an invariant definite article, *de*, instead of the three-way gender distinction found in standard German (cf. *der Baum* 'tree', *das Haus* 'the house', and *die Katze* 'the cat'). This article does not take any case marking and the infinitive forms of verbs are often used instead of the standard inflected forms, e.g. *Wenn de Baby weinen, de Mama muss aufpicken* 'If/when the baby cries, the mother must pick (it) up'. Pidgins and creoles also have few prepositions. In Tok Pisin, for instance, two forms, *long* and *bilong*, indicate all grammatical relations, as in *Mi go long taun* 'I went to town'; *Em givim tupela pik long mi* 'He gave me two pigs'; and *Haus bilong papa bilong mi i stap long hap* 'My father's house is over there'. Others such as Bislama have up to five prepositions, but none appears to have a range anything like its superstrate language.

Other grammatical distinctions lacking in pidgins appear to be more essential to the adequate functioning of language and will be reconstituted as part of the process of creolization. Lexical forms will usually be recruited from the superstrate language to perform these functions. As we saw in the case of tense-mood-aspect systems, there are many similarities in the lexical resources used by creoles to mark these functions. Thus, for English-based creoles the indefinite article is usually derived from the numeral *one*, as in Hawai'i Creole English *I got one dog* 'I have a dog', a future marker from a verb meaning 'go', e.g. *I go leave om outside for you* 'I will leave it outside for you', the completive marker from a verb meaning 'finish', as in Tok Pisin *mi toktok pinis* 'I have finished speaking', etc.

Question words are usually composed of two elements, e.g. Guyanese Creole *wisaid* (< which side) 'where', Cameroon Pidgin *wetin* (< what thing) 'what', and Tok Pisin *wanem* (< what name) 'what'. Creoles tend not to show any difference in syntactic structure between questions and statements. If a creole has special question particles, they are sentence final and optional. In Guyanese Creole an utterance such as *i bai di eg dem* 'He bought the eggs' is not formally distinguishable as an interrogative or declarative. The difference is marked by intonation.

Phonology

On the whole, the phonology of creoles has been less well investigated than their syntax, and within the domain of phonology, there is scant information on suprasegmental phenomena such as tone, stress, and intonation. Many have commented that the suprasegmental phonology of the Atlantic English-based creoles has been influenced by the tonal systems of the African substrate languages. In Jamaican Creole, tone is lexical in a few minimal pairs. Thus, /at/ with a high level tone means 'hat' or 'hurt', while with a high falling tone it means 'heart'. Another contrastive set is /bit/, which with a high level tone means 'bit' and with a high falling tone means 'beat' or 'beet'.

As in syntax, the relative contribution of universals v. substratum influence needs further investigation in particular cases before more general conclusions can be stated. It is not always possible to trace the origin of a particular creole feature to a unique source. For example, I noted earlier the tendency towards a simple syllable structure. The preference for open syllables which end in vowels rather than consonants may, however, derive from universal developmental tendencies as well as from substratum influence. Compare, for example, Tok Pisin /giraun/ from English *ground*, Negerhollands /filis/ from Dutch *vleis* 'meat', West African Pidgin English /sikin/ from English *skin*, and Jamaican Creole /taki/ from English *talk* and /habi/ from English *have*.

Many scholars have commented on the small size or reduction of pidgin and creole phonological inventories when compared to both their lexifier and substratum languages. Although it has been sometimes argued that creoles represent the lowest common denominator of the source languages, this is not always true. Pidgins and creoles may also have segments which are not found in the superstrate. The Tok Pisin consonantal system used by Usarufa speakers actually has a much greater range of diversity than the Usarufa system both in terms of distribution and phonetic variety. Many speakers of Tok Pisin, for example, particularly those from the Highlands, have prenasalized stops, e.g. *ngut* 'gut'.

In Saramaccan, a creole English spoken by some 20,000 'Bush Negroes' or Maroons, whose ancestors escaped into the interior part of Suriname from plantations nearer the coast during the late seventeenth and early eighteenth centuries, the double stops /kp/ and /gb/ have been retained from the African substratum languages. The same is true for some varieties of West African Pidgin English.

Sounds that are typically absent or infrequent in creole phonologies are often those that are absent or vary in phonological status in the substrate languages. Both Jamaican Creole and Tok Pisin, for instance, do not regularly contrast /p/ and /f/. In Tok Pisin as well as Sranan /r/ and /l/ are not distinct. This has been attributed to the fact that in the substratum languages for Jamaican Creole and Sranan and many of the languages of Papua New Guinea there is no systematic contrast between /p/ and /f/ and /r/ and /l/.

In Tok Pisin, for example, /p/ is used in words deriving from English /p/ such as *pik* 'pig', *planti* 'many, plenty'. Tok Pisin /p/ derived from English /f/ is pronounced in one of three ways: as English /pf/, as English /f/, or as /p/. This means that some Tok Pisin speakers use /p/ for every use of English < p > and < f > , e.g. /pik/ 'pig', /prut/ 'fruit'. Other speakers use English /pf/ only for words derived from /p/ and they use English /f/ or /p/ for words deriving from English /f/, e.g. *pik, frut*. Most speakers use /f/ for words written with ⟨f⟩, e.g. /fut/ 'foot'.

Nevertheless, at the same time as creole phonology reflects pressures from the substratum, there are also universal tendencies of first and second language acquisition which will tend to eliminate marked (i.e. highly unusual, infrequently occurring) sounds and to reduce the overall number of phonological contrasts. We can note, for instance, the general avoidance of fricatives and affricates in pidgin phonological inventories. From a markedness perspective, fricatives are more marked than stops. Their presence in a language presupposes the existence of stops. This is a good example of how substratum influence and universal pressures may converge on a common solution. However, other sounds commonly not found may be due to superstratum influence. For example, the fact that /h/ is generally absent in Jamaican Creole and Tok Pisin is probably due to the variable omission of initial /h/ in non-standard varieties of English of the kind we examined in Chapter 3, to which creole speakers were exposed. In other respects, creoles have been conservative in preserving phonological patterns found in the superstrate during the time of creole formation. For example, in Jamaican Creole the palatalization of /k/ and /g/ as in /kyar/ 'car' and /gwain/ 'going' were customary in some of the varieties of British English transported to Jamaica in the eighteenth century.

Pidgins and creoles do not have a single phonology and phonology remains the least stable system in otherwise stabilized pidgins. As I have shown, phonological variability may be due to substratum and/or superstrate influences as well as universal developmental tendencies, but it is also affected by external factors such as education, sex, age, acquisitional history. This means that variant pronunciations may be found for the same items even within a small group of speakers. Expansion of a pidgin usually involves a steady increase in phonological distinctions. During decreolization, when the superstrate exerts pressure on the creole, the creole phonological system may merge partially with that of the superstrate language. Thus, the phonology of individual speakers of Tok Pisin varies from heavily Anglicized to what some have called a 'core phonology'. The core phonology is shared by all speakers of the language, while the

Anglicized phonology makes the most of the consonant and vowel distinctions in English.

In principle, the fluent bilingual speaker of Tok Pisin and English has the whole phonological inventory of English to draw on when speaking Tok Pisin. By virtue of increasing exposure to English, where contrasts such as that between /p/ and /f/ and /r/ and /l/ are significant, speakers are beginning to remodel Tok Pisin forms on their English cognates. This is the phonological dimension of decreolization. New phonological distinctions are being introduced, particularly in the Tok Pisin spoken by the younger generation of speakers in urban areas. There is an interesting phenomenon going on at the same time in rural areas, which is also motivated by exposure to English, but it has the opposite effect. Some young rural speakers now say /fig/ instead of /pig/ and /fikinini/ instead of /pikinini/. This is the result of a process known as 'hypercorrection', discussed in Chapter 3 in connection with a sociolinguistic pattern in which young lower middle-class women, in particular, produce more standard forms than the middle class. The Tok Pisin case is somewhat different. These speakers know that where they have forms beginning with /p/ many English speakers have /f/, but they do not know English well enough to know how English speakers make use of this contrast between /p/ and /f/. So in attempting to correct their use of /p/ to /f/, they overcorrect and produce forms which are not English at all. This kind of hypercorrection occurs in English too, as in the Brooklyn shibboleth *terlet* for *toilet* noted in Chapter 3, and probably in most cases where two varieties of differing prestige are in contact.

Lexicon

As noted earlier, pidgins and creoles generally take their names from their lexifier language, even though there is a great deal of variation in terms of the extent to which a particular language draws on its so-called lexifier for its vocabulary, and there is a variety of problems in determining the sources of words, due to phonological restructuring of the kind we have just examined. Compare, for instance, the lexical composition of Sranan and Saramaccan, two of six so-called English-based creoles spoken in Suriname, in what was formerly the Dutch-controlled part of Guyana. In Saramaccan 50 per cent of the words are from English (e.g. *wáka* 'walk'), with 10 per cent from Dutch (e.g. *strei* 'fight' ⟨*strijd*⟩, 35 per cent from Portuguese (e.g. *disá* 'quit' ⟨*deixar*⟩, and 5 per cent from the African substrate languages (e.g. *totómbotí* 'woodpecker'). In Sranan only 18 per cent of the words are of English origin, with 4.3 per cent of African origin, 3.2 per cent of Portuguese, and 21.5 per cent of Dutch; 4.3 per cent could be derived from either English or Dutch. Innovations comprise another 36 per cent, and 12.7 per cent have other origins.

Not surprisingly, African words are concentrated in the semantic domains of religion, traditional food, music, diseases, flora, and fauna. Words from the other languages do not concentrate in particular semantic domains. Numbers, for instance, draw on both English and Dutch. Sranan and Saramaccan are not mutually intelligible and neither is mutually intelligible with any of the input languages. Other languages show a more equal distribution between two main languages, such as Russenorsk, a pidgin once spoken along the Arctic coast of northern Norway from the eighteenth until the early twentieth century, whose vocabulary is predominantly Russian and Norwegian.

Depending on the circumstances, a creole may adopt more items from the superstrate language due to intense contact. Tok Pisin, for instance, takes from 11 per cent to 20 per cent of its lexicon from indigenous languages such as Tolai, spoken in New Britain, and at least 5 per cent from German, as well as some words from Malay such as *binatang* 'insect'. Some of the 200 German elements, as well as words from indigenous languages, are now being replaced by English words. Thus, *beten* (German 'pray') is giving way to English *pre*, and Tolai *kiau* to English *egg*. In Hawai'i Creole English some Hawaiian words like *mahea* 'where', *pio* 'to extinguish or put out', and *hemo* 'to take off/remove' were once common expressions, but few speakers over 40 know or use them today. Others still in common use such as *haole* 'foreigner' go back to the earliest contacts between Hawaiians and Europeans.

It is not always possible to trace creole lexical items to a unique source, e.g. Tok Pisin *gaden* may be equally from German *Garten* or English *garden*. Similarly, *bel* 'stomach' may be derived from English *belly* or Tolai *bala* 'stomach'. The residue of faulty analyses is particularly evident in the lexicons of pidgins and creoles. Tok Pisin, for example, has incorporated *bow and arrow* as one lexical item, *bunara*. Compare also *trausel* from *tortoise shell* and *tasol* from *that's all*. French-based creoles are notable for such fused forms in which the noun is agglutinated to the article, as Haitian Creole *dlo* 'water', which corresponds to the French sequence of words *de l'eau*. Such forms result from faulty boundary segmentation of the kind also found in first and second language acquisition, but persist in pidgins and creoles partly through lack of access to correct target models.

The number of items in the lexicon of a pidgin is highly restricted. Estimates of size vary from about 300 to 1,500 words, depending on the language. In the case of the younger generation of Tok Pisin speakers, for example, it ranges from about 800 in rural areas to about 2,500 in urban areas, where a greater number of English words have been incorporated and where the language is being nativized and expanded. Where there is intense contact between a pidgin/creole and its lexifier, and a high degree of bilingualism, it can be difficult to decide where the pidgin/creole lexicon ends and that of the lexifier begins because bilingual speakers freely incorporate words from the lexifier into the pidgin/creole.

There are a number of consequences which follow from the fact that pidgins and creoles have a rather small number of lexical items: semantic generality, multifunctionality, circumlocution, and greater lexicalization. The degree to which these tendencies are manifested in a particular language depends on its degree of expansion and structural stability.

Reduction of number of items does not in itself simplify a language, though it entails certain adjustments in lexical structure which may make a language more regular, as illustrated above in my discussion of gender. Lexical items in pidgin languages tend to cover a wider semantic domain than in the base language. Tok Pisin has the term *pisin* (< English *pigeon*) for 'bird'. Historically, this represents a case of extension of reference from the English term *pigeon* which refers to a specific kind of bird in English to a term with more general reference.

Consider also Pidgin Fijian, where the general term *kato* covers a domain lexicalized by four different items in Fijian: *kato* 'case, box, basket', *noke* 'fishing basket', *su* 'coconut leaf basket', *i lalakai* 'woven leaf tray'. Similarly, Saramaccan *búka* (< Portuguese *boca* 'mouth') also means 'beak', while Portuguese has another word *bico*.

Due to their small inventory of items pidgins associate different grammatical information with the same semantic and phonological items. This is generally referred to as multifunctionality, i.e. use of the same lexical item in more than one grammatical function. For example, in Tok Pisin *askim* can function as both noun and verb: *mi gat wanpela askim* 'I have a question', *Mi laik askim em* 'I want to ask him/her/it'. The existence of multifunctionality also calls into doubt the extent to which traditional grammatical categories such as noun or verb are applicable to creoles.

Gaps in the pidgin lexicon, especially in the early stages of its development, may be filled by borrowing or circumlocution. Only at a later stage in its development does the pidgin develop productive internal resources for expanding its lexicon. Circumlocution is a strategy which involves letting the syntax make up for the lack of productive morphological processes which would be used to form words in the lexifier language. Stable pidgins often develop phrase-like formulas for the description of new concepts. Consider the formula Object + Verb + *gauna* 'thing for doing something to an object' found in Hiri Motu, a pidgin based on the indigenous language, Motu, of Papua New Guinea, e.g. *kuku ania gauna* [smoke eat thing] 'pipe', *lahi gabua gauna* [fire burn thing] 'match'.

Europeans have been eager in the past to cite mythical circumlocutions to demonstrate the inadequacy of pidgin, one of the most notable being that for 'piano' in Melanesian Pidgin, e.g. *big fellow bokkes, suppose missis he fight him, he cry too much* 'the big box, if the European woman hits it, it cries a lot'. Although it is possible that such a description was used in the first encounter with the piano, it is highly unlikely that it persisted. Once an innovation has caught on and is used, it will become conventionalized and shortened. Initially these expressions served as descriptions. As the lexicon expands, the clumsy but motivated compounds and periphrastic expressions disappear, e.g. Tok Pisin *kot bilong ren* 'raincoat' is now *kotren* or *renkot* and *bel bilong mi hat* [stomach of me hot] is now *mi belhat* 'I am angry'.

Pidgins and creoles exhibit a high degree of motivation and transparency in compounding as a direct consequence of their small vocabulary. Many aspects of the lexicon and grammar of Tok Pisin reflect a semantic orientation which is basically non-European, while other aspects draw on universal principles which determine maximum regularity of encoding of grammatical categories and lexical distinctions. In some areas of the lexicon we see a conspiracy between these factors. As an example, Table 6.1 illustrates the semantic field lexicalized by the Tok Pisin term *gras* (〈English *grass*), which can be used to refer to 'head hair', 'body hair', 'fur', 'feathers', 'moustache', and makes a partial comparison with Warapu, a non-Austronesian language spoken in north west New Guinea, etc.

The fact that meanings such as 'grass, 'beard', 'feather', and 'weed' are all expressed by separate, unrelated lexemes in English is an indication of its greater degree of lexicalization. Note too that we would not even consider this to be a coherent semantic field in English. In Tok Pisin, however, there is a kind of iconic relation between these items, which is expressed by the fact that they are all encoded by means of constructions incorporating the word *gras*. In other words, the terms in Tok Pisin are motivated, whereas in English they are

Table 6.1 The conceptual field expressed by Tok Pisin *gras* compared with Warapu

Tok Pisin	English	Warapu
Gras	'hair'	pei
Gras bilong fes	'beard'	
Mausgras	'moustache'	
Gras antap long ai	'eyebrow'	
Gras bilong pisin	'bird's feather'	ndru pei
Gras bilong dog	'dog's fur'	naki pei
Gras nogut	'weed'	

arbitrary. This represents a good illustration of what is called diagrammatic iconicity, i.e. a systematic arrangement of signs, none of which necessarily resembles its referent, but whose relationships to each other mirror the relationships to their referents. Thus, one could say that *grass* has the same relationship to the ground or earth that feathers have to a bird, a beard to a face, etc. They are all covering on different surfaces. In this particular semantic domain the optimal solution to the problem of encoding is reinforced by the existence of a similar system in the indigenous languages.

Many of the languages of Papua New Guinea (both Austronesian and non-Austronesian) have the same lexical item for 'feather' and 'hair'. Often 'fur' and 'leaf' are included within the scope of reference of this same term. In Warapu, a single lexical item is used for 'head hair' and 'leaf'. The same item in Warapu also means 'body hair', 'fur', and 'feathers', as seen above. This is also true of Karam, a New Guinea Highlands language. This distribution of domains is not uncommon in Austronesian languages of New Guinea, but a more normal set for non-Austronesian languages is to have one word for all kinds of hair and a separate word for 'leaf'. We can now see how Tok Pisin serves to channel an alien conceptual system into a native conceptual system, while constituting at the same time a simplified means of expression which creates pressure for the grammatical complexities often found in other languages to be eliminated or sharply reduced.

Nevertheless, there is an inverse correlation between the lexical expansion of a language and the iconicity of its grammar. Now English terms like *feda* are increasingly used, especially by the younger generation of urban speakers, who are rapidly expanding the vocabulary of Tok Pisin. In such cases borrowing from English is making the structure of Tok Pisin more irregular and complex.

Names for body parts such as *ai* 'eye' and *maus* 'mouth' are used as metaphors in many pidgins and creoles, and occur quite often in compounds. Compare, for example, Tok Pisin *aipas* 'blind' (< 'close' + 'eye') and Cameroon Pidgin *lokai* (< 'close' + 'eye'). Tok Pisin also has *mauspas* 'silent' (< 'mouth' + 'close') and *yaupas* 'deaf' (< 'ear' + 'close'), as well as *ai bilong sua* 'head of a sore', *ai bilong botol* 'lid of a bottle', and *ai bilong kokonas* 'hole of a coconut'.

Of course, English has metaphorical extensions of body parts too such as 'eye of a storm', and 'ear of corn', but the fact that it has many more arbitrary terms like 'blind', 'deaf', and 'dumb' to encode meanings which are all formally linked in Tok Pisin is an indication of the greater degree of lexicalization of English.

Another more general process of grammaticalization is probably at work here too. Body parts provide the most important source domain for spatial concepts in language. Thus, pre- and postpositions expressing location in many languages are cognate with or derived from body parts. Thus, mouth and eye frequently provide the source for the spatial dimension of 'front'. In Tok Pisin *sanap long ai bilong ol* means 'to stand up in front of everyone'. Similarly, the word for 'head' in many languages comes to encode the dimension of 'on' or 'front'; back, the location of 'behind'; the buttocks or anus, the location of 'under'.

Consider these Tok Pisin compounds containing *as* (< *arse*): *as bilong diwai/flaua* 'the base of the tree', *asples* 'one's place of origin', and *as bilong kros* 'the reason/cause for anger', where we have a metaphorical extension from the concrete domain of body parts to a more abstract concept which does not have an inherent spatial dimension of 'bottomness' or 'under'. Body part compounds are also widely used in the expression of emotions, e.g. Sranan *dek'ati* 'courage' (< Dutch *dik* 'thick' and English *heart*), *atibron* 'anger' (< *heart* + *burn*), etc.

In pidgins and creoles these metaphorical uses are an important means of extending a restricted vocabulary with limited syntactic means. Extensions such as these may also represent a conspiracy between coding preferences in indigenous languages and universal pressure for semantic generality and regularity. Borrowing from English, however, is threatening to disrupt the unity of a great many semantic fields which are linked by these metaphors. While the borrowing of *lid* represents an economy at one level over periphrastic *maus/ai bilong pot* 'mouth/eye of the pot', at another level it leads to complexity. The price that has to be paid when a concept is fully lexicalized is that it has to be learned as a totally new item.

The creole continuum

The boundary between pidgins and creoles cannot be defined in purely linguistic terms. Thus, some languages such as Tok Pisin and West African Pidgin English, spoken widely in West Africa, may exist in both pidgin and creole forms, which display different degrees of structural expansion and stability depending on whether they are used by first or second language speakers. Creolization can take place at any point during the pidgin's life cycle, ranging from a jargon to an expanded pidgin. The term 'jargon' refers to a speech variety with a minimal linguistic system and great individual variation used for communicating in limited situations between speakers of different languages, e.g. trade, while a pidgin has a certain degree of stability. Three possible routes to creolization are depicted in Fig. 6.4.

Once creolization has occurred, the evolutive changes that take place thereafter may make it impossible to identify a prior creole or pidgin stage, as in the case of Black English in the United States, which many linguists believe to be a variety in the late stages of decreolization. The term *decreolization* is used to refer to changes which bring a creole closer to its superstrate language, and there is some dissatisfaction with it because some changes may not be motivated by influence from the lexifier language. In other words, not all changes are unidirectional; some may make the creole more different from its superstrate, and some may make it only superficially more similar, such as the case of *had* in Hawai'i Creole English.

The terms 'basilect', 'mesolect', and 'acrolect' are used to describe the range of varieties often found after creolization, as shown in Fig. 6.5 illustrating the

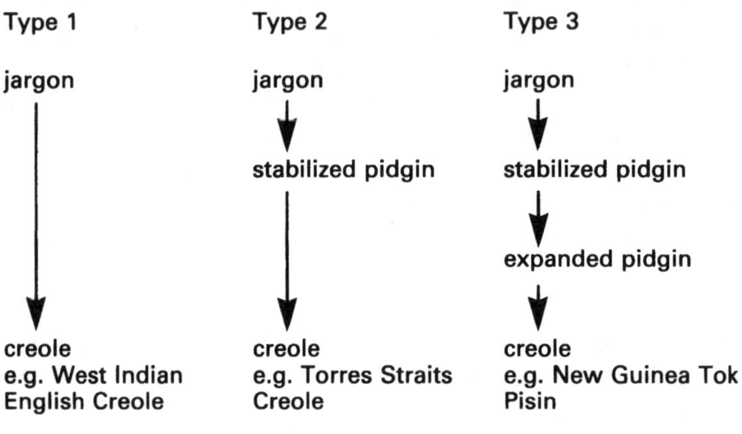

FIG 6.4 Three types of creolization

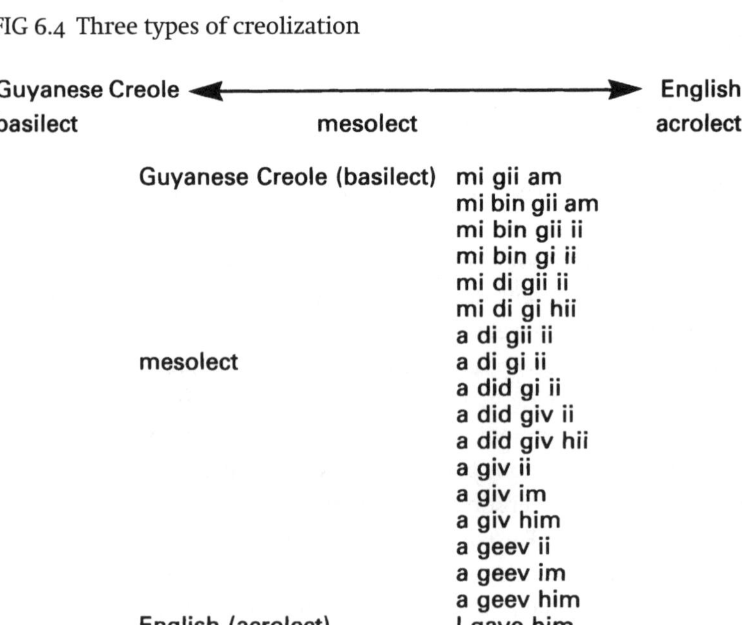

FIG 6.5 The Guyanese creole continuum

Guyanese creole continuum. They are arranged along a post-creole continuum which has acrolectal (those varieties closest to the superstrate) at one end and basilectal (those varieties furthest from it) at the other. Mesolectal varieties are intermediate. This can be illustrated with the set of eighteen variants from the Guyanese post-creole continuum shown in Fig. 6.5.

The ordering of the varieties in the model presented here makes no claim about their diachronic development since it seems likely that in many cases mesolectal and acrolectal varieties were present even in the earliest phases of creole formation and do not always develop after creolization in adaptation to the superstrate. Thus, acrolectal varieties cannot be regarded as necessarily 'later' than basilectal ones. Creolization and decreolization can be coexistent, as they are for instance in Papua New Guinea. Tok Pisin is in the process of being nativized by the younger generation at the same time as increased accessibility to English schooling is creating a range of varieties which are neither Tok Pisin nor English.

Because creolization can occur at any stage in the development continuum from jargon to expanded pidgin, different kinds and degrees of structural repair may be necessary to make the pidgin fully adequate to meet the demands placed on it for use as a primary language. Pidgin grammars tend to be shallow, with no syntactic devices for subordination or embedding. Distinctive marking of structures such as relative clauses comes later in the stabilization or expansion phase of the pidgin life cycle, or arises in the process of creolization. Sources for new structures vary too. Some whose primary interest is in the first type of creolization, where a pidgin is abruptly transformed into a creole within one generation, believe that bioprogram universals provide the most important input into the newly emerging creole.

Pidgins and creoles in social context

Although pidgins and creoles are often widely used by the majority of the population in the countries where they are spoken, throughout their history most have not had any official status. In the Pacific, for instance, only Tok Pisin and Bislama have received some official recognition. Tok Pisin is a de facto official language in Papua New Guinea spoken by more than half of the population of 4 million. However, English is still the most widely used official medium of education, despite initiatives in the 1990s to introduce education in a number of vernacular languages. There is also another pidgin language, Hiri Motu ('trade Motu'), based on the indigenous language, Motu, which shares the same de facto official status as Tok Pisin. In practice, all this means is that Hiri Motu and Tok Pisin may be used in the House of Assembly, the country's main legislative body. In fact, most business is conducted in Tok Pisin, the most widely shared language among the members.

Although Bislama is recognized by the constitution of Vanuatu as the national language of the country, paradoxically it is forbidden in the schools. Thus, Vanuatu may be the only country in the world which forbids the use of its national language! English and French, the languages of the former colonial powers, are still the official languages of education. Although Australian Kriol does not have any official status, it has been used in bilingual education programs in parts of Australia. While many linguists in both the Caribbean and Pacific have argued for an increase in status and standardization of the pidgins and creoles spoken in these regions so that they can be used in education, the governments concerned have generally ignored these issues and preferred instead simply to continue the colonial legacy of using the metropolitan European language already in place.

French-based Haitian Creole is one of the few which appears to have been given serious attention by government planners. In 1983 the constitution declared both Haitian Creole and French to be Haiti's national languages, with French serving as the official language. The 1987 constitution declared Haitian Creole to be official as well. Although French still dominates most public and formal domains, Haitian Creole has been making steady advances into new domains of use in teaching and literacy programs.

The low status of pidgin and creole languages is generally a consequence of the fact that they have not been regarded as fully-fledged languages, but as corrupt and bastardized versions of some other language. As recently as 1986 the *Times Higher Educational Supplement* (17 Jan. 1986) carried a report from a newspaper in Ghana complaining about the use of Pidgin English on Ghanaian campuses and recommending that stern measures be taken against it. The report notes that in no other case do the future leaders of a country talk 'a mixture in which all tenses are thrown to the wind, and words are picked from far and wide, making no sense to the listener'.

The lack of written matter also fuels popular ideas that pidgins and creoles are not 'real' languages. In the majority of countries where pidgins and creoles are spoken the very act of writing itself is a largely a middle-class occupation restricted to those who have not only a sufficient degree of education, but also time to write. Not surprisingly, most pidgins and creoles are not written languages and therefore not standardized, and written material has been scant. Indeed, popular belief in many creole-using societies has it that these languages CANNOT be written. This comment made by a speaker of Kwéyôl, a French creole originally from the eastern Caribbean, and now used in the UK, is typical: 'It's broken French, you can't write it down. No, it's not a language.'

For most creole speakers in Hawai'i it is a revelation, if not downright heresy to some, that the speech variety they call simply 'pidgin' can be regarded as a language in its own right and that the study of pidgin and creole languages constitutes a legitimate academic discipline. In a survey of attitudes towards the use of creole in the classroom, even those who were tolerant to some extent about the use of spoken pidgin, especially if it is the child's only way of communicating, were negative about writing. One teacher at an elementary school, for example, said pidgin should not be written because it had no grammar. Or, as another woman put it: 'That's why you go to school for, so you don't write pidgin English.'

These responses underline the close linkage in many people's minds between the school and standard English, or, for that matter, between schooling and the use of a dominant language, whatever that language happens to be. As mentioned in Chapter 2, introduction of Quechua in Peruvian schools has encountered resistance, despite the fact that it is everyone's vernacular language. In a similar study in Papua New Guinea, most of the teachers surveyed wanted to retain English, despite the fact that they regarded themselves as more proficient in their vernacular languages and Tok Pisin, and agreed that the use of Tok Pisin would enhance communication in the classroom, as well as help their pupils to read better in English.

In the 1950s UNESCO (United Nations Educational, Scientific, and Cultural Organization) was set up to address a variety of economic, social, political, and educational issues. Its volume entitled *The Use of Vernacular Languages in Education* (1953) arose from a conference of specialists who were supposed to tackle the question of how to raise levels of education around the world, particularly among the underprivileged, whose illiteracy made participation in national development difficult or impossible. In their belief that the key to economic and cultural development lay in the extension of literacy, they concluded:

> Every child of school age should attend school and ... every illiterate should be made literate. We take it as axiomatic, too, that the best medium for teaching is the mother tongue of the pupil ... all languages ... are capable of becoming media of school teaching.

The UNESCO monograph reflects the ambivalence of the time towards pidgin and creole languages. In May of that same year, for instance, the United Nations Trusteeship Council sent a mission to New Guinea to report on the Australian administration of the territory. They urged Australia to take 'energetic steps' to stop the use of Tok Pisin as a language of instruction in the schools. At the time, Tok Pisin was one of the few pidgin or creole languages to have been standardized and used as a medium of education. For the Christian missionaries who standardized the language and used it in their schools, the motivation was purely pragmatic. Tok Pisin was not seen as a means for social or national development, but as a practical tool in converting people to Christianity. It was the most widespread language of a highly linguistically diverse population.

The UN report was the subject of much controversy in the Australian media. One writer of a letter to the *Sydney Morning Herald* said, 'the greatest objection to pidgin is that it has no literature and never can have any'. Of course, at this time most of what was written in Tok Pisin was written by missionaries and government officials. Although some indigenous people used Tok Pisin for writing informal letters, they had not yet appropriated the written language as a means for literary expression. Nowadays, virtually anything can be written in Tok Pisin from newspapers, political broadsides, to plays.

Although devising a writing system for any language is a fairly straightforward exercise from a linguist's point of view, the writing of pidgins and creoles can present some problematic choices between alternative systems. Many of those who tried to develop orthographies for creoles assumed they were dealing with a version of English or other European language. As a result of these perceived similarities, writing systems based on European languages often did the creoles a disservice in suggesting that they were inferior and amusing versions of European languages. Devising distinctive orthographies for creoles helps increase their autonomy and people's awareness of them as languages distinct from rather than parasitic on their lexifier languages.

For example, in one of the orthographies proposed for the French-based creole spoken in the Dominican Republic, 'Today I am sick' would be written as *zordi mwe malad*, while in French, this would be *aujourd'hui je suis malade*. The first person singular pronoun in the creole is from the French unstressed pronoun *moi* 'me', and many people object to spelling it in creole in such a way as to obscure its French origin.

Such resistance to developing orthographies which follow the norms of the creole rather than those of the superstrate is usually strongest among those already literate in the superstrate. Unfortunately, such negative attitudes are unhelpful in promoting initial literacy in countries such as Haiti and Papua New Guinea, where literacy rates are still very low, and learning to read in creole offers the quickest, most meaningful, and often only option for people to become literate. This is especially true for adults. Nearly one-third of the world's adult population is still not literate, and literacy is inaccessible to more than 100 million children. Even in Hawai'i, studies have shown that comprehension of written standard English is still a problem even for fifth grade students.

One linguist who devised an orthography for Carriacou Creole English spoken in Grenada found that creole speakers learned to read more easily using material produced in their own language. Even those already literate in English adjusted to the new creole system within five minutes. Moreover, he found that reading in creole written according to English orthographic norms was just as difficult as reading in standard English. Some of the strongest critics of this project were trained educators.

Here again, we must consider the larger context. Spelling reform has been a consistent theme in the history of English for well over a hundred years, but each time calls for a simplification and a break from etymology have been resisted. Etymologies are irrelevant for most speakers of English too, especially when there are so many false etymological spellings such as *island*. Because English orthography is based on a number of different systems which apply to different sets of words, it may take English-speaking children up to two years longer to learn to read than children who are speakers of other European languages. Educators may remember the debate about the so-called ITA, initial teaching alphabet, which relied on a more phonemic spelling, with the aim of helping children to learn to read more quickly. Yet, because people have invested a considerable amount of time in learning English spelling, it serves as a useful mark of being educated. People are unwilling to abandon this. The popularity of spelling bees in the English-speaking world attests to its continuing importance. In the next chapter, I explore other kinds of problems children face in learning to read.

If the point of teaching people to read in their own language is to make them literate more easily and quickly, we must also not forget that there is no point in devising a written standard language if there is nothing considered worth reading. Even in cases where a creole has status as a national or official language, as Bislama, for instance, does in Vanuatu, or Haitian Creole French does in Haiti, this does not guarantee the use of creoles in wider society. Similarly, in the Central African Republic, no action has been taken to extend the use of Sango to reading and writing, despite the fact that in 1984 both French and Sango were declared the languages of the school, and despite the existence of an official orthography.

The few pidgins and creoles such as Tok Pisin which have been reduced to writing and undergone some degree of standardization have been used primarily by missionaries for proselytization, and most of the written material available was and still is religious in nature. The general lack of written material outside the religious domain was also taken as evidence by some that pidgins and creoles were not suitable vehicles for serious literature and artistic expression.

To get an idea of how widely varied the written uses of pidgin and creole languages *can* be, we can compare two Pacific pidgins/creoles which differ quite dramatically in terms of their functions: Tok Pisin and Hawai'i Creole English. Hawai'i Creole English, spoken in the Hawaiian islands, a former United States territory and since 1959 the fiftieth state, has no official status and no written norms, despite the fact that it is the first language of probably the majority of children in Hawai'i. It arose on sugar plantations, where workers from many different nationalities (and hence language backgrounds), in particular, Japanese, Chinese, and Filipinos, were imported.

Hawai'i Creole English is far more decreolized than Tok Pisin due to the greater and more rapid metropolitanization of the Hawaiian islands, particularly through the influence of the United States, which annexed the islands not too long after white planter interests succeeded in overthrowing the Hawaiian monarchy in 1893. It was never used as a language of education and the local Department of Education has actively campaigned against it for many years in an effort to eradicate it completely. Although there is no official orthography for Hawai'i Creole English and therefore no standard, some writers have attempted to use it as the medium for poetry, short stories, and drama.

All these genres exist in Tok Pisin too. In addition, however, there are Tok Pisin versions of the Old and New Testaments plus a weekly newspaper with comics, advertising, etc. and a wide range of other secular material. Although most of the classics of the emerging literature of Papua New Guinea were written in English, there is some creative writing in Tok Pisin in the forms of poem and plays. Some of the country's first playwrights were politicians, such as Rabbie Namaliu, one of Papua New Guinea's recent prime ministers. Drama in Tok Pisin has been particularly popular thanks to the formation of groups such as The Raun Raun Theatre in Goroka, who perform in a sort of folk opera style. Addressing themselves to village audiences and carrying on the tradition of oral literature, they use Tok Pisin exclusively and do not rely on scripts.

The advertisement in Fig. 6.6 is a good example of how Tok Pisin is used creatively in the media. The slogan says literally 'It bun belong me straight', a colloquial expression which means that it is just the thing to serve as the foundation of a good diet. In its literal sense *bun* means 'bone' or 'skeleton', and one who is *bun nating* (literally 'bone nothing'), for example, is a skinny person. Tok Pisin can also be heard on the radio and was for many years used as a language of education by missionaries, who still make use of it in some church-supported schools.

Writers who want to use Tok Pisin can simply use the existing orthography, but writers using Hawai'i Creole have worked out their own ad hoc systems. The following poem in Hawai'i English Creole was composed by Joseph Balaz, a local writer who is the author of *Ramrod*, a literary publication. 'Da History of Pigeon' takes its motivation from what he calls the 'phonic' association between the linguistic term 'pidgin' and the bird 'pigeon'. The poem was written for oral presentation at a colloquium on pidgin and creole languages at the University of Hawai'i at Mānoa in Honolulu in 1986.

FIG 6.6 An advertisement for Sun Flower tinned fish in Tok Pisin. The slogan says 'It's my very foundation'

Da History of Pigeon
(in phonic association to pidgin)

Like different kind words, da world was full of different kind birds: yellow birds, blue birds, red birds, love birds—and den came da pigeon.

Da history of da word pigeon is li'dis—Wen da French-speaking Normans wen conquer England in da year ten-six-six, dey wen bring along wit dem da word pigeon, for da type of bird it was. Da resident Anglo-Saxons used da word dove, or D-U-F-E, as dey used to spell 'um, to mean da same bird. It just so happened dat terms in Norman-French wen blend wit Old English sentence structure, to form what we know as Middle English. In da process, da French word became da one dat referred to da pigeon as food. Today in England, if you look for dem, you can find recipes for pigeon pie.

Food for taught, eh—Even back then, da word pigeon wen blend with pigeon for get some moa pigeon.

So now days get pigeon by da zoo—get pigeon on da beach—get pigeon in town—get pigeon in coops—and no madda wat anybody try do, dey cannot get rid of pigeon—I guess wit such a wide blue sky, everything deserves to fly.

A number of the phonological features specific to Hawai'i Creole English that have been represented in Balaz's spelling, e.g. *da* ('the'), *dis* ('this'), *den* ('then'), *dey* ('they'), *dem* ('them'), *dat* ('that'), *wit* ('with'), *taught* ('thought'), *everything*

('everything') illustrate the tendency for the English interdental fricatives to become stops in the creole. Spellings such as *moa* ('more') and *madda* ('matter') indicate the absence of postvocalic /r/ in creole. Hawai'i Creole English does not mark case, gender, or number, so *'um* (probably from a phonetically reduced form of 'him' or 'them') can mean 'him/her/them/it'. Such orthographies usually make rather liberal use of apostrophes, as in Balaz's spelling of *li'dis* suggesting its link with English *like this*. The overuse of apostrophes suggesting elided consonants and vowels fosters the view that the language being represented is simplified and reduced by comparison with the standard.

There are also some syntactic features specific to the creole such as the use of *wen* (from English 'went') to mark the simple past as in *wen conquer*. The construction *for get moa pigeon* is also characteristic; other English-based creoles use *for* where English would use 'to' or 'in order to'. Another feature is the use of *get* in existential constructions, e.g. *get pigeon by da zoo* 'there are pigeons at the zoo'. Because the creole does not mark plurals, the plural form of 'pigeons' and the term for the language, 'pidgin', are homophonous. This allows Balaz to make the humorous point that because both pidgins and pigeons are everywhere, they are hard to get rid of!

Although linguists have for a long time used a phonemic orthography for writing Hawai'i Creole English, most creative writers are either unaware of it or have chosen not to use it. One of the few poets to depart radically from English spelling is Jozuf Hadley. In this extract from his poem 'ma kat stanlee', we can see how he has created his own quasi-phonetic orthography.

ma ket stenle	My cat Stanley—the Blue
da blu kraws wen sen om	Cross sent him one
wang krismes kad e	Christmas card, yuh?
hi no ste nau bat	He's not here now but—
he ste fri eswai	he's free that's why.

Elsewhere, writers have faced similar problems to those of Balaz. In Sierra Leone, for example, Thomas Decker was convinced of the need to use Krio more widely and translated the Bible and the works of Shakespeare both to demonstrate the serious capabilities of Krio as a literary language and to make these works available to a Krio-speaking audience. The performance of his translation of *Julius Caesar* in the grounds of the State House by the National Theatre League in 1964 heralded the birth of drama in Krio.

Subsequent plays such as Dele Charley's one-act traditional African dance-drama *Fatmata* took the development of Krio as a dramatic medium even further since they were not translations, but original works with local themes. Like Raun Raun Theatre's productions, this drama draws on oral narrative traditions, in this case on the Anansi stories known throughout the Afro-Caribbean region. In this extract from *Fatmata*, Charley uses a traditional African pattern of call and response, where a narrator calls out and a chorus replies.

Narrator: Wan dey ya, wan titi bin dey
[Once there was a girl]
Chorus: Wey naym Fatmata
I fain lek bohl yai.
[Whose name was Fatmata.
She was as beautiful as an eyeball.]
Narrator: Plenti man bin want Fatmata.
[Many men wanted Fatmata.]
Chorus: But dis Fatmata
bin praud lek pikokh
I leys leke fat.
Noh sabi natin sef.
[But this Fatmata
Was as proud as a peacock.
She was as lazy as a lump of lard
And she knew nothing.]
Narrator: Boht i fain lek bohl yai
En i bin sabi dres.
[But she was as beautiful as an eyeball
And she knew how to dress.]
Chorus: Boht na bin ekspensiv gial
En im mama bin pwel am.
[But she was an expensive girl
And her mother spoiled her.]

Such plays are often full of proverbial wisdom, which is used to deliver morals. In this particular case, Fatmata is too choosy and stubborn when it comes to accepting suitors. When she finally accepts the attention of a stranger and marries him, he turns out to be a devil in disguise. The moral of this play is summed up in the proverb 'Tranga yeys noh gud' (Stubbornness is a bad thing).

The use of pidgin and creole languages in the quest for a distinctive voice shows how the very act of writing in a marginalized language whose status as a language is denied by the mainstream is symbolic of the appropriation of the power vested in the written word. Writing in Hawai'i Creole English, Krio, or Tok Pisin becomes an 'act of identity'. Rejecting the term *dialect* because it suggested inferiority, Edward Kamau Brathwaite argued for the use of what he called 'nation language' (i.e. Jamaican Creole English) in poetry as a way of capturing the sounds and rhythm of oral traditions of performance. Inspired by hearing a recording of T. S. Eliot reading from *The Waste Land*, Brathwaite urged poets to model their poetry on the African-derived rhythms of calypso in order to break the pentameter, which other New World poets before him such as Walt Whitman had also sought to undermine.

The creole voice which is grounded in the oral tradition has found it easier to penetrate the literary domain in speech-based genres which are composed primarily to be performed, e.g. drama and poetry. In certain respects the use of pidgins and creoles has been fuller and easier in these genres due to conventional associations between them and modes of narration. Drama is a genre which is heavily oriented to the first person present, a narrative form associated with subjective experience and inner feelings. The affinity between music, poetry, and drama as performance genres can be clearly seen in the Caribbean in so-called Yard Theater and the work of Jamaican dub poets like the late Michael Smith and Linton Kwesi Johnson, whose sound poems were on the British reggae music charts in the late 1970s and early 1980s.

Dub poets such as Jean Binta Breeze would carry on the process of legitimizing nation language by writing it down. In this print version of her performance 'Dubbed out', the spacing of the lines jerking to a halt enacts the beating down of sense and lyricism.

I
search for words
moving
in their music

not

broken
by

the

beat

Through the commercial success of performers such as Mikey Smith, Benjamin Zepphaniah, or Mutabaruka the once historically devalued Caribbean popular culture has become part of multicultural Britain. The message of protest went out from Kingston and London around the world making the Afro-Caribbean region one of the vibrant areas in the world producing literature in English as well as creole. Further evidence of its vitality and excellence can be seen in the fact that Nobel prizes and other prestigious awards have gone to some of its writers such as Wole Soyinka from Nigeria and Derek Walcott from St Lucia, some of whose works draw on pidgin and creole Englishes.

Nothing prevents the codification of a standard orthography for creoles such as Hawai'i Creole English, or, for that matter, any other language. The emergence of standard languages, as well as literary forms, is intimately connected with socio-political context. No language, literary or otherwise, can develop without support.

Annotated bibliography

There are a number of good surveys of the field of pidgin and creole studies, e.g. John Holm's two volumes (1989), the first of which is an overview of theory and structure, while the second includes sample texts and short descriptions of these languages. Mark Sebba's (1997) book is also a good overview as is the one edited by Jacques Arends, Pieter Muysken, and Norval Smith (1995). A general bibliography, now somewhat outdated, can be found in John Reinecke et al. (1975). Other surveys include Peter Mühlhäusler's (1986) and Suzanne Romaine's (1988). These latter two focus more on the Pacific, while Holm's volumes treat the Atlantic. Useful collections of articles can be found in Hymes (1971), Valdman and Highfield (1980), Highfield and Valdman (1981), Hill (1979), Valdman (1977), Rickford and Romaine (1999), Woolford and Washabaugh (1983), Muysken and Smith (1986), Gilbert (1987), Spears and Winford (1997), Baker and Syea (1996).

The bioprogram hypothesis was first put forward in detail in Derek Bickerton's book (1981) and subsequently modified. An overview of some of the issues can be found in Romaine (1988: ch. 7) and Bickerton's article (1988). The example from Pidgin Yimas is taken from William Foley's article (1988). The story of the mutiny on the *Bounty* can be found in Charles Nordhoff and James Norman Hall's trilogy (1960); for further linguistic and historical details see Ross and Moverley (1964). Further information on African-American English varieties is found in the collection by Mufwene and Rickford (1998). See also the papers in Mufwene (1993) on the African substrate in the Atlantic creoles, and Keesing (1988) on the Oceanic substrate in Melanesian Pidgin. Thomason and Kaufman (1988) discuss some of the problems in applying traditional models of historical change to varieties produced by language contact.

The Guyanese Creole example is taken from William O'Donnell and Loreto Todd (1980). Terry Crowley's (1990) book is a history of Bislama. A discussion of the problems surrounding the use of Hawai'i English Creole can be found in Charlene Sato's articles (1985, 1991) and in Suzanne Romaine's articles (1994 *a* and 1994 *b*, 1999 *b*). Further information on the structure, social status, and uses of Tok Pisin can be found in Suzanne Romaine's articles (1990, 1992 *a*, 1994 *c*) and her book (1992 *b*), as well as the collection of papers in Wurm and Mühlhäusler (1985). Suzanne Romaine's (1996) article discusses some of the literary uses of four English-based pidgins and creoles. The quote about Kwéyôl not being a real language is cited in Morris and Nwenmely (1993: 261), and the quotation from the *Sydney Morning Herald* is reported by Hall (1955: 103). The quotation about Hawai'i Creole English is from Romaine (1999 *b*: 294). The collection of papers in Tabouret-Keller et al. (1997) offers a re-evaluation of the issues surrounding vernacular literacy. Michael Stubbs's (1980) book considers the sociolinguistics of literacy.

For information on socio-political issues in the Caribbean, Hubert Devonish's (1986) book is useful. Jean Binta Breeze's poem is taken from Morris (1988: 29). The collection of papers in Jones et al. (1992) discusses some of the uses of Krio in Sierra Leone. The extract from *Fatmata* is in Dele Charley (1983: 4–6).

Diana Eades and Jeff Siegel's article (1999) discusses initiatives undertaken in Australia's legal and educational system to increase the use of creoles. Ronald Kephart's (1992) article describes his study of reading among Carriacou Creole-speaking children. Joseph Nidue's (1988) article describes negative attitudes towards Tok Pisin among Papua New Guinean teachers. Susan Bauder Reynolds's (1999) article investigates the difficulties of creole-speaking children in Hawai'i in comprehending standard English.

Chapter 7

Linguistic Problems as Societal Problems

> A senior professor of education visited a London comprehensive school and discussed with one class the languages they spoke at home. One boy put up his hand and said that his family spoke a French Creole. In an unguarded moment the professor replied, 'That's nice'. 'What's nice about it?', asked the boy.

SOCIOLINGUISTIC research, in particular on social dialects and minority languages, has had many practical implications because it is concerned with fundamental inequalities in language use. In the last chapter I showed how pidgins and creoles have generally been excluded from use in education, despite evidence which shows that children learn best in their own language. Although linguists have increasingly appreciated the importance of these languages, as illustrated in the opening quotation to this chapter, they still suffer from low prestige among their speakers.

There are many areas of public life where language has an impact, such as the medical and legal professions, but particularly in the school. Sociolinguists have been actively engaged in studying the problems which arise from language use in these contexts, and especially what happens when there is a mismatch or difference in language involved between the participants such as doctor and patient, teacher and student. In this chapter I will focus on some of the types of problems arising in school which are language-related.

Language and educational failure

Language has often been cited as the main cause for the greater rate of school failure among minority children. As one of society's main socializing instruments, the school plays a powerful role in exerting control over its pupils. It endorses mainstream and largely middle-class values and language. Children who do not come to school with the kind of cultural and linguistic background supported in the schools are likely to experience conflict. This is true even of working-class children belonging to the dominant culture, but even more so for children of ethnic minority background.

In Britain, for example, there is a hierarchy of educational success or failure. White middle-class children do best, while children of West Indian origin do worst. Data from 1969 and 1975 from the Toronto Board of Education showed that students of non-English-speaking background who immigrated to Canada performed worse academically and were in lower academic streams than those born in Canada.

In the United States grade twelve Hispanic students are about 3.5 years behind national norms in academic achievement. Similarly, a survey of the performance of students in fifty large urban public school districts, including many hundreds of schools, indicated that although white students showed steady improvement in their reading achievement scores as they got older, African-American students showed a steady decline. More specifically, 60.7 per cent of the white students read above the 50th percentile norm at the elementary school level in 1992–3, and 65.4 per cent did so by high school, while only 31.3 per cent of the African-Americans read above the 50th percentile norm at the elementary school level, and only 26.6 per cent did so by high school. Data from the 1994 National Assessment of Educational Progress show the same depressing trend: on a 500-point scale, African-American students at the age of 9 are an average of 29 points behind the scores of their white counterparts; by the age of 13 they are 31 points behind; and by the age of 17, they are 37 points behind. Thus, the longer African-Americans stay in school, the more they fall behind.

Much the same has been found elsewhere, for example, in Europe. To begin with, however, it should be noted that a percentage of minority children do not attend school anyway. In what was West Germany, for example, about 25 per cent do not attend school, and more than 50 per cent do not obtain any kind of leaving certificate. Drop-out rates for immigrant children in the secondary schools are higher than for indigenous pupils. In Denmark during the years 1975–8, not a single child of Turkish or Pakistani origin (the two largest minority groups in Denmark) finished secondary school.

After leaving school, these minorities also have a greater chance of being unemployed than indigenous children. In 1982, for example, the unemployment rate for foreigners in Sweden was twice as high as for Swedes. The economic returns from schooling are in general much greater for those who are advantaged, i.e. middle class, to begin with. Moreover, even if minority children achieved better in school and were able to complete their education, it would not necessarily guarantee employment. Minorities in most countries have access to a smaller percentage of the available economic resources than the majority. This is reflected in the fact that ethnic minorities are over-represented in almost every category that can be used to measure educational, psychological, economic and social failure, e.g. rates of crime, alcoholism, mental disturbances.

Native Hawaiians, for example, fare far worse than any other ethnic group in the state of Hawai'i on most statistics relating to health, social welfare, education, etc. They have the shortest life expectancy in a state which has the highest life expectancy for the whole USA. They have the highest incidence of heart disease, diabetes, and cancer, the lowest incomes, and highest unemployment. Although Hawaiians make up about 12.5 per cent of the population, only 6 per cent of students at the University of Hawai'i at Mānoa are of Hawaiian ancestry.

Such dismal statistics, however, mask a lot of important differences among various distinctive minority groups. Some south-east Asian minority students in both the United States and Britain have managed to perform better than their white mainstream classmates. Their success has been hard won and such individuals and the groups they belong to have suffered backlash from the dominant group with whom they are competing for places in higher education, jobs, etc.

For some time there has been an unacknowledged relationship between bilingualism and special education. There are many reasons why disproportionate numbers of minority language children have been placed into special education classes and vocational programs in many countries. The indiscriminate use of psychological tests on newly arrived immigrants to the United States in the early part of this century resulted in the deportation of persons who were assessed to be feeble-minded, largely because they did not understand English. The number of foreigners deported for this reason increased by approximately 350 per cent in 1913 and 570 per cent in 1914.

The misguided use of psychological assessment is also in considerable part to blame for the over-representation of ethnic minority students in classes for the mentally retarded. Constructs such as intelligence, learning disability, language proficiency, and bilingualism are poorly understood by many educators. In Britain, for example, a government inquiry into the special educational needs of children contained only one paragraph devoted to the assessment of minority children. It states that whenever a child is being assessed whose first language is not English, at least one of the professionals involving in assessing the child's needs must be able to understand and speak the child's language. However, the formal recommendations of the report make no mention of the needs and rights of minority students.

FIG 7.1 Images of standard English and Hawai'i Creole English (HCE)

Because schools measure success in terms of mastery of standard English (or whatever the accepted language of society is), non-standard speech is seen as illogical, and bilingualism as a problem. Negative attitudes towards languages such as Hawai'i Creole English (HCE), for example, regularly become part of public controversy in Hawai'i, particularly when the annual achievement test results are announced. 'Pidgin' is blamed for the poor performance of Hawai'i's students on the verbal ability section of the Stanford Achievement Test (SAT). Hawai'i has consistently ranked in the bottom three or four states in the USA in terms of the achievement of its students. Half of Hawai'i's public school students in rural, poorer economic areas regularly score below average on the reading comprehension portion of the SAT.

The results are not surprising because a much greater percentage of HCE speakers reside in these areas, where they have less exposure to standard English. However, these facts also have to be seen in their proper social and historical context. The Department of Education needs to be honest in recognizing the 'pidgin problem' as a social and political problem, and not simply hide behind the excuse that it is a language problem.

It is important to note, in particular, the state's abysmal level of funding for public education. In 1995, the results of a national evaluation of the quality of public schools showed that the state ranked as the second lowest in the USA, and its funding per student had actually declined between 1985 and 1995. Hawai'i spends only $4,724 per student compared to New Jersey, for instance, the best funder of public education, which spends almost twice that amount ($8,118).

Hawai'i's teachers are also paid the lowest salaries in the USA adjusted for cost of living and the state provides few opportunities for professional development. Interestingly, the report's findings appeared on the front page of the newspapers at the same time as the teachers were threatening a strike because they had worked without a contract since 1995.

There is also a long history of discrimination against creole-speaking children in Hawai'i through education in a school system which originally was set up to keep out those who could not pass an English test. In this way it was hoped to restrict the admission of non-white children into the so-called English Standard schools set up in 1924, and attended mainly by Caucasian children, locally called *haoles* (from Hawaiian 'foreigner'). By institutionalizing what was essentially racial discrimination along linguistic lines, the schools managed to keep creole speakers in their 'place' and maintain distance between them and English speakers until after the Second World War. The relative isolation of creole speakers from speakers of mainstream varieties of English actually strengthened HCE for a time. Normally, schooling in the colonial language accelerates decreolization. Generations of children were punished and made to feel ashamed for speaking creole.

It was also not too long ago that minority children in countries like Australia, the United States, Britain, and Sweden were subjected to physical violence in school simply for speaking their home language. Some Finnish schoolchildren in the Tornedal area of Sweden had to carry heavy logs on their shoulders or wear a stiff collar because they had spoken Finnish. In other parts of Sweden, like Norrbotten, there were workhouses which poor children attended, earning their keep by doing most of the daily domestic work. When one of the children spoke Finnish, they were all lined up and had their ears boxed one by one. In Wales, a child caught speaking Welsh at school had to wear a wooden sign (the so-called Welsh 'not') around his or her neck.

Unfortunately, such abuse still occurs in a number of countries today. There is a great deal of difference between democratic countries and oppressive regimes with respect to the degree of compliance with international agreements and covenants relating to the rights of minorities and indigenous peoples. Norway, for instance, has taken a number of steps to strengthen and protect the Saami language, such as the Saami Language Act of 1992, and the USA passed the Native American Languages Act in the same year, while Turkey continues a long history of human rights abuses against the Kurds and their language, despite the fact that Turkey is signatory to many international covenants and treaties, as well as an aspiring member of the European Union.

Kurdish is banned from public use. The Turkish census does not count Kurds because the government denies their very existence. Kurds have been sent to prison even for saying they were Kurds, and Kurdish children are forced to learn Turkish at school. Many linguists have pressed for international recognition of linguistic human rights because present international covenants on human rights make provision for a basic right to education, though not necessarily in one's own language. Unless the child understands the language of education, however, basic education cannot function at optimal levels.

Much of the early literature appeared to indicate that bilingualism exerted a negative influence on children's development. Beliefs about the harmful and undesirable effects of bilingualism have been used to support policies of monolingual instruction in the majority language, in particular for children of minority language background. Bilingualism was, and still is, often cited as an explanation for the failure of certain groups of children. It has been argued that it is counter-productive to the child's welfare to develop and maintain proficiency in more than one language. Linguists, however, have argued that learning two languages need not be a handicap. If that were so, then the rich would not consider it an advantage to send their children to private schools in Switzerland, where they learn French or German and are exposed to another culture. Why is it considered a disadvantage for a British child to know and maintain Panjabi?

As I noted in Chapter 2, in most parts of the world schooling is virtually synonymous with learning a second language. The idea that the home language is inappropriate for school can be so deeply ingrained in community members' perceptions that they may resist its introduction in school, even when its use would benefit both teachers and students. We have seen several examples of these attitudes which have worked against the incorporation of languages such as Quechua into Peru's schools and pidgins and creoles in places as diverse as Hawai'i and Papua New Guinea.

Educators have also fought against the use of dialects in school because they were regarded as substandard forms of speech. Based on studies of the language of minority groups, sociolinguists have, however, argued that nonstandard speech forms are just as structurally complex, rule-governed, and capable of expressing logical arguments as standard English. Moreover, because such varieties play an important role in speaker identity, change towards standard English may be resisted. Generations of school teachers

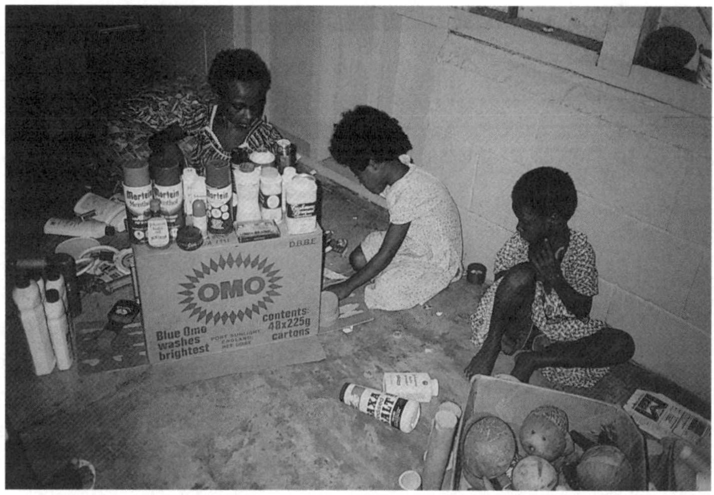

FIG 7.2 Papua New Guinean children playing in facilities provided by a mobile pre-school unit 'Skulnabaut' which operates in Tok Pisin

have not managed to eradicate the use of common features of non-standard English such as multiple negation. Indeed, the use of non-standard English may become stronger during adolescence as a marker of peer group allegiance.

In a study of self-esteem and academic achievement among girls, one African-American girl told the researcher: 'You got to have something that blends in the way you talk, the way you dress, if you have something to talk about, something like that. If you talk white, you a schoolgirl, you a nerd.' This girl sanctioned another African-American girl, an honor roll student, for acting white and not speaking according to black norms. One day when the girl greeted her with 'Hi, LaRhonda', she corrected her by saying, 'It's L! You call me L and it's "Yo, wahddup!" Not "Hi".' Recall from Chapter 4 that inner city area black youths who socialized in street gangs were those who used the most non-standard forms of speech and were most opposed to the value system of the school. Not only did they have the highest rate of failure, but they were also regarded as those most likely to fail by their teachers.

As the case of Hawai'i shows, many factors are responsible for the poor achievement of some schoolchildren, e.g. lack of exposure to the school language, linguistic/cultural mismatch between home and school, inferior quality of education provided to minority students, socio-economic status, disrupted patterns of intergenerational cultural transmission as a result of minority/majority status relations, and attitudes of the majority to the minority and vice versa. Many linguists now conclude, however, that in many cases negative attitudes towards non-standard speech and bilingualism are more decisive in determining school outcomes than actual linguistic differences themselves. They lead to low esteem among students and serve to perpetuate a cycle of failure.

Studies show that teacher expectations are closely tied to student achievement and that teachers already tend to have negative expectations of minority children. In one study teachers were asked to evaluate samples of speech, writing, drawing, and photographs of some school pupils. In particular, they were asked to say how successful they thought a child was likely to be based on the evidence from the samples. The experimenters obtained independent ratings of all the samples and then presented them in various combinations. Thus, one hypothetical child might have a speech sample independently judged as sloppy, paired with a photograph and writing sample judged to be good, etc. Assessment of students' likely success in school was linked most strongly to the speech sample. Those who had speech samples judged to be poor were stereotyped as underachievers, even though they might have produced written work and drawings independently rated as good.

In another experiment, prospective elementary teachers' perceptions of the relative standardness of children's speech were also affected by the children's race; the same recording, when accompanying a videotape of an African-American or Mexican-American child, was rated as less standard than when accompanying a videotape of a white child.

In another study, kindergarten teachers in Toronto were asked to pick three students whom they felt were likely to fail by grade 3 and three whom they felt would be highly successful. Those who had English as a second language were regarded as likely to fail about twice as often as other students. Once a label such as 'limited English proficiency' or 'learning disabled' is given to these children, this is seen as the explanation for their problems. It then deflects attention from other possible contributions in the school and larger social environment. It has also been shown that teachers' assumptions about students' proficiency in English affects the quality of the instruction given to them. In one case non-English-speaking students were made to focus on more mechanical tasks associated with reading rather than activities associated with promoting comprehension.

Difference v. deficit

In the 1950s a very influential theory about the connection between language and school success distinguished between a so-called 'restricted code' and an 'elaborated code'. The elaborated variety was alleged to have greater syntactic complexity, as evidenced, for example, by a greater proportion of subordinate clauses, conjunctions, etc. It makes meaning explicit, and one does not have to be in a particular situation to understand the meaning. The meaning is in the text, not the context. These codes are believed to be acquired by socialization into different classes and family structures. The failure of working-class children in school was explained in terms of their lack of access to the elaborated code.

As samples, we can take the following types of stories told by 5-year-old schoolboys when asked to describe what they saw in a series of pictures. Of particular interest here is how the participants in the picture are referred to by the choice of pronouns or nouns. The elaborated version explicitly states who did what and can be immediately understood without seeing the pictures.

Elaborated version

Three boys are playing football and one boy kicks the ball and it goes through the window the ball breaks the window and the boys are looking at it and a man comes out and shouts at them because they've broken the window so they run away and then that lady looks out of her window and she tells the boys off.

Restricted version

They're playing football and he kicks it and it goes through there it breaks the window and they're looking at it and he comes out and shouts at them because they've broken it so they run away and then she looks out and she tells them off.

For many, the implication of this theory was that speakers of underprivileged groups could succeed if they could be taught the elaborated code. This became known as 'deficit theory', and programs of so-called 'compensatory' education were launched in the USA and elsewhere to provide deprived preschool children with compensating experience and exposure to middle-class culture so that they could start school on an equal footing with middle-class children who had exposure to the elaborated code at home. Between 1965 and 1970 $10 billion was spent on these kinds of programs, the best known of which was Project Headstart. In some cases educational programs were proposed which used methods designed for teaching English as a second language because it was argued that the children lacked a language.

When results were not as good as had been hoped for, some suggested that preschool intervention programs came too late because mothers were not socializing their children into the kind of environment which would lead to school success. Thus, some argued it was mothers who had some deficit. Obviously, if this sort of argument is carried to its extreme, we are no longer talking about environmental differences but genetic ones, and indeed some did believe that the IQ differences found between children of different social class and ethnic backgrounds were genetically determined.

Sociolinguists who have attacked deficit theories have argued instead that different groups have different ways of using language, but no one's language is deficient. Evidence against verbal deficit comes from many sources. For one thing, it can easily be shown that non-standard varieties of language are just as structurally complex and rule-governed as standard varieties and just as capable of expressing logical arguments as standard speech. Indeed, the last chapter revealed not only some of the structural regularities of creole languages but also the expressive possibilities of some creole languages which have been used for a variety of literary purposes. In fact, increasing use of HCE in so-called 'local' literature has provided a lot of material that can and should be used effectively in the classroom. Logicality, however, has become linked with middle-class language because it is middle-class children who do best at school, as we will see in the next example.

Language differences in the classroom

In a study done of 'sharing time', a common speech event at many schools, we can see how the teacher's assumptions about what is a good contribution are not made explicit. This activity usually begins with the teacher asking, 'Who has something important, special, or exciting to share?' The teacher defines what is 'important', though it is not made explicit to the children, and it is obvious from remarks made by some children that they do not know what the teacher will consider important. The teacher asked one child who volunteered a story, 'Is this very, very important because we don't have much time this morning?' The child replied, 'I don't know if it is or not, but I want to say it anyway.' From analysing the contributions made by different children and the teacher's reactions to them, we can get an idea of what the teacher wanted.

A good story should have a simple statement of one topic and a series of comments leading to the resolution of some action concerning it. Certain topics are thus not so much inherently important or trivial. What was important was to talk about a topic in such a way as to make it sound important. But some of the children used styles of speaking which made it seem to the teacher that there was no topic at all. The narratives expected by the teacher were book-like in that all the details had to be fully spelled out and made explicit as in the elaborated code discussed above. Minimal background knowledge was to be assumed on the part of the audience. Objects had to be named even when they were in plain sight.

Let's examine how one teacher reacts to two different styles of narration, one by a black child and another by a white child. In the following extract, the black child is labelled D and the teacher T.

T: I want you to share some one thing that's important.

D: In the summer, I mean, when I go back to school in September, I'm gonna have a new coat and I already got it and it's got a lot on it and when I got it yesterday and when I saw it, my brother was going somewhere. When I saw it on the couch and I showed my sister and I was reading something out on the bag and my big sister said: 'Deena, you have to keep that away from Keisha' 'cause that's my baby sister and I said 'no' and I said the plastic bag because when she was with me and my cousin and her—

T: Wait a minute. You stick with your coat now. I said you could tell one thing.

D: this was about my—

T: OK. All right. Go on.

D: And yesterday when I got my coat my cousin ran outside and he tried to get him and when he got in the house he laid on the floor and I told him to get up because he was crying.

T: What's that got to do with your coat?

D: Because he wanted to go outside.

T: Why?

D: Cause my mother wanted us to stay in the house.

T: What does that have to do with your coat?

D: Because . . . I don't know.

T: OK. Thank you very much, Deena.

In terms of the teacher's notions of sharing time, a story like this one is difficult to follow. It seems to have no single topic, no beginning, and no end. The focus of the story has to be inferred from links that are never made explicit. At the point where the teacher interrupts, she tries to bring Deena back to develop what she thinks is the topic, i.e. the coat. When the child was interviewed later about her story, she explained the link between her cousin and the coat by saying that she was trying to keep him from putting his dirty hands on it.

The other topic had to do with the coat and the plastic bag. In one case the child was protecting her baby sister from the bag the coat was in and in the other topic she was protecting the coat from the messy hands of her cousin. The outcome of this mismatch in styles and expectations between teacher and child is that the teacher cannot see her way into the narrative and consequently does not help the child to produce the kind of narrative considered appropriate for sharing time. She cannot follow the transitions between topics. The child said afterwards she felt frustrated by the teacher's interruptions, which she took as a sign of her lack of interest in what she had to say.

The next extract is from a white child, M, who uses a style which is more like what the teacher wants. Here when the teacher interrupts, she does so in a way that helps the child to expand the narrative.

M: When I was in camp, we made these candles.
T: You made them?
M: I tried it with different colors with both of them but one just came out. This one just came out blue and I don't know what this color is.
T: That's neat-o. Tell the kids how you do it from the very start. Pretend we don't know a thing about candles. OK. What did you do first? What did you use? Flour?
M: There's some hot wax, some real hot wax that you just take a string, tie a knot in it and dip the string in the wax.
T: What makes it have a shape?
M: You just shape it.
T: Oh, you shaped it with your hands.
M: But you have first you have to stick it into the wax and then water and then keep doing that until it gets to the size you want it.

The teacher and the child are in synchrony in this story. The teacher prompts the child and gives her guidelines as to what is important in order for the story to proceed. When she asks the child to pretend 'we don't know anything about candles', she is instructing her to assume no knowledge and to be explicit. The child picks up her clues and builds on them. Children are either aided or hindered in their transition from home to school by the stories that are told at home, and the functions they have in particular communities. In one study done of two communities fictitiously referred to as Roadville (working-class white) and Trackton (working-class black), it was found that although both groups spent a lot of time telling stories, they had different ideas about what stories were and what they were for.

In Roadville, stories stick to the truth and are factual. They end with a summary and a moral. Any fictionalized account is not a 'story' at all, but a lie. What Trackton people call stories are, however, hardly ever serious. The best stories are 'junk' and those who are the best storytellers talk the best junk, i.e. make the most wildly exaggerated comparisons. Neither Roadville's factual accounts nor stories from the Bible would be called 'stories' in Trackton. For Roadville people, Trackton's stories would be lies, while for Trackton, Roadville's stories would not even count as stories. These different ideas about stories derive partly from varying literacy practices. The Trackton parents do not read books with their children and have no reason to talk about the stories in books. Roadville children are used to looking at books at home. Yet neither community prepares its children for the uses of written and spoken language they will encounter at school. At school, they must learn not just how to tell and write stories, but how to talk about them.

Similarly, questions these children hear at home are not like those which teachers use at school. Most of the teachers' questions are about things to which the teacher already has the answer, or are requests to name things, e.g. *what color is that?* Another frequent type is really a rhetorical question about things in isolation from their context, e.g. *I wonder why he did that*. One of the teachers' complaints was that Roadville and Trackton children seemed unable to answer even the simplest questions. One local grandmother noticed the difference between questions at home and school when she commented, 'We don't talk to our children like you folks do; we don't ask them about colors' names and things.'

Literacy is acquired in the context of schooling. In Chapter 3 I showed how what goes by the name of 'logic' in language is mainly an acquired way of talking and thinking about language which is made possible largely by literacy. There are many school uses of language which derive their mode of interpretation from literate uses of language. Take, for example, the type of test or quiz in which children are given a question such as: Henry VIII had two wives. True or false? Why is it that the correct answer is false? Henry, of course, had more than two wives but that means he had at least two. Nevertheless, the conventional interpretation of this utterance is that Henry VIII had only two wives, although there is nothing in the linguistic form to indicate that this should be so.

It is hard to have judgements about speech independently of notions of correctness we are taught in school when we learn to read and write. Studies have shown that teachers routinely correct children in school for using forms that are quite acceptable in speech. Moreover, they use these forms themselves in the classroom. Not surprisingly, the children are confused about what the teacher wants. An example can be taken from a French study, where a teacher is trying to get a child to be explicit. In this extract she is asking the child about a story which has been read in class. The teacher is labelled T and the child, P.

T: Que fait le Papa de Daniel?
[What's Daniel's father doing?]
P: Il promène la chèvre.
[He's walking the goat.]
T: Bon. Alors elle répond: 'il promène la chèvre.' Qui est-ce il? Elle m'a dit 'il'. Moi, je sais pas qui c'est il. [Good, well, she's answered: he's walking the goat. Who is this he? She told me 'he'. I don't know who this he is.]
P: promène la chèvre le–
[walks the goat the]

T: Qui?
[Who?]
P: le fermier
[The farmer]
T: Alors je repose ma question: 'Que fait le papa de Daniel'? [Now I'll ask my question again. What's Daniel's father doing?]
P: Le fermier promène la chèvre.
[The farmer is walking the goat.]
T: Oui. Est-ce je t'ai demandé ce que fait le fermier? J'ai demandé ça? J'ai demandé ça les petits filles?
[Did I ask you what the farmer's doing? Did I ask that? Did I ask that, girls?]

The answer the teacher wants is, *Le papa de Daniel promène la chèvre* 'Daniel's father is walking the goat', but she fails to elicit it. She rejects various answers. At first, when the child fails to make the subject explicit, using instead the pronoun *il* 'he' to refer to *le papa de Daniel*, she tries to get the child to repeat *le papa de Daniel* by claiming she doesn't know who 'he' refers to. The teacher prompts again before the child tries something else which is more explicit, but the teacher rejects it too without saying why, and then repeats her original question. The child interprets this as a prompt to repeat a complete sentence, but this still does not satisfy the teacher.

It is not clear why only *le papa de Daniel promène la chèvre* is the 'right' answer. Both *le fermier* and *il* accomplish the same thing, and it is clear from the context who these words refer to. In replying to the teacher's question, the pupil is using a rule which is quite acceptable and normal in both spoken and written discourse; namely, a referent known by speaker and hearer can on second mention be referred to as 'he' or 'she'. Imagine that this exchange took place in the teacher's home between the teacher and a friend, with the two of them talking about Daniel's father, and the teacher suddenly says, 'I don't know who this *he* is.' The friend would certainly think the teacher did not know how to carry on a conversation! Only in the classroom could such an abnormal use of language count as a legitimate exchange. By 'abnormal' I mean that there is nothing ungrammatical, but what has been said violates the rules governing communicative competence. The teacher is trying to impose on the child a language which is in fact too explicit for the context without explaining why it is 'better' to do so.

Testing: who decides what is right?

We have seen that standards of language use and standard languages are essentially arbitrary conventions which can be learned only by going to school. This is precisely why they are so effective in maintaining barriers between groups. Knowledge of the standard is unevenly distributed. There has been much discussion in the popular press and academic professions about the problem of declining standards. Standards change. This is true of language no less than other cultural products like fashion. People have complained about the decline of English since at least the fifteenth century. In 1989 Prince Charles angered British school teachers when he complained publicly that his staff could not read or write English properly. Around the same time, the *Times Higher Education Supplement* carried a front-page article in which several Oxford professors complained about the low standards of English used by students at Oxford University and suggested the possibility of introducing remedial instruction. Interestingly, these remarks came in the wake of the British government's inquiry into the teaching of English, which was full of recommendations for tolerance of pupils' varieties of English. The same report also stressed the need for standard English to play a part in a new national curriculum.

There can be no doubt that whatever knowledge it is schools test, it is unevenly distributed among schoolchildren in a way which follows patterns of social class stratification and ethnic divisions in society. When some test scores are looked at longitudinally, it also appears that the population is doing less well than in previous years. In the United States, for instance, some have expressed alarm that scores on college entrance exams such as the SAT (Scholastic Achievement Test) are declining. At one level, there is, however, no reason to panic about this. When the SAT was normed, its population represented a small minority of college-bound white middle-class students. It tests the extent to which those who take it have acquired the middle-class norms necessary for success in higher education. No wonder standards appear to have declined when the same set of norms is being used to test an ethnically more diverse population! This apparent crisis in language proficiency is in some respects an academic problem created when definitions of literacy, competence, etc. have been narrowed to such an extent that they make children's experience with language at school discontinuous with everyday communicative competence.

Given the inherent bias in the school's curriculum towards the language and culture of the dominant group in society, it would be surprising if minority children managed to score better than mainstream children, even when a foreign language background is not an intervening variable. Research has shown that when tests are devised which are aimed specifically at the kinds of knowledge minority children have, but which majority children lack, the minority children do well. A black high school group averaged 36 points higher than a white group on a test called BITCH-100 (Black Intelligence Test of Cultural Homogeneity), which contained 100 vocabulary items in use in Afro-American slang. This difference in scores reflects the fact that the white students had less opportunity to acquire the words than the blacks through previous cultural experience.

I showed in Chapter 3 that just because children do not choose the answers which the testers decide are the correct ones does not mean that their early experience is deprived or that they are unintelligent. It just means they have not had the experiences which the tests focus on. There is no unequivocal relationship between any one set of cultural experiences and the abstract concept we call intelligence. IQ tests are designed to exclude any culturally specific ways in which minority children have gained intelligence. Because many aspects of intelligence are learned or mediated through specific cultural experiences in a particular language or variety, it is impossible to devise a test of intelligence which is context-free and culture-independent. This means that all tests need to be interpreted in the light of the effect of a particular child's minority background, and knowledge about bilingualism, where another language is involved.

In an IQ test given to low-income Portuguese-speaking children in Massachusetts, many children are unable to answer the question: *From what animal do we get bacon?* Despite the fact that pork is a staple food for most Portuguese families, children are not familiar with the term *bacon*. If the question had been rephrased so as to ask: *From what animal do we get sausages?*, children would have been able to answer it. In another item, children are asked whether it is better to give money to a well-known charity or to a beggar. Within the children's culture, organized charities are almost non-existent, so the only real choice is to give the money to the beggar. The testers, however, want the child to pick the charities. The cultural bias in testing procedures such as these has led some researchers to recommend alternative means of assessment which rely less heavily on formal tests.

Taking appropriate action

Political mobilization of linguistic minorities and legislation prompted by equality of opportunity has led in some places to the development and funding of programs aimed at rectifying linguistic inequalities. In some cases, however, the courts have become battlegrounds for issues, which, although not primarily linguistic, have had fundamental linguistic implications. The Ann Arbor decision on Black English (or African-American Vernacular English as many linguists now prefer to call it) in 1979 is an example of litigation brought under equality of opportunity legislation, which actually makes no mention of language. It guarantees simply that no one shall be denied equal educational opportunity on account of race, color, sex, or national origin. Black parents in Ann Arbor, Michigan, filed a suit against the school board for failure to take into account the linguistic background of their children.

The issue of language, in particular the autonomy of African-American English, became salient in this case because it was argued that a language group, i.e. speakers of this variety, coincided with a racial group. The Ann Arbor case probably could not have occurred or been won without the research done on social dialects in the 1960s and 1970s, which supported the argument that African-American English was not a deficient, but only different, linguistic system. The judge, who ruled in favor of the black parents and their children, was clearly influenced by the expert testimony of sociolinguists.

In December 1996 the issue erupted again even more loudly when Oakland School District in California announced that it was recognizing Ebonics (a blend of *ebony* + *phonics* meaning 'black sounds', a term coined in 1973 to refer to African-American English) as the primary language of its students, and would teach them through a program incorporating Ebonics as a means of helping the children improve their mastery of standard English. African-Americans constitute a slight majority in this school district, but have performed at lower levels than any other group. The announcement drew immediate fire from the state's governor, who vowed not to fund it, all the way up to Washington, DC, where the Secretary of Education said that Ebonics was a dialect, not a distinct language, and would therefore not be eligible for money intended for bilingual education programs. Meanwhile, some prominent African-American community leaders decried the decision as an attempt to hold the children back and keep them from learning standard English. A feature story in *Newsweek* (1997) characterized the Oakland resolution as a 'muddled plan'.

Much of the great volume of public discussion in the newspapers, radio, and on the internet focused on the largely irrelevant, but nonetheless inflammatory, question of whether Ebonics was a language, a dialect, incorrect English, or slang. By now, the many examples offered in this book should make it clear that the question of whether Ebonics (or any other variety for that matter) is a language or a dialect is a political and not a linguistic issue. Moreover, the act of bestowing recognition on a variety will not make it a language unless it has the power of institutional support. Although the Linguistic Society of America passed a resolution at its annual meeting in January 1997 supporting the

Oakland school board's decision as 'linguistically and pedagogically sound', California State Assemblywoman Diane Martinez successfully introduced on 28 February 1997 Assembly Bill 1206, which 'prohibits school districts from utilizing, as part of a bilingual education program, state funds or resources for the purpose of recognition of, or instruction in, any dialect, idiom, or language derived from English'.

Many of the critics, however, misunderstood the intention of the Oakland resolution and interpreted it as a plan to teach Ebonics (or at worst, 'slang'!) rather than to use it as a tool to increase proficiency in standard English. More specifically, the resolution was essentially a proposal to expand the SEP (Standard English Proficiency) program in use in over 300 California schools, supported by federal government funds under Title I.

Evidence from a variety of studies, however, shows that ignoring or condemning the child's home language, whether it is Ebonics, Hawai'i Creole English, or Spanish, is not a particularly successful strategy. The futility of constant correction of non-standard language in the classroom also receives support from academic research. One researcher found that children's use of African-American English increased in direct proportion to how much they were corrected. In classrooms where teachers corrected children, the more they continued to use non-standard speech. Reading scores were also low in such classrooms, compared to classrooms where children were allowed to express themselves and read orally in African-American English.

Constant correction may lead to loss of self-esteem, as explained by a 64-year-old Hawaiian man, who explained how he hated school because he was made to feel dumb: 'I was corrected so often dat I neva even talk any more, I hated school so much all I wanted to do was stay on the ranch with my fada because nobody correct me all the time dea.' He left school in the fifth grade. Many other people have stories about specific incidents which revealed the deep embarrassment they felt at being corrected for speaking 'pidgin'. One male student attending the University of Hawai'i at Hilo talked about how one fellow student at Konawaena School on the leeward coast of the Big Island was corrected. The student asked the teacher, 'I can go batroom?' The teacher insisted that the student repeat the question over and over again in front of the class until he produced it in standard English, 'May I go to the bathroom?' A female school counselor recalled a teacher who would thank students for telling her something in pidgin but not respond to their questions unless they asked them in standard English.

As indicated in the previous chapter, studies show that the use of the home language in early literacy is effective. A very early study with dramatic findings was done between 1948 and 1954 in fourteen schools in Iloilo Province in the Philippines. Half of the children were taught completely in English for four grades while other children were taught first for two years in Hiligaynon, their native language, before switching to English. The children who began in their own language very rapidly caught up with the children who started in English, and even surpassed them. Similar results have been found where the vernacular is a non-standard variety. In Norway and Sweden, for instance, studies show the advantage of teaching children to read first in their own variety before switching to the standard.

A study done in the early 1980s involving 540 students in twenty-seven different schools in five different parts of the United States demonstrated the advantage in using African-American English as a language of initial literacy. Four hundred and seventeen of the students were taught with an experimental series of 'Bridge' readers which began with narratives and exercises written in African-American English, went through a transitional series written in a variety intermediate between African-American English and English, and ended up with a final series written entirely in standard English. At the same time a control group of 123 was taught entirely in standard English using conventional methods, without the 'Bridge' readers.

After four months of instruction and testing, the children taught only in standard English showed only 1.6 months of reading gain. By contrast, the group taught with the 'Bridge' readers showed 6.2 months of reading gain. Despite the fact that the results strongly supported the use of the 'Bridge' readers as a way of increasing reading levels, the publisher was overwhelmed with negative reactions similar to those expressed by critics of the Oakland resolution and decided against continuing production of the 'Bridge' series. Thus, in the 1990s the debate has erupted again because schools continue to take in children who have fewer advantages than others to begin with and give them fewer in school too.

Other methods of taking students' language into account, such as the one the Oakland school board proposed, involve drawing students' attention specifically to the differences between the vernacular and the standard language. A study done in inner city Chicago with African-American students showed that those taught for eleven weeks with conventional methods making no reference to African-American English showed an 8.5 per cent increase in their use of Ebonics speech in their writing while others exposed to the contrastive approach showed a 59 per cent decrease in their use of Ebonics features in their writing.

Indeed, at the time of the Oakland controversy a contrastive approach was already being used quite successfully with fifth and sixth grade students in Georgia to help them switch between home and school speech. Students in the program had improved scores at every school. Why then do the results of these studies not seem to make much impact on public education policy, despite the efforts of linguists to make them known?

One flag—one nation?

One reason is that the division between standard and non-standard is symbolic of other very deep fault lines in society. Debates about language are thus really about issues of race, gender, class, or culture, and about whose norms will prevail. This can be seen in discussions of the issue of students' right to their own language, and the backlash against it. Some still regard the concept of language rights as 'regressive' because they are seen as encouraging the persistence of ethnic and other differences leading to antagonisms. As we saw in Chapter 2, a fear of divided loyalties and identities—supposedly the result of unassimilated ethnic groups—has underlain the formation of most nation-states.

In the USA such attitudes have also formed the historical context in which bilingual education has been discussed. As we have just seen, the Ebonics issue touched some sensitive nerves when some critics saw its recognition as a language as a ploy to get funding earmarked for bilingual education, at a time when many people are opposed to it.

After the United States federal government passed the Bilingual Education Act of 1968, over $7 million were appropriated for 1969–70 to support educational programs which were aimed at the special educational needs of children of 'limited English-speaking ability' in schools having a high concentration of such children from families with low incomes. The budget for bilingual education increased steadily until in 1980 it had reached its peak of $191.5 million. The money was intended to support initiatives in bilingual education that would later be financed through state and local funds. In the first few years the emphasis was on elementary education.

Although the Bilingual Education Act provided opportunities for schools to set up bilingual education programs, it did not place individual schools under any legal obligation to do so. Litigation brought to the courts on behalf of various groups of minority students led in some cases to court-mandated bilingual education programs. The most famous precedent-setting case was that of *Lau* v. *Nichols*. In this instance a class action suit was brought against the San Francisco Unified School District by Chinese public school students in 1970. It was argued that no special programs were available to meet the linguistic needs of these students. As a consequence, they were prevented from deriving benefit from instruction in English and were not receiving equal treatment.

The plaintiffs made their appeal not on linguistic grounds, but on the basis of the Civil Rights Act of 1964, which states that: 'no person in the United States shall, on the ground of race, color or national origin, be excluded from participation in, be denied the benefits of, or be subject to discrimination under any program or activity receiving Federal financial assistance.' In their case against the school board, the plaintiffs requested a program of bilingual education. Although the case was lost, the Supreme Court overturned the decision of the federal district court in 1974. It concluded that: 'the Chinese-speaking minority receives fewer benefits than the English-speaking majority from respondents' school system which denies them a meaningful opportunity to participate in the educational program—all earmarks of discrimination banned by the regulations.' This was a landmark decision because it meant that for the first time in the United States the language rights of non-English speakers were recognized as a civil right.

By this stage, however, the Chinese students had dropped the request for bilingual education. Like the Ann Arbor ruling which said simply that the school board had to 'take appropriate action' to ensure equal participation for all students in its educational programs, the Supreme Court decision did not press for any specific remedy. It pointed out only two possibilities: namely, teaching English to the students or teaching them in Chinese. They requested only that the school board rectify the situation of inequality of educational opportunity. The remedy taken by the San Francisco school board was to set up bilingual education programs for Chinese, Filipino, and Spanish-language groups, who made up over 80 per cent of the students with little or no English. Instruction in English as a second language was offered to all other minority groups.

The *Lau* decision led to other cases. It also encouraged expansion of the services and eligibility provided through the Bilingual Education Act. Moreover, many states passed bills which mandated bilingual education. This followed the precedent set by Massachusetts in 1971. The Lau decision was also instrumental in setting up policy guidelines at the federal level which would allow the US Office of Education to decide whether a school district was in compliance with the Civil Rights Act and the *Lau* case. A document was produced which is referred to as the 'Lau Remedies'. It directed school boards to identify students with a primary or home language other than English and to assess their proficiency in English and the home language. Elementary school students were to be taught in their dominant language until they were able to benefit from instruction entirely in English.

The significance of the Lau Remedies is that they prescribed a transitional form of bilingualism and specifically rejected the teaching of English as a second language as a remedy for elementary students. When the Bilingual Education Act came up for renewal in 1978, a large number of school systems had implemented the Lau Remedies and set up bilingual education programs.

In 1975 the United States Civil Rights Task Force examined a number of school systems around the country which were receiving federal assistance. In the case of Dade County in Florida, for instance, it stated that the constitutional rights of over 10,000 elementary pupils of various language backgrounds (Portuguese, Greek, Arabic, Korean, etc.) were being violated. Since the Lau Remedies had ruled out instruction in English as a second language as an acceptable educational program, the county was directed to provide bilingual education to all non-English speaking students; otherwise, it would lose all federal funds.

The model of bilingual education prescribed by the federal government, however, was opposed in its aim and principles to the kind of enrichment program Dade County had pioneered in the early 1960s. The federal regulations supported only transitional bilingualism, which meant that the students and school board would be judged on how proficient the students had become in English so that they could switch to mainstream English-only instruction. There was no intention or provision to maintain the students' home language. The latter presumably would fade of its own accord through lack of opportunity for use and support by the schools. Instead of receiving equal instruction in both languages as they would in a maintenance program, the students would be given increasingly less instruction in their native language until they finally left the program.

The result has been that although Cuban-American children fare better in Dade County's public schools than other Hispanics in public schools elsewhere in the United States, they still experience greater failure than Anglo students. There are, however, some private, low-tuition schools for children of working-class background in Dade County (and elsewhere in the United States). There a different approach is taken to bilingual education. The schools are staffed mostly by Cuban teachers, who in most cases were born and educated in pre-Castro Cuba. Classroom instruction reinforces the values that prevail in Miami's predominantly Cuban neighborhoods, and Spanish is the social language of these schools. Despite the fact that most subjects are taught in English, development of Spanish skills is, nevertheless, central. Literacy in Spanish according to monolingual Cuban standards is expected and obtained. The success of these schools can be attributed to the prestigious status accorded to Spanish. The concept of language dominance is not useful in these schools because no curricular decisions are based on it.

The actual number of children in the United States who at present receive bilingual education represents only a quarter of the population for whom it is intended. Most of these schools do not attempt to maintain the native language of the children and over half do not provide any content area instruction in the native language.

Litigation in US courts during the late 1960s and early 1970s has also led to the clarification of rights of bilingual students to non-biased assessment and appropriate placement procedures. A landmark case was decided in California in 1970 (*Diana* v. *State Board of Education*). A suit was filed on behalf of nine Mexican-American children who had been placed in classes for the mentally retarded on the basis of the results of IQ tests administered in English. The court ruled that the inherent cultural bias of the tests discriminated against the plaintiffs.

An out-of-court settlement was reached in which the following provision was made:

> All children whose home language is other than English must be tested in both their primary language and English . . . Such children must be tested only with tests or sections of tests that do not depend on such things as vocabulary, general information, and other similarly unfair verbal questions. Mexican-American and Chinese-American children already in classes for the mentally retarded must be retested in their primary language and reevaluated only as to their achievement on non-verbal tests or sections of tests . . . Any school district which has a significant disparity between the percentage of Mexican-American students in its regular classes and those for the retarded must submit an explanation for this disparity.

In the years that followed this decision, close to 10,000 minority children were reinstated in regular classrooms in California. However, a first language assessment of children who show discrepancies between verbal and non-verbal IQ is appropriate only within the first few years of a child's residence in the new country. Testing in the first language after this period is likely to be invalid because of possible attrition of ability in that language due to increasing exposure to the second language.

As has been typical with legislation concerning language rights of minorities, court recommendations have been made in advance of the technology and expertise required to carry them out. In the 1960s and 1970s no one had had much experience in devising adequate tests for minority students in their own language or for determining when speakers were 'of limited English proficiency', and therefore eligible for education under the provisions of the Lau Remedies.

Bilingual education: maintenance or assimilation?

In some respects it is ironic that one of the reasons why bilingual education has been viewed so negatively by many people in the United States is the fear that it aims to maintain languages, and by implication cultures, other than English.

Often the most outspoken opponents are those of immigrant background for whom no provision was made, and who were eager to assimilate as quickly as possible to the mainstream American way of life. One such person, who emigrated from Germany at age 9 and was put into regular English schooling, wrote a letter to the *New York Times* (18 Feb. 1981) in which he said: 'I am convinced a bilingual education would have impeded my integration into American society.' Another, who was Yiddish-speaking, wrote (*New York Times*, 3 Nov. 1976): 'The bilingual method is probably more confusing than helpful to many. Exposure to English throughout the day results in more rapid and more effective progress than dilution in a bilingual process.'

Former President Reagan also spoke out strongly against the desirability of maintaining native languages. He condemned the idea as un-American. In a speech made to a group of mayors he said (as reported in the *New York Times*, 3 Mar. 1981): 'It is absolutely wrong and against the American concept to have a bilingual education program that is now openly, admittedly dedicated to preserving their native language and never getting them adequate in English so they can go out into the job market.' President Reagan's remarks echo those of one of his predecessors, Theodore Roosevelt, who in 1918 said: 'We have room for but one language here, and that is the English language, for we intend to see that the crucible turns our people out as Americans, of American nationality, and not as dwellers in a polyglot boarding house and we have room for but one loyalty, and that is a loyalty to the American people.'

American unity has never rested primarily on language, but rather on common political and social ideals. Nevertheless, the current movement called 'US English', a multimillion-dollar lobby group with links to the immigration-restriction lobby, seeking to obtain a constitutional amendment making English the official language of the USA, is trying to stir up support for a language-related national identity politics. Founded by former Senator Hayakawa, US English wants to repeal laws mandating multilingual ballots and voting materials, and to restrict government funding for bilingual education to short-term transitional programs. A number of states such as California have passed English-only legislation.

In 1983 President Reagan proposed to cut the federal budget for bilingual education and to relax restrictions on the remedies used by local school districts in educating children who were of limited proficiency in English. The Congress took testimony from the National Association for Bilingual Education (NABE) and US English. In its testimony NABE argued that there were demonstrable gains from bilingual education, as evidenced by improved test scores, enhanced self-esteem, and community involvement. They also stressed the value of languages other than English as a natural resource, which should be built upon and expanded. US English, on the other hand, claimed that bilingual education retarded the acquisition of English, and the integration of the student into the mainstream.

Although members of US English legitimize the organization's existence as a way of breaking down supposed language barriers and facilitating minority access to the material and other benefits of mainstream America, the irony is that most ethnic minorities do not actually want a self-contained ethnic group where no English would be spoken. Nor, however, do they want to assimilate linguistically or culturally. A majority want to maintain their ethnicity and language while also being American. An unfounded fear of diversity itself and thinly disguised racism lies behind the backlash against bilingual education in the USA, and a similar denial of home language instruction to the children of migrant workers in many European countries.

Despite propaganda from US English to the contrary, there were actually 4.5 times as many non-English speakers recorded in the 1890 US census, when immigration reached its highest point, as in the 1990 census. The assimilative forces that absorbed those immigrants and their languages are in fact even more powerful today. Although the number of non-English speakers is increasing, so is the rate of shift to English. Languages other than English are the ones under threat—not English. Spanish is fast approaching a two-generation pattern shift rather than the three-generation model typical of immigrant groups in the past. Without the replenishing effects of continuing immigration, Spanish would scarcely be viable in the USA over the long term.

Another irony in the resistance to providing support in the form of bilingual education is that opposition to it in the USA and UK has occurred side by side with increasing concern over the lack of competence in foreign languages at a time when it is seen as critical to American defense interests. Thus, while foreign language instruction in the world's major languages in mainstream schools has been seen as valuable, both economically and culturally, bilingual education for minority students has been equated with poverty, and loyalties to non-mainstream culture which threaten the cohesiveness of the state. The Defense Language Institute in Monterey, California, which teaches more than 40 languages to 6,000 students, spends about $12,000 to provide a 47-week course in Korean. A graduate of such a course can be expected to achieve a lower level of grammatical proficiency than a 5-year-old native speaker. In 1986 there were 10,000 Korean students in California's public schools lacking opportunities and encouragement to develop their native language skills. Most of them will lose their knowledge of Korean before reaching adulthood.

The reason there is little enthusiasm for the languages of immigrant minorities, even when the language concerned is a world language such as Spanish (as is the case in the USA) or Arabic (as is the case in France and the Netherlands), reflects status differences between the majority and minority populations.

Distinctive food, dress, song, etc. are often accepted and allowed to be part of the mainstream (witness the popularity of Mexican food in the USA, or Indian restaurants in the UK) but language seldom is.

This ostensible concern over language differences masks the fear many middle-class whites have of losing their majority status as projections indicate that Hispanics alone may comprise over 30 per cent of the US total population soon after the turn of the century; by 2050, 58 per cent of schoolchildren will be non-white. Likewise, in Europe estimates suggest that one-third of the urban population under the age of 35 will be composed of ethnic minorities, the result of widespread migration in the 1950s and 1960s when Europe experienced an acute labour shortage. If we calculate the long-range social and economic cost of continuing the present pattern of undereducating these minority children in Europe, the USA, and elsewhere, the results are enormous. It is these children who will become the majority and upon whom the economic burden will fall of caring for the next generation of children and the previous generation soon to be retirees. At the same time the highly developed technological economies in Europe and the USA will require an increasingly highly educated workforce. New member states in the European Union are almost certain to bring with them their own unresolved language problems and tensions between majority and minorities. Thus, conflicts will increase rather than decrease.

Immersion or submersion?

Many politicians and educators in the United States have inappropriately cited the success of the Canadian immersion programs as justification for English immersion as a suitable form of education for linguistic minorities in the United States. However, the issues are different in the two countries and so are the contexts in which acquisition takes place. In Canada, the students are predominantly of English-language background and the language of instruction is the minority language of the society as a whole (i.e. French), although in the wider international context it is a language of considerable prestige and importance. Despite their superficial similarity, submersion of minorities in English-only programs in the USA and Canadian immersion programs are different and they lead to different results. In the United States there is no intention of giving wider institutional recognition to the students' minority languages. Just because some groups of minority students can survive in immersion or submersion programs does not mean they are necessarily the most appropriate means of education for all students.

The type of program chosen will typically, though not always, have different consequences in different contexts. Immersion programs usually result in additive bilingualism. They seek to add a second language without threatening the first. The child's native language is intact and develops, even though the child has not had the same amount of instruction as its monolingual peers in majority language schools. Most of the positive results of bilingualism have been obtained by researchers in Canada from this kind of acquisitional context. The outcome of the so-called language shelter programs in Scandinavia could also be described as additive bilingualism.

In submersion programs a second language gradually undermines proficiency in the first. This has been called subtractive or disruptive bilingualism because the development of the child's first language has been disrupted and is incomplete. Many researchers, particularly in Scandinavia, have claimed that the development of the children in both languages is fragmentary and incomplete. They are thus referred to as 'semilingual', or 'doubly semilingual'. The negative results for bilingualism, e.g. lower IQ, poorer achievement in language tests, have been obtained largely in connection with subtractive bilingualism in submersion-type programs. The political implications of this are clear, although they continue to be ignored.

In practice, the situation in individual countries is complex and often several different options are available for different kinds of children, depending on a variety of circumstances, which vary from place to place. We can compare German and Swedish policy for the education of the children of migrant workers who entered western Europe in large numbers in the 1960s and 1970s to provide labor during a period of economic expansion. In Germany, there are six different types of classes in which guest workers' children receive their education. They can attend ordinary German classes with minimal or no consideration given to their lack of ability in German. They can also attend special classes for guest workers' children only. These follow the ordinary German curriculum. The main difference is that the children are segregated from other German-speaking children. If they attend international preparatory schools they can obtain intensive training in German as a second language. Here the aim is transitional because the children are expected at a later stage to be integrated into the ordinary German classes.

Another type of transitional program provides instruction in the native language for several years and German as a second language. Some of these lead to compulsory transfer to ordinary German classes after grade 6. Some of the classes, however, have an optional transfer. Often the mother tongue teachers do not want the children moved because they fear they will lose their jobs. The German teachers may also feel pressure from German parents who do not want their children in the same classes with foreign children. In practice, many children drop out after the sixth year or are not transferred. Finally, some children have the option of attending mother tongue classes which follow the curriculum of the home countries and are organized by them. This is also a segregationist model, and does not aim at bilingualism, although at the same time it is the only program which attempts maintenance of the native language and culture. From the perspective of the child's chances of returning to the home country and reintegrating, only the last option is a reasonable one. The German classes segregate them and alienate them most by assimilating them into German values and ideology.

We can see how the education which the children of migrant workers receive contributes to the reproduction of the powerless status of the parents at the same time as it allows the host country to maintain control over the migrants' destiny. When economic expansion began to decline in the 1970s, it was more profitable to export capital to underdeveloped countries where wages were low, than to import workers. As unemployment rates began to rise in the European countries, many people began to argue that the guest workers should be sent home because they were a drain on the social services and prevented nationals from getting jobs.

Education for foreign children in Sweden falls into three categories. The most common provides instruction in Swedish in ordinary Swedish classes. The child may have already had some teaching in Swedish as a second language. There may also be supplementary tuition given in some subjects in Swedish and/or the mother tongue. The school decides whether the child needs supplementary tuition in Swedish, and if so, it is compulsory. Teaching of and in the mother tongue is, however, voluntary, except in areas where there are sufficient numbers of students who want it. There is also an option whereby a child attends classes with one Swedish teacher and one immigrant teacher in classes which contain Swedish children and children from one immigrant group only. These are called compound or cooperation classes. The groups are taught separately, each by its own teacher through the medium of the native language for part of the time, and then in Swedish together with the other children for the rest of the time. In practice, the amount of mother tongue teaching is limited and decreases gradually because the aim is that by grade 4, the immigrant children should be able to be taught in Swedish only. Thus, this is a traditional assimilationist model of transitional bilingualism.

Finally, there is also the possibility of attending classes where the instruction is done mainly through the medium of the mother tongue with Swedish as a second language. The classes consist of children of the same nationality. This continues for the first three years with the amount of time given to Swedish steadily increasing. Only 10 per cent of all immigrant pupils attended such classes in 1981. Since this is the model preferred by many immigrant groups themselves, there has been increasing pressure to set up more of these programs. This model has as its goal maintenance of the mother tongue.

It is not possible to evaluate policies except within the context of the relationship between the host and sending countries, and the status and function of minorities in the host country. Thus, while monolingualism in the minority language in segregation programs may make the children linguistically equal to their peers in the home country, within the context of the host country they are being educated to be kept in the same weak position as their parents. They are unable to demand any rights, and are potentially ready to be sent back.

Monolingualism in the majority language by submersion programs prevents the children from going back and tries to assimilate them to the dominant culture. Given the different political status of minorities in Germany, where guest workers are not treated as immigrants with the possibility of obtaining citizenship, and Sweden, where they are, different policies for education prevail. It is not surprising therefore to find that German and Swedish researchers do not agree on what the best educational strategy for these children is. In Scandinavia it is recommended that immigrant children should be taught through their home language with the majority language as a second language. Researchers, along with the minority groups themselves, are opposed to putting children directly into the normal majority classes. In Germany, however, many researchers recommend rapid integration into the German classes and are opposed to native language instruction. The minority groups themselves are divided in their opinion. In Berlin, for example, Turkish parents want instruction for their children in German from the beginning of primary school onwards, while Greeks prefer their children to be taught for the first few years in Greek only. The attitudes of different minority groups towards mother tongue teaching and language maintenance reflect general views on cultural assimilation. In both Sweden and Germany, however, researchers believe they are recommending what is best for the children under the present socio-political circumstances. The German researchers want to ensure non-segregation, and the only way to do that in the German system is to send the children to ordinary German classes.

Semilingualism: a new deficit theory

In Sweden policy has been partly influenced by some controversial research findings concerning 'semilingualism'. This term has been used to describe what some researchers believe to be the less than complete linguistic skills of some bilinguals. From a historical and political perspective, it is significant that the term has emerged in connection with the study of the language skills of ethnic minorities. The term has since become widely used in the Canadian debate about bilingualism, and it has become more popular in the UK too. The terms 'semilingualism' and 'double semilingualism' are, however, usually defined with reference to some idealized and rather narrow notion of 'full competence' in one language or another. Individuals are said to be semilingual, for instance, if they have a smaller vocabulary, compared with monolinguals who are of the same social group and educational background. In addition, the semilingual can be expected to deviate from the norm in the two languages.

Here we see a number of basic misconceptions about the nature of language and about what constitutes competence in a language, as they have been applied specifically to bilinguals. Linguistic competence has been conceptualized in terms of an implicit container metaphor: a container which can be either 'full' or 'partially full'. From the perspective of the history of science, it is perhaps not surprising that the container metaphor should be applied to notions of linguistic competence since the container metaphor is a basic one in the human conceptual system. It has been a dominant mode of conceptualizing human intellectual capacities in other scientific fields as well. One needs only to think of craniometry, i.e. the measure of brain size and volume, as a good example of the literal application of the metaphor 'the mind is a container'. Once the notion becomes reified that the mind is located in the brain and the brain is the center of intelligence, it is easy to see why some scientists in the nineteenth century believed that one could measure intelligence by measuring the volume of the brain.

The controversies concerning craniometry were not confined just to the more academic journals. They became a subject of interest in the popular press, particularly when the results were used to prove that the alleged inferiority of some racial groups, and women too, was genetically determined. The work of anthropologists was influential in dismissing cranial indices as measures of mental worth by showing that they varied widely both among adults of a single group and within the life of individuals.

What craniometry was for the nineteenth century, intelligence testing has become for the twentieth. The misuse of mental tests is not inherent in the idea of testing itself, but arises largely through the fallacy of reification. Craniometry was based on the illusion that a measure of what filled the cranial space told us something of the value of the contents. IQ testing can be thought of as a more sophisticated attempt to reify the container metaphor. Although the measures it relies on are considerably more abstract, their relation to the general concept of intelligence is not clear; nor is the latter notion well understood. Even though many are aware of this, the results of IQ testing have been misused, particularly in the case of minority language groups.

We see too the container metaphor interacting with a spatial metaphor so that the idea is fostered that there is a relationship between form and content. We expect that more of form equals more of content. Linguistic expressions are seen as containers and their meanings are the contents of those containers. The container metaphor becomes problematic when it is translated into measures developed by the testing industry. When notions like the 'ability to extract meaning' become operationalized as scores on, say, reading tests, a child who fails is then labelled as one who is 'unable to extract meaning'. Similarly, when the cognitive aspects of language are tested in terms of being able to produce synonyms or create new words, the child who can't is branded as 'lacking in the cognitive aspects of language development'. Then it becomes easy to believe that abstract, and usually quantitative, measures, such as size of vocabulary, response time, must express something more real and fundamental than the data themselves. Once certain features like the mastery of complex syntax, accurate spelling, and punctuation, etc. become established measures of language proficiency, it is hardly questioned what is actually meant by language ability and what role these features play in it. The kinds of tests used in schools are only indirectly related to common sense notions of what it means to be a competent language user, as I have already shown.

Many minority students can develop communicative skills in a new language within two years, while lagging behind in other areas of proficiency, which might take up to seven years to develop to the appropriate level attained by monolingual students. Part of the reason why conversational skills are acquired more easily is because they are context-embedded. Children learn these aspects of language through interaction with peers. The kind of knowledge required to do well on tests is considerably more abstract and is learned largely through classroom instruction. Most testing instruments rely on the assumption that it is possible to separate analytically different aspects of language competence without reference to the context of use. This is a highly questionable assumption.

Although it is true that some of the surface features of language can be easily measured, there is an inverse relationship between what can be easily measured and assessed quantitatively and its importance for effective communicative skills. More visible and highly recurrent features, such as pronunciation and vocabulary, are measured and quantified throughout a child's school career without regard for their interrelationship with other levels of linguistic organization. These features tend to be the ones that are measured, rather because we think we know what they are and their inventory is easier to delimit than because of what they tell us of language learning and development. Often children's progress is measured longitudinally by comparing scores obtained on the same or similar tests from year to year. This practice assumes that because a feature measures something meaningful at one stage, it continues to do so. It has, however, been shown that this is clearly not the case for reading, a skill which is essential for school success. Different levels of language take on significance at different stages in the process of learning how to read.

Just as it is not clear who is semilingual, it is not easy to locate the ideal bilingual. I showed in Chapter 2 that where bilingualism exists at the societal or individual level, the two languages are functionally differentiated and coexist in a diglossic relationship. In such situations, the same competence does not develop in both languages or varieties, although together they bear the same functional load as one language does in a monolingual community. In much of the research on bilingualism, the notion of balanced bilingualism has, however, functioned as an implicit synonym for 'good' or 'complete' bilingualism. It has been used as a yardstick against which other kinds of bilingualism have been measured and stigmatized as inadequate or underdeveloped. Much of this terminology reflects the ideological bias of a linguistic theory which has been concerned primarily with the idealized competence of monolingual speakers in the speech communities of western Europe and the United States: communities which, on the whole, have a high degree of stability and autonomy, and also possess highly codified standard languages and prescriptive traditions.

The term 'balanced bilingual' also reveals a static conception of language. Where languages are in contact, there is usually considerable intergenerational variation in patterns of language use and often quite rapid change in communicative repertoires. We can see how notions like 'half', 'full', etc. rely on some sort of assessment procedure. At this stage, however, there is no general agreement among child language researchers about the 'normal' course of development among monolingual, let alone bilingual, children. Most of the studies of both groups focus on the middle-class child. Although it could be argued that some language contact phenomena reflect the consequences of incomplete language acquisition, it is impossible to define the notion of complete acquisition. If we assumed that complete acquisition included knowledge of the monolingual standard variety, then the Spanish of second- and third-generation bilinguals in California would have to be considered an incompletely acquired variety, in spite of the fact that these speakers are able to communicate fluently in Spanish in all the domains where they are expected to use the language. One could not test the competence of these speakers by measuring their control over the categories and rules of the monolingual code, some of which do not exist in their own speech. A realistic assessment of bilinguals must be based firmly on a knowledge of developmental norms for the two languages, and typical patterns of interference as well as patterns of socialization.

The social and linguistic consequences of using two or more languages for different functions are not the same everywhere. Communicative competence is differentially shaped in relation to patterns of language use, as well as community attitudes and beliefs about competence. Certain types of bilingualism can become 'problematic' when a society perceives certain complexes of skills as 'inadequate' or 'inappropriate' relative to the things that have to be done and the conventionalized linguistic means for doing so. Clearly the notion of language proficiency needs to be defined in such a way as to allow us to look at the productive skills of bilingual children as strategic accomplishments in performance rather than as deficits in competence.

We must ask what goals different societies have when they try to make various children bilingual or monolingual (see Chapter 2). Often children are caught in a vicious circle. Because the school fails to support the home language, skills in it are often poor. At the same time they do not progress in the new language at school, and are labelled semilingual. Often it is argued that bilingualism impedes development in the second language. Thus, the failure of the school to let children develop further in their mother tongue is often used to legitimize further oppression of it.

We have seen that the term 'bilingual education' can mean different things in different contexts. If we take a common sense approach and define it as a program where two languages are used equally as media of instruction, many so-called bilingual education programs would not count as such. Moreover, the 'same' educational policy can lead to different outcomes, depending on differences in the input variables.

Proponents of maintenance programs have certain social and political assumptions about the value of cultural pluralism and the negative aspects of enforced assimilation. They rest on the view that the right to one's own language is a basic human right. Unfortunately, speaking a non-standard variety of English or another language is still firmly linked in the public's perception with a socially unacceptable set of social, racial, and ethnic characteristics. In the mid-1980s in Hawai'i, James Kahakua, a speaker of Hawai'i Creole English and English and a meteorologist with twenty years of experience, was denied promotion because he spoke with a local accent. When Kahakua sued his employer under the Civil Rights Act on the basis of language traits linked to national origin, the judge who ruled against him said that there was no racial or physiological reason why Kahakua could not have used standard English pronunciation. The speech pathologist who testified on behalf of the employer urged Kahakua to get professional help in lessening his 'handicap' to control his use of pidgin.

Annotated bibliography

The story at the beginning of this chapter is taken from Ralph Grillo's book (1989). For discussion of minority education issues in Canada, see Jim Cummins's book (1984), and more generally, Paulston (1994), and the papers in Cenoz and Genesee (1998) and Tollefson (1991). The data on SAT results in Hawai'i come from reports in the *Honolulu Star-Bulletin* (1997); see also Donnelly (1997) and Watson-Gegeo (1994) for discussion. The statistics on the reading scores of white and black students in the USA are reported in Rickford (1998), which contains a discussion of evidence relating to the Oakland resolution on Ebonics. The studies of teacher attitudes are reported in Frederick Williams's (1976) book.

One of the most important articles demonstrating the grammaticality of Black English is William Labov's (1972 *b*) article. The examples of restricted and elaborated code were taken from P. R. Hawkins's paper (1973). Kenji Hakuta's book (1986) and Tove Skutnabb-Kangas's book (1984) provide good overviews of the political implications of bilingualism. A critical review of semilingualism can be found in Marilyn Martin-Jones and Suzanne Romaine's article (1985). The study of sharing time is in Sarah Michaels's article (1981); see also Cazden (1986). George Lakoff and Mark Johnson's book (1980) shows how metaphor influences human conceptual processes. Stephen J. Gould's book (1981) discusses some of the misconceptions behind IQ testing. The Roadville and Trackton study is found in Shirley Brice Heath's book (1983). The study of girls' self-esteem and school achievement is described in Peggy Orenstein's book, from which the quotations are taken (1994: 157; 156).

The papers in Geneva Smitherman's (1981) collection represent some of the reactions to the Ann Arbor decision; see especially the paper by Simpkins and Simpkins on the use of 'Bridge' readers. John Leland and Nadine Joseph's (1997) article summarizes some of the official and popular reactions to the Oakland school board's decision to recognize Ebonics. Hanni Taylor's (1989) book is a study of the contrastive approach to teaching African-American children to read, and Piestrup's paper (1973) shows some of the disadvantages of constant correction; see Romaine (1999 *b*) for examples of correction in Hawai'i, from whom the quotations are taken (pp. 292; 294). For similar evidence on the efficacy of using pupils' home languages in teaching, see Tove Bull's (1990) article on the use of dialect readers in Norway, Tore Österberg's (1961) book on Sweden, and Pedro Orata's (1953) study on the use of vernacular languages in the Philippines. Rosina Lippi-Green's (1997) book documents many cases of accent discrimination in the USA such as that of James Kahakua; see also the papers in Schieffelin, Woolard, and Kroskrity (1998) on language ideology.

Further information about human rights abuses against the Kurds is contained in Tove Skutnabb-Kangas and Sertaç Bucak's (1994) article: on language rights more generally, see the chapters in Skutnabb-Kangas and Phillipson (1994), and the useful appendix of selected extracts from UN documents and other legislation dealing with linguistic human rights. The quotation from Theodore Roosevelt is from James

Crawford's book (1989: 23), as is the information about the costs of language training at the Defense Language Institute. See also Crawford's account of the English-only movement in his (1992) book. Calvin J. Veltman's books (1983, 1988) provide evidence for rapid shift to English among immigrants to the USA.

Chapter 8

Conclusions

WITHIN the perspective adopted in this book I have claimed that language has no existence apart from the social reality of its users. Although language is a precondition for social life, it does not exist on its own and it does not simply reflect some pre-existing reality. I have tried to show how social and linguistic knowledge are intertwined by looking at some of the various ways in which social differences are encoded in speaker's choices both of variants within what is thought of as one language as well as between languages.

I commented in my preface that sociolinguistics lacked a convincing theoretical model within which to situate and explain its findings. While sociolinguists have shown the importance of heterogeneity and developed methods for analyzing it, they have not really 'explained' it. There has been some confusion in sociolinguistic discussions about cause and effect, particularly in studies making use of quantitative analysis which establishes correlations between certain social and linguistic variables. In fact, it is almost paradoxical that for many this kind of work (discussed in Chapter 3) is synonymous with sociolinguistics because in many cases once a sample of speech data has been obtained from a group of speakers representing particular social categories, the emphasis is subsequently almost entirely on quantifying, formalizing, and analyzing the linguistic variables. The social categories such as class or gender are taken as givens and the social context which motivated the collection of data in the first place is often lost sight of in the final product. Within such statistical studies it is often easy to forget that speakers create and interpret language rather than merely respond passively to variables such as style, social class membership, gender, race.

This kind of sociolinguistics does not really challenge the current paradigm of Chomskyan linguistics, except in so far as it draws its data from real-life speakers in actual speech situations rather than from introspection and judgements about the grammaticality of utterances isolated from context. Thus, it could be seen as simply a different way of collecting data rather than a radically different way of constructing a theory of language. This raises the question of what relationship a social theory of language would have to current linguistic theory.

Not all scholars are agreed on the boundaries and relationship between linguistics and sociolinguistics. One sociolinguistics textbook, for instance, argues that sociolinguistics is that branch of linguistics which studies 'just those properties of language and languages which require reference to social, including contextual factors, in their explanation'. Another comments that 'sociolinguistics proper' should be aimed at 'improving linguistic theory and at developing our understanding of the nature of language', but very definitely not at making linguistics a social science. Others would be unhappy with this limited and narrow characterization of sociolinguistics as a subdiscipline of linguistics and have proposed instead a 'socially constituted' theory of language. Similarly, another sociolinguist professes that he has resisted the term 'sociolinguistics' because it 'implies that there can be a successful linguistic theory of practice that is not social'. In order to make sociolinguistics 'socially constituted', its findings will have to be interpreted within a social theory, but this brings us back to the charge that there is no such convincing framework. What are the prospects then for developing one?

It seems reasonable to suppose that one goal of sociolinguistics would be to explain patterns of variation in language by identifying some social force(s) or agent(s) which caused them. This would be similar to what a physicist might, for instance, want to say about the regular relationship between pressure and the volume of a gas; namely, that differences in pressure explain the differences in volumes of gases because they cause them. In fact, this regularity goes by the name of Boyle's Law. We might formalize the physicist's kind of reasoning as follows, where *x* is the pressure of a gas and *y* its volume:

x correlates with *y*
x explains (causes) *y*

Now let's try to develop a sociolinguistic analogy to this type of explanation. In Chapter 3 I examined how a person's network had an effect on speech. I compared, in particular, two working-class Belfast women, Paula and Hannah, who behaved quite differently, and explained their linguistic choices in terms of the different social networks they had. Many other sociolinguistic studies discussed in this book establish correlations between language use and social factors, e.g. social class, gender, style. But can these social factors in any sense be said to 'cause' the language behavior in question? We can try fitting this sort of finding into my formal explanatory schema above and replace *x* now with a concept like social network or social class, and *y* with a particular linguistic behavior, such as using glottal stops, or choosing Spanish instead of English.

It becomes immediately obvious that sociolinguistic correlations are not explanatory in the same sense as Boyle's Law. In other words, the fact of being middle class instead of working class, or being female instead of male, or having a dense social network, does not 'cause' a person to speak in a particular way. Such correlations between language and social categories do not tell us what kind of language a person will choose on any particular occasion, or why. By contrast, knowing the pressure of a gas permits a precise prediction about its volume. The reason why social explanations are of a different character is that human beings are to a certain extent free agents and can exercise choice within certain limits. Humans are also able to reflect on their actions and modify them in the light of decisions they take.

While I cannot, for instance, defy the laws of gravity and jump to the top of a fifty-storey building, I can, if I wish, decide that henceforth I will start using more glottal stops in my speech, or, even more arbitrarily, that I will refer to all cats as dogs. The existence of choices such as these means that any study of human behavior must allow for the fact that the outcome of any event will not be entirely governed or predictable by the same kinds of laws which apply to inanimate objects or substances such as gases. Inanimate objects do not have a choice, nor do they contemplate what actions they will take.

Human choices are also meaningful. It is highly unlikely, for example, that I would choose to start using more glottal stops in my speech, unless I had a reason for doing so; for example, I might want to identify with people who do speak in that way. I regularly change certain words in my vocabulary depending on whether I am in Britain or the USA, saying *lift* instead of *elevator*, for instance. One could say there is a regular correlation between my being in the USA and saying *elevator*, but it is not a necessary one. I can always choose to say *lift*, if I want to, though I may risk being misunderstood. And, on occasion, I have forgotten where I was and said the 'wrong' word. Neither does the simple fact of my being in one country or the other explain why I make the choice. My choice of one over the other is a kind of act of accommodation motivated by my desire to be understood.

The outcome of any linguistic event will be determined locally by the choices of speakers, as well as prevailing social, economic, and political conditions. There are, of course, other limitations posed on my choices by the language I speak, as well as by my physical and mental capabilities. I showed in Chapter 1 how some languages require the encoding of certain distinctions of gender, politeness, and deference. These are difficult, if not impossible, to avoid. Imagine how difficult it would be to avoid using the distinctions of T/V when speaking French. Similarly, I may wish to start speaking like a New Zealander, but this would be very difficult because I rarely have any exposure to New Zealand models of speech.

For some, the alleged failure of sociolinguistics (and the social sciences in general) to be explanatory in the way that the physical sciences are believed to be was and is bad news. It meant that linguistics was not and could not be a science. However, on closer examination regularities such as Boyle's Law are not entirely satisfying as explanations either, unless we know something about molecular structure and have a theory about how molecules behave under pressure. Furthermore, Boyle's Law predicts the behavior of 'ideal' gases under 'ideal' conditions—in other words, under carefully controlled experimental conditions where the temperature of the gases, for example, is constant. Much the same applies to our linguistic examples. The correlations between language and social structure do not explain anything unless they can be fitted into a more general theory about how humans behave.

Concepts such as social class and social network do not satisfactorily explain the origin, maintenance, and change of speech patterns unless fitted into some more general theory of social behavior and the meaningfulness of human action. The findings of social class-based approaches to language have often assumed a consensus-based theory of society. The explanation offered for hypercorrection in Chapter 3 is a good example. It is assumed that people in a speech community share norms of evaluation. Many sociolinguists working in urban areas took the city as a relevant unit of analysis roughly coterminous with the notion of speech community.

In the case of New York City, for instance, it is assumed that everyone acknowledges the greater prestige of using postvocalic /r/ regardless of what class they belong to because the middle-class speech style uses postvocalic /r/. This is why the working class tries to aim at this norm in its more formal style. However, the normative pressure of the standard does not explain why the working class still maintains its own way of speaking over the long term and continues not to use postvocalic /r/ in its everyday informal speech. Furthermore, if everyone agreed on the same norms all the time, language could never change at all. Thus, the coexistence of different norms within a speech community is a prerequisite for change.

The persistence of both non-standard speech and minority languages suggests, in contrast to the consensus model, that there are conflicts and divisions in society. Speech communities may reveal discontinuities of different types. I showed in Chapter 3 how sociolinguistic patterns can also be seen as indices of inequality and differing degrees of access to prestige languages. Indeed, there is evidence that the differences between white and black speakers in US cities may be increasing rather than decreasing, partly as a result of educational inequality and partly as a result of segregation. Similarly, diglossia is symptomatic of power differences between groups of speakers. Varieties such as Hawai'i Creole English, African-American English, Hungarian in Oberwart, Quechua in

Peru are not considered appropriate for the public domain, despite the obvious value they have among their own speakers.

I have also shown here how languages such as Ebonics are brought into being by acts of political and social power on the part of their speakers and how linguistic differences enact and transmit inequalities in power and status. It is interesting in this regard that Chomsky professed to be puzzled when he was asked to speak on the topic of language and freedom. Despite having devoted his life to the study of language, and being heavily committed to political activism, he found the proposed title of the lecture troublesome. ‘In what way’, he wondered, ‘are language and freedom to be interconnected?’

Speakers of minority languages whose right to speak their own language has been denied would have many answers for Chomsky. In Quebec, for instance, the controversial law which required all signs to be in French only represented the symbolic ability of the Quebec government to control and maintain the Frenchness of Quebec in the midst of a predominantly anglophone Canada. Anglophones in Quebec and elsewhere felt that the signs represented an assault on individual rights. The Canadian Supreme Court indeed ruled against such signs in French only in 1988, regarding them as a violation of Quebec's own Charter of Human Rights.

Not surprisingly, signs carry a lot of symbolic freight. They do more than identify places and things. They reveal social hierarchies. Jerusalem's political history is encapsulated in the city's multilingual signs. Trilingual signs with English on top and Arabic and Hebrew underneath date from the period when Palestine was ruled under British mandate. When the Jordanians conquered the Old City, their use of Arabic–English signs with Arabic on top signaled the political pre-eminence of Jordan. The absence of Hebrew in effect declared Jewish claims to be illegitimate. When the Israelis captured the Old City in 1967, they put up trilingual signs, this time with Hebrew on top, and English and Arabic underneath.

Languages and language varieties are always in competition, and at times in conflict, as the cases of Quebec and Jerusalem show. Conflict-based social theories therefore deserve further examination within sociolinguistics. One such approach has made use of the notion of a linguistic market-place. This model takes as its starting point the idea that language is a form of social and cultural capital that can be converted into economic capital. In most of the western urban societies studied by sociolinguists the use of the standard language functions as the ‘leading currency’ in the linguistic market-place.

In the formerly divided city of Berlin, however, standard German could not usually be converted into economic capital in what was East Berlin because professionals had neither the prestige nor the earning power that their counterparts did in West Berlin. In West Berlin the local dialect was associated with

FIG 8.1 New languages as acts of identity

FIG 8.2 Jerusalem street signs

a value system that was virtually non-existent in the East, where even white-collar workers used dialect. Because social prestige was not linked with the professional classes, the acquisition of the standard did not entail significant economic gains. At most, it had some cultural capital under the socialist regime. The reunification of the city under a capitalist democracy and the resiting of the capitol there provides sociolinguists with an interesting opportunity to observe interactions between language and changing social structures.

Another alternative to class-based consensus approaches is based on the concept of life modes and different types of network structures that arise in social and economic subgroups. The life modes of most academics in western societies, for example, are characterized by loose networks. They are highly mobile socially and geographically as they pursue their careers, often at an international level. In the course of their contacts with other academics through conferences and electronic mail links, they contract a lot of weak ties to others whom they know in a professional capacity, but with whom they do not interact on a daily personal basis.

An important idea missing in earlier network studies which figures in the life-mode model is the varying potential of different kinds of networks to exercise power that is the source of conflict and inequality. More powerful networks are better able to impose their norms on others. The ability of networks to exert this power will vary in different kinds of societies, depending on political structure, etc., as I have already indicated in my example of Berlin. Within this view of social structure, networks operate on a consensus basis, while class differences generate conflict.

Although there are no ready-made social theories for sociolinguists to plug their data into which will cover all the aspects of language use I have discussed in this book, there is also no reason to dismiss the enterprise of sociolinguistics. As a discipline, sociolinguistics is still rather young and more empirical research is needed in non-western societies. As I pointed out in my Preface, most sociologists have preferred to ignore the role of language in constructing society, so major developments on the theoretical front will probably have to proceed on the basis of closer collaboration between sociologists and sociolinguists.

At the same time, it is equally clear to me that there is little point in trying to formulate a satisfying social theory of language by attempting to graft a sociolinguistic methodology onto a mainstream linguistics which seems determined to remain basically asocial with its fundamental distinction between knowledge of language (i.e. competence) and its use (i.e. performance). That is why I have called this introduction to sociolinguistics language *in* society rather than language *and* society.

Annotated bibliography

Some definitions of sociolinguistics and its relation to linguistics can be found in William Downes's book (1984), Peter Trudgill's (1978) article, Dell Hymes's book (1974), and the preface in Labov (1972 *a*). Noam Chomsky's remarks on language and freedom can be found in his book (1970). The analysis of signs in Jerusalem is in Bernard Spolsky and Robert L. Cooper's book (1991). Glyn Williams's (1992) and J. K. Chambers's (1995) books offer critical evaluations of sociolinguistic theory. Suzanne Romaine's article (1984 *c*) examines the explanatory status of sociolinguistic theory.

The notion of the linguistic market-place has figured in sociolinguistic research done in Montreal, as in the article by David Sankoff et al. (1989), and in Berlin, as in the articles by Norbert Dittmar et al. (1988 *a* and 1988 *b*). Lesley and James Milroy's (1992) article explores the use of conflict models and the notion of life mode in attempting to reconcile social class-based and network-based approaches.

References

Aikio, Marjut (1992). 'Are Women Innovators in the Shift to Second Language? A Case Study of Reindeer Saami Women and Men', *International Journal of the Sociology of Language*, 94: 43–61.

Alford, Henry (1864). *A Plea for the Queen's English: The Queen's English: a Manual of Idiom and Usage*. London: Longman & Green.

Ammon, Ulrich, Dittmar, Norbert, and Mattheier, Klaus (eds.) (1987–8). *Sociolinguistics: An International Handbook of the Science of Language and Society*. 2 vols. Berlin: Walter de Gruyter.

Anderson, Benedict (1991). *Imagined Communities: Reflections on the Origin and Spread of Nationalism*, rev edn. London: Verso.

Arends, Jacques, Muysken, Pieter, and Smith, Norval (eds.) (1995). *Pidgins and Creoles: An Introduction*. Amsterdam: John Benjamins.

Atkinson, Donna (1987). 'Names and Titles: Maiden Name Retention and the Use of Ms', *Journal of the Atlantic Provinces Linguistics Association*, 9: 56–83.

Bailey, C.-J. (1973). *Variation and Linguistic Theory*. Arlington, VA: Center for Applied Linguistics.

Bailey, Richard W. (1991). *Images of English*. Ann Arbor: University of Michigan Press.

Baker, Philip, and Syea, Anand (eds.) (1996). *Changing Meanings, Changing Functions: Papers Relating to Grammaticalization in Contact Languages*. London: University of Westminster Press.

Baker, Sidney J. (1945). *The Australian Language*. Melbourne: Sun Books.

Barbour, Stephen, and Stevenson, Patrick (1990). *Variation in German: A Critical Approach to German Sociolinguistics*. Cambridge: Cambridge University Press.

Bauman, Richard (1983). *Let your Words be Few: Symbolism of Speaking and Silence among 17th Century Quakers*. Cambridge: Cambridge University Press.

Bell, Alan (1984). 'Language Style as Audience Design', *Language in Society*, 13: 145–204.

Bergvall, Victoria L., Bing, Janet M., and Freed, Alice F. (eds.) (1996). *Rethinking Language and Gender Research: Theory and Practice*. Harlow: Longman.

Bickerton, Derek (1981). *Roots of Language*. Ann Arbor: Karoma.

—— (1988). 'Creole Languages and the Bioprogram', in Newmeyer 1988: 268–84.

Blom, Jan Petter, and Gumperz, John J. (1972). 'Social Meaning in Linguistic Structures: Code-Switching in Norway', in John J. Gumperz and Dell Hymes (eds.), *Directions in Sociolinguistics*. New York: Holt, Rinehart & Winston: 407–35.

Bolinger, Dwight (1980). *Language: The Loaded Weapon*. London: Longman.

Bortoni-Ricardo, Stella (1985). *The Urbanization of Rural Dialect Speakers: A Sociolinguistic Study in Brazil*. Cambridge: Cambridge University Press.

Brathwaite, Edward Kamau (1984). *The History of the Voice: The Development of Nation Language in Anglophone Caribbean Poetry*. London: New Beacon Books.

Britto, Francis (1986). *Diglossia: A Study of the Theory with Application to Tamil*. Washington: Georgetown University Press.

Brouwer, Dédé, and van Hout, Roeland (1992). 'Gender-Related Variation in Amsterdam Vernacular', *International Journal of the Sociology of Language*, 94: 99–122.

Brown, Roger, and Gilman, Albert (1972). 'The Pronouns of Power and Solidarity', in Giglioli 1972: 252–82.

Bull, Tove (1990). 'Teaching School Beginners to Read and Write in the Vernacular', in *Tromsø Linguistics in the Eighties*, 11. Oslo: Novus Press: 69–84.

— (1991). 'Women and Men Speaking: The Roles Played by Women and Men in the Process of Language Shift', *Working Papers on Language, Gender and Sexism*, 1: 11–24 (International Association of Applied Linguistics).

Burton, Pauline, Dyson, Ketaki Kushari, and Ardener, Shirley (eds.) (1994). *Bilingual Women: Anthropological Approaches to Second Language Use*. Oxford: Berg.

Butler, J. (1894). *Memoir of John Gray of Dilston*. Edinburgh.

Calvet, Louis-Jean (1974). *Linguistique et colonialisme: petit traité de glottophagie*. Paris: Payot.

Cameron, Deborah (1985). *Feminism and Linguistic Theory*. London: Macmillan.

— and Coates, Jennifer (eds.) (1988). *Women in their Speech Communities: New Perspectives on Language and Sex*. London: Longman.

Carroll, John B. (ed.) (1956). *Language, Thought and Reality: Selected Writings of Benjamin Lee Whorf*. Cambridge, MA: MIT Press.

Cazden, Courtney (1986). *Classroom Discourse: The Language of Teaching and Learning*. Portsmouth, NH: Heinemann.

Cenoz, Jason, and Genesee, Fred (eds.) (1998). *Beyond Bilingualism: Multilingualism and Multicultural Education*. Clevedon: Multilingual Matters.

Chambers, J. K. (1992). 'Dialect Acquisition', *Language*, 68: 673–705.

— (1995). *Sociolinguistic Theory*. Oxford: Blackwell.

— and Trudgill, Peter (1980). *Dialectology*. Cambridge: Cambridge University Press.

Charley, Dele (1983). *Fatmata*, ed. Neville Shrimpton. Krio Publications Series 2. Umeå: Umeå University Press.

Chen, Matthew, and Wang, William S. Y. (1975). 'Sound Change: Actuation and Implementation', *Language*, 51: 255–81.

Chomsky, Noam (1970). *For Reasons of State*. New York: Pantheon.

Clyne, Michael G. (1982). *Multilingual Australia*. Melbourne: River Seine Publications.

Coates, Jennifer (1988). *Women, Men, and Language: A Sociolinguistic Account of Sex Differences*. London: Longman. 2nd edn. 1993.

— (1996). *Women Talk: Conversation between Women Friends*. Oxford: Blackwell.

Cooper, Carolyn (1995). *Noises in the Blood: Orality, Gender, and the 'Vulgar' Body of Jamaican Culture*. Durham, NC: Duke University Press.

CORFIELD, PENELOPE J. (1991). 'Class by Name and Number in Eighteenth Century Britain', in PENELOPE J. CORFIELD (ed.), *Language, History and Class*. Oxford: Blackwell: 101–49.

COUPLAND, NICHOLAS (1980). 'Style Shifting in a Cardiff Work Setting', *Language in Society*, 9: 1–12.

CRAWFORD, JAMES (1989). *Bilingual Education: History, Politics Theory and Practice*. Trenton, NJ: Crane Publishing Company.

—— (1992). *Hold your Tongue: Bilingualism and the Politics of English Only*. Reading, MA: Addison-Wesley.

CROWLEY, TERRY (1990). *Beach-La-Mar: The Emergence of a National Language in Vanuatu*. Oxford: Oxford University Press.

CULLUM, JANE (1981). 'Peer Influence on Choice of Some Linguistic Variants', M. A. thesis, University of Birmingham.

CUMMINS, JIM (1984). *Bilingualism and Special Education: Issues in Assessment and Pedagogy*. Clevedon: Multilingual Matters.

DALY, MARY (1978). *Gyn/Ecology: The Metaethics of Radical Feminism*. London: The Women's Press.

DANA, RICHARD HENRY, Jr. (1840). *Two Years before the Mast: A Narrative of Life at Sea*. New York: Harper & Brothers.

DANNEQUIN, CLAUDINE (1977). *Les enfants baillonnés* [Gagged Children]. Paris: CEDIC, Diffusion Nathan.

DAS GUPTA, JYOTIRINDRA (1970). *Language Conflict and National Development: Group Politics and National Language Policy*. Berkeley and Los Angeles: University of California Press.

DECKER, THOMAS (1988). *Juliohs Siza*, ed. Neville Shrimpton and Njie Sulayman. Krio Publications Series 4. Umeå: Umeå University Press.

DEVONISH, HUBERT (1986). *Language and Liberation: Creole Language Politics in the Caribbean*. London: Karia Press.

DITTMAR, NORBERT, and SCHLOBINSKI, PETER (eds.) (1988). *The Sociolinguistics of Urban Vernaculars: Case Studies and their Evaluation*. Berlin: Walter de Gruyter.

—— and WACHS, INGE (1988 *a*). 'The Social Significance of the Berlin Vernacular', in Dittmar and Schlobinski 1988: 19–43.

—— (1988 *b*). 'Components for an Overarching Theoretical Perspective in Sociolinguistics', in Dittmar and Schlobinski 1988: 114–44.

DIXON, R. M. W. (1972). *The Dyirbal Language of North Queensland*. Cambridge: Cambridge University Press.

DONNELLY, CHRISTINE (1997). 'Hawaii Second Worst in Funding Public Education', *Honolulu Star-Bulletin*, 16. Jan: 1, 10.

DORIAN, NANCY C. (1982). 'Defining the Speech Community to Include its Working Margins', in Romaine 1982: 25–33.

—— (ed.) (1989). *Investigating Obsolescence: Studies in Language Contraction and Death*. Cambridge: Cambridge University Press.

Downes, William (1984). *Language and Society*. London: Fontana.

Dubois, Betty Lou, and Crouch, Isabel (1975). 'The Question of Tag Questions in Women's Speech: They Don't Really Use More of Them, Do They?', *Language in Society*, 4: 289–94.

Eades, Diana, and Siegel, Jeff (1999). 'Changing Attitudes towards Australian Creoles and Aboriginal English', in Rickford and Romaine 1999: 265–79.

Eckert, Penelope (1988). *Jocks and Burnouts: Social Categories and Identity in High School*. New York: Teachers College Press.

—— (1989). 'The Whole Woman: Sex and Gender Differences in Variation', *Language Variation and Change*, 1: 245–67.

Edelsky, Carole (1977). 'Acquisition of an Aspect of Communicative Competence: Learning what it Means to Talk like a Lady', in Susan Ervin-Tripp and Claudia Mitchell-Kernan (eds.), *Child Discourse*. New York: Academic Press: 225–43.

Edwards, John (1994). *Multilingualism*. London: Routledge.

Edwards, Viv (1986). *Language in a Black Community*. Clevedon: Multilingual Matters.

Ehrlich, Susan, and King, Ruth (1994). 'Feminist Meanings and the (De)politicization of the Lexicon', *Language in Society*, 23: 59–76.

Ellis, Sarah S. (1839). *The Women of England: Their Social Duties, and Domestic Habits*, 3rd edn. London.

Etiquette for Ladies and Gentlemen (1839). London.

Fasold, Ralph (1984). *The Sociolinguistics of Society*. Oxford: Blackwell.

—— (1990). *The Sociolinguistics of Language*. Oxford: Blackwell.

Ferguson, Charles (1972). 'Diglossia', in Giglioli 1972: 232–52.

Finegan, Edward, and Biber, Douglas (eds.) (1994). *Perspectives on Register: Situating Register Variation within Sociolinguistics*. New York: Oxford University Press.

Fishman, Joshua (1967). 'Bilingualism with and without Diglossia: Diglossia with and without Bilingualism', *Journal of Social Issues*, 23: 29–38.

—— Cooper, Robert L., and Ma, Roxanna (1971). *Bilingualism in the Barrio*. Bloomington: Indiana University Press.

Foley, William (1986). *The Papuan Languages of New Guinea*. Cambridge: Cambridge University Press.

—— (1988). 'Language Birth: The Processes of Pidginization and Creolization', in Newmeyer 1988: 162–83.

Friedan, Betty (1963). *The Feminine Mystique*. New York: Norton.

Friedman, Victor A. (1996). 'Observing the Observers: Language, Ethnicity and Power in the 1994 Macedonian Census and Beyond', in Barnett R. Rubin (ed.), *Toward Comprehensive Peace in Southeast Europe: Conflict Prevention in the South Balkans*. New York: Twentieth Century Fund Press: 81–107.

—— (1997). 'Macedonia', in Hans Goebl, Peter Nelde, Zdenek Stary, and Wolfgang Wölck (eds.), *Contact Linguistics*, vol. ii. Berlin: Walter de Gruyter: 1442–51.

—— (1998). 'The Implementation of Standard Macedonian: Problems and Results', *International Journal of the Sociology of Language*, 131: 31–57.

GAL, SUSAN (1979). *Language Shift: Social Determinants of Linguistic Change in Bilingual Austria*. New York: Academic Press.

GEERTZ, CLIFFORD (1972). 'Linguistic Etiquette', in Pride and Holmes 1972: 167–79.

GIGLIOLI, PIER PAOLO (ed.) (1972). *Language and Social Context*. Harmondsworth: Penguin.

GILBERT, GLENN G. (ed.) (1987). *Pidgin and Creole Languages: Essays in Memory of John E. Reinecke*. Honolulu: University of Hawai'i Press.

GILES, HOWARD (ed.) (1984). *The Dynamics of Speech Accommodation: International Journal of the Sociology of Language*, 46.

GOODWIN, MARJORIE HARNESS (1980). 'Directive-Response Speech Sequences in Girls' and Boys' Task Activities', in SALLY MCCONNELL-GINET, RUTH BORKER, and NELLY FURMAN (eds.), *Women and Language in Literature and Society*. New York: Praeger: 157–73.

—— (1990). *He Said–She Said: Talk as Social Organization among Black Children*. Bloomington: Indiana University Press.

GORDON, G. (1970). 'The Status Areas of Edinburgh: A Historical Analysis', Ph.D. thesis, University of Edinburgh.

GOULD, STEPHEN JAY (1981). *The Mismeasure of Man*. New York: Norton.

GRADDOL, DAVID, and SWANN, JOAN (1989). *Gender Voices*. Oxford: Basil Blackwell.

GRILLO, RALPH D. (1989). *Dominant Languages: Language and Hierarchy in Britain and France*. Cambridge: Cambridge University Press.

GUIGO, DENIS (1991). *Libération* (Paris), 5 Feb, 1991.

GUMPERZ, JOHN J. (1982). *Discourse Strategies*. Cambridge: Cambridge University Press.

H., HON. HENRY (1866). *Poor Letter H: Its Use and Abuse*, 40th edn. London: John F. Shaw and Co.

HADLEY, JOZUF (1974). 'Ma ket stenle', in *Hawaiian Stories: An Introduction to Hawaii's Pidgin English*. Lihue: Kauai Printers: 1–5.

HAKUTA, KENJI (1986). *Mirror of Language: The Debate on Bilingualism*. New York: Basic Books.

HALL, ROBERT A., JR. (1955). *Hands off Pidgin English*. Sydney: Sydney & Melbourne Publishing Company Pty, Ltd.

HARRIS, MARTYN (1987). 'Developing one's Haspirations', *Daily Telegraph*, 23 Dec.: 14.

HARVEY, PENELOPE (1994). 'The Presence and Absence of Speech in the Communication of Gender', in Burton et al. 1994: 44–64.

HAUGEN, EINAR (1953). *The Norwegian Language in America: A Study in Bilingual Behavior*. Philadelphia: University of Pennsylvania Press.

—— (1966). *Language Conflict, and Language Planning: The Case of Modern Norwegian*. Cambridge, MA: Harvard University Press.

—— (1972). 'Semicommunication: The Language Gap in Scandinavia', in ANWAR DIL (ed.), *The Ecology of Language: Essays by Einar Haugen*. Stanford, CA: Stanford University Press: 215–36.

HAWKINS, P. R. (1973). 'Social Class, the Nominal Group and Reference', in BASIL

BERNSTEIN (ed.), *Class, Codes and Control*, ii: *Applied Studies towards a Sociology of Language*. London: Routledge & Kegan Paul: 81–92.

HEATH, SHIRLEY BRICE (1983). *Ways with Words: Language, Life and Work in Communities and Classrooms*. Cambridge: Cambridge University Press.

HEFNER, W., and URELAND, P. STURE (1980). 'Areale und soziolinguistische Variation: die p-/pf Isoglosse im Raum RHEIN-NECKAR-MAIN', in Ureland 1980: 51–94.

HELLER, MONICA (1992). 'The Politics of Code-Switching and Language Choice', in CAROL EASTMAN (ed.), *Codeswitching*. Clevedon: Multilingual Matters: 123–42.

HELLINGER, MARLIS (ed.) (1985). *Sprachwandel und feministische Sprachpolitik: internationale Perspektiven* [Language Change and Feminist Language Politics: International Perspectives]. Opladen: Westdeutscher Verlag.

—— (1990). *Kontrastive feministische Linguistik: Mechanismen sprachlicher Diskriminierung im Englischen und Deutschen* [Contrastive Feminist Linguistics: Mechanisms of Linguistic Discrimination in English and German]. Munich: Max Hueber Verlag.

HERBERT, R. K. (1986). 'Say 'Thank You'—or Something', *American Speech*, 61: 76–88.

HIGHFIELD, ARTHUR, and VALDMAN, ALBERT (eds.) (1981). *Historicity and Variation in Creole Studies*. Ann Arbor: Karoma.

HILL, GEOFFREY (1902). *The Aspirate, or The Use of the Letter 'H' in English, Latin, Greek and Gaelic*. London: T. Fischer Unwin.

HILL, JANE H. (1987). 'Women's Speech in Modern Mexicano', in SUSAN U. PHILIPS, SUSAN STEELE, and CHRISTINE TANZ (eds.), *Language, Gender and Sex in Comparative Perspective*. Cambridge: Cambridge University Press: 121–60.

—— and HILL, KENNETH C. (1980). 'Mixed Grammar, Purist Grammar, and Language Attitudes in Modern Nahautl', *Language in Society*, 9: 321–48.

HILL, KENNETH C. (ed.) (1979). *The Genesis of Language*. Ann Arbor: Karoma.

HINDLEY, REG (1990). *The Death of Irish: A Qualified Obituary*. London: Routledge.

HOLM, JOHN (1989). *Pidgin and Creole Languages*, 2 vols. Cambridge: Cambridge University Press.

HOLMES, JANET (1994). *Women, Men and Politeness*. London: Longman.

—— (1995). 'Glottal Stops in New Zealand English: an Analysis of Variants of Word Final /t/', *Linguistics*, 33: 433–65.

Honolulu Star-Bulletin (1997). *SAT Scores for Hawai'i's Public Schools*. Jan.

HORNBERGER, NANCY H. (1988). *Bilingual Education and Language Maintenance: A Southern Peruvian Quechua Case*. Dordrecht: Foris Publications.

HOWELL, JAMES (1659). *Lexicon Tetraglotton*. London.

HUDSON-EDWARDS, ALAN (ed.) (1992). *Studies in Diglossia*. Denton: University of Texas Press.

HYMES, DELL (ed.) (1971). *Pidginization and Creolization of Languages*. Cambridge: Cambridge University Press.

—— (1972). 'On Communicative Competence', in Pride and Holmes 1972: 269–93.

—— (1974). *Foundations in Sociolinguistics*. Philadelphia: University of Pennsylvania Press.

JESPERSEN, OTTO (1922). 'The Woman', in *Language, its Nature, Development, and Origin*. London: Allen & Unwin: 237–54.

JOHNSON, SAMUEL (1755). *A Dictionary of the English Language*, 2 vols. London.

JONES, DANIEL (1917). *An English Pronouncing Dictionary*. London: Dent.

JONES, ELDRED D., SANDRED, KARL I., and SHRIMPTON, NEVILLE (eds.) (1992). *Reading and Writing Krio*. A workshop held at the University of Sierra Leone. Uppsala: Almqvist & Wiksell International.

JOSEPH, JOHN E. (1987). *Eloquence and Power: The Rise of Language Standards and Standard Languages*. London: Pinter.

KANFER, STEFAN (1972). 'Sisspeak: A Msguided Attempt to Change Herstory', *Time*, 23 Oct.: 79.

KARAKASIDOU, ANASTASIA N. (1997). *Fields of Wheat, Hills of Blood: Passages to Nationhood in Greek Macedonia 1870–1990*. Chicago: University of Chicago Press.

KEENAN, ELINOR (1974). 'Norm Makers, Norm Breakers: Use of Speech by Men and Women in a Malagasy Community', in JOEL SHERZER and RICHARD BAUMAN (eds.), *Explorations in the Ethnography of Speaking*. Cambridge: Cambridge University Press: 125–43.

KEESING, ROGER (1988). *Melanesian Pidgin and the Oceanic Substrate*. Stanford, CA: Stanford University Press.

KEPHART, RONALD (1992). 'Reading Creole English Does not Destroy your Brain Cells', in JEFF SIEGEL (ed.), *Pidgins, Creoles and Nonstandard Dialects in Education*. Applied Linguistics Association of Australia Occasional Paper 12: 67–86.

KESHAVARZ, MOHAMMAD H. (1988). 'Forms of Address in Post-revolutionary Iranian Persian', *Language in Society*, 17: 565–76.

KHOSROSHASHI, FATEMEH (1989). 'Penguins Don't Care, but Women Do: A Social Identity Analysis of a Whorfian Problem', *Language in Society*, 18: 505–26.

KIPARSKY, PAUL (1972). 'Explanation in Phonology', in STANLEY PETERS (ed.), *Goals of Linguistic Theory*. Englewood Cliffs, NJ: Prentice-Hall.

KIPERS, PAMELA S. (1987). 'Gender and Topic', *Language in Society*, 16: 543–57.

KULICK, DON (1992). *Language Shift and Cultural Reproduction: Socialization, Self and Syncretism in a Papua New Guinean Village*. Cambridge: Cambridge University Press.

LABOV, WILLIAM (1963). 'The Social Motivation of Sound Change', *Word*, 19: 273–307.

—— (1966). *The Social Stratification of English in New York City*. Washington, DC: Center for Applied Linguistics.

—— (1971). 'The Notion of "System" in Creole Languages', in Hymes 1971: 447–72.

—— (1972 *a*). *Sociolinguistic Patterns*. Philadelphia: University of Pennsylvania Press.

—— (1972 *b*). 'The Logic of Non-standard English', in *Language in the Inner City*. Philadelphia: University of Pennsylvania Press: 201–40.

—— (1990). 'The Intersection of Sex and Social Class in the Course of Linguistic Change', *Language Variation and Change*, 2: 205–54.

—— (1994). *Principles of Linguistic Change Volume I, i: Internal Factors*. Oxford: Blackwell.

LAKOFF, GEORGE (1987). *Women, Fire and Dangerous Things: What Categories Reveal about the Mind*. Chicago: University of Chicago Press.

— and JOHNSON, MARK (1980). *Metaphors We Live By*. Chicago: University of Chicago Press.

LAKOFF, ROBIN (1975). *Language and Woman's Place*. New York: Harper & Row.

LEECH, GEOFFREY (1974). *Semantics*. Harmondsworth: Penguin.

LELAND, JOHN, and JOSEPH, NADINE (1997). 'Hooked on Ebonics', *Newsweek*, 13 Jan.: 78–80.

LE PAGE, R. B., and TABOURET-KELLER, ANDRÉE (1985). *Acts of Identity: Creole-Based Approaches to Language and Ethnicity*. Cambridge: Cambridge University Press.

LIEBERSON, STANLEY (1969). 'How Can we Describe and Measure the Incidence and Distribution of Bilingualism?', in LOUIS G. KELLY (ed.), *Description and Measurement of Bilingualism*. Toronto: University of Toronto Press: 286–95.

LIPPI-GREEN, ROSINA (1997). *English with an Accent: Language, Ideology and Discrimination*. London: Routledge.

LUCAS, J. (1972). 'Lae—a Town in Transition', *Oceania*, 42: 260–84.

MACAULAY, R. K. S. (1977). *Language, Social Class, and Education: A Glasgow Study*. Edinburgh: University of Edinburgh Press.

— (1991). *Locating Dialect in Discourse*. New York: Oxford University Press.

MCDONALD, MARYON (1994). 'Women and Linguistic Innovation in Brittany', in Burton et al. 1994: 85–110.

MÅRTENNSSON, EVA (1986). 'Det nya niandet' [The New Ni-Trend], *Nordlund*, 10: 35–79.

MARTIN-JONES, MARILYN, and ROMAINE, SUZANNE (1985). 'Semilingualism: A Half-Baked Theory of Communicative Competence', *Applied Linguistics*, 6: 105–17.

MATTHEIER, KLAUS (1980). 'Sprachveränderungen im Rheinland', in Ureland 1980: 121–38.

MENCKEN, H. L. (1919). *The American Language*. New York: Knopf.

MICHAELS, SARAH (1981). 'Sharing Time: Children's Narrative Styles and Differential Access to Literacy', *Language in Society*, 10: 423–43.

MILL, JOHN STUART (1869). *The Subjection of Women*. No place: no publisher.

MILROY, JAMES (1991). *Linguistic Variation and Change: On the Historical Sociolinguistics of English*. Oxford: Blackwell.

— and MILROY, LESLEY (1985 *a*). *Authority in Language: Investigating Language Prescription and Standardisation*. London: Routledge & Kegan Paul.

— — (1985 *b*). 'Linguistic Change, Social Network and Speaker Innovation', *Journal of Linguistics*, 21: 339–84.

— — (1992). Social Network and Social Class: Toward an Integrated Sociolinguistic Model', *Language in Society*, 21: 1–26.

MILROY, LESLEY (1980). *Language and Social Networks*. Oxford: Blackwell.

— (1987). *Observing and Analysing Natural Language*. Oxford: Blackwell.

— and MUYSKEN, PIETER (eds.) (1995). *One Speaker, Two Languages: Cross-disciplinary Perspectives on Code-Switching*. Cambridge: Cambridge University Press.

MONTAGUE, ASHLEY (1968). *The Natural Superiority of Women*. London: Macmillan.

MORRIS, CAROL, and NWENMELY, HUBISI (1993). 'The Kwéyòl Language and Literacy Project', *Language and Education*, 7: 259–70.

MORRIS, MERVYN (ed.) (1988). *Jean Binta Breeze Riddym Ravings and Other Poems*. London: Race Today Publications.

MUFWENE, SALIKOKO (ed.) (1993). *Africanisms in Afro-American Language Varieties*. Athens, GA: University of Georgia Press.

—— and RICKFORD, JOHN R. (eds.) (1998). *African-American English: Structure, History and Use*. London: Routledge.

MUGGLESTONE, LYNDA (1995). *'Talking Proper': The Rise of Accent as a Social Symbol*. Oxford: Oxford University Press.

MÜHLHÄUSLER, PETER (1986). *Pidgin and Creole Languages*. Oxford: Blackwell.

MURDOCH, RUPERT (1994). 'Power of Technology to Liberate', *Australian*, 21 Oct.: 11.

MUYSKEN, PIETER, and SMITH, NORVAL (eds.) (1986). *Substrata vs. Universals in Creole Genesis*. Amsterdam: John Benjamins.

MYERS-SCOTTON, CAROL (1992). *Motivations for Code-Switching: Evidence from Africa*. Oxford: Oxford University Press.

—— (1993). *Duelling Languages*. Oxford: Oxford University Press.

NETTLE, DANIEL, and ROMAINE, SUZANNE (2000). *Vanishing Voices: The Extinction of the World's Languages*. New York: Oxford University Press.

NEWMEYER, FREDERICK (ed.) (1988). *The Cambridge Survey: Language: The Socio-cultural Context*, vol. iv. Cambridge: Cambridge University Press.

NICHOLS, PATRICIA (1983). 'Linguistic Options and Choices for Black Women in the Rural South', in BARRIE THORNE, CHERIS KRAMARAE, and NANCY HENLEY (eds.), *Language, Gender and Society*. Rowley, MA: Newbury House: 54–68.

NIDUE, JOSEPH (1988). 'A Survey of Teachers' Attitudes towards the Use of Tok Pisin as a Medium of Instruction in Community Schools in Papua New Guinea', *Papua New Guinea Journal of Education*, 24: 214–31.

NORDBERG, BENGT (1990). 'Svensk sociolingvistisk bibliografi 1989' [Swedish Sociolinguistics Bibliography]. FUMS Rapport 152.

—— (ed.) (1994). *The Sociolinguistics of Urbanization: The Case of the Nordic Countries*. Berlin: Mouton de Gruyter.

NORDHOFF, CHARLES, and HALL, JAMES NORMAN (1960). *The Bounty Trilogy*. Boston: Little, Brown & Company.

OAKLEY, ANN (1982). *Subject Women*. London: Fontana.

O'DONNELL, WILLIAM, and TODD, LORETO (1980). *Variety in Contemporary English*. London: George Allen & Unwin.

ORATA, PEDRO T. (1953). 'The Iloilo Experiment in Education through the Vernacular', in UNESCO 1953: 123–31.

ORENSTEIN, PEGGY (1994). *Schoolgirls: Young Women, Self-Esteem, and the Confidence Gap*. New York: Doubleday.

ÖSTERBERG, TORE (1961). *Bilingualism and the First School Language: An Educational*

Problem Illustrated by Results from a Swedish Dialect Area. Umeå: Västerbottens Tryckeri.

PAULSTON, CHRISTINA BRATT (1976). 'Pronouns of Address in Swedish: Social Class Semantics and a Changing System', *Language in Society*, 5: 359–86.

—— (1994). *Linguistic Minorities in Multilingual Settings: Implications for Language Policies*. Amsterdam: Benjamins.

PIESTRUP, ANN M. (1973). *Black Dialect Interference and Accommodation of Reading Instruction in First Grade*. Berkeley: Monographs of the Language Behavior Research Laboratory.

POPLACK, SHANA, and SANKOFF, DAVID (1988). 'Code-Switching', in Ammon, Dittmar, and Mattheier 1987–8: vol. ii.

PRIDE, JOHN, and HOLMES, JANET (eds.) (1972). *Sociolinguistics*. Harmondsworth: Penguin.

PULLUM, GEOFFREY (1991). *The Great Eskimo Vocabulary Hoax and Other Irreverent Essays on the Study of Language*. Chicago: University of Chicago Press.

REINECKE, JOHN, DECAMP, DAVID, HANCOCK, IAN, and WOOD, RICHARD E. (1975). *Bibliography of Pidgin and Creole Languages*. Honolulu: University of Hawai'i Press.

REYNOLDS, SUSAN BAUDER (1999). 'Mutual Intelligibility? Comprehension Problems between American Standard English and Hawai'i Creole English in Hawai'i's Public Schools', in Rickford and Romaine 1999: 303–19.

RICKFORD, JOHN R. (1986). 'The Need for New Approaches to Social Class Analysis in Sociolinguistics', *Language and Communication*, 63: 215–21.

—— (1998). 'Using the Vernacular to Teach the Standard', in GERDA DEKLERK (ed.), *Proceedings of the California State University Long Beach [CSULB] Conference on Ebonics*. Long Beach, CA: CSULB.

—— and ROMAINE, SUZANNE (eds.) (1999). *Creole Genesis. Attitudes and Discourse*. Amsterdam: John Benjamins.

ROMAINE, SUZANNE (ed.) (1982). *Sociolinguistic Variation in Speech Communities*. London: Edward Arnold.

—— (1984 *a*). *The Language of Children and Adolescents: The Acquisition of Communicative Competence*. Oxford: Blackwell.

—— (1984 *b*). 'The Sociolinguistic History of t/d Deletion', *Folia Linguistica Historica*, 5: 221–55.

—— (1984 *c*). 'The Status of Sociological Models and Categories in Explaining Language Variation', *Linguistische Berichte*, 90: 25–38.

—— (1988). *Pidgin and Creole Languages*. London: Longman.

—— (1990). 'Pidgin English Advertising', in CHRISTOPHER RICKS and LEONARD MICHAELS (eds.), *The State of the Language*. Berkeley and Los Angeles: University of California Press: 189–203.

—— (ed.) (1991). *Language in Australia*. Cambridge: Cambridge University Press.

—— (1992 *a*). 'The Status of Tok Pisin in Papua New Guinea: The Colonial Predicament', in ULRICH AMMON and MARLIS HELLINGER (eds.), *Status Change of Languages*. Berlin: Mouton de Gruyter: 229–53.

—— (1992 *b*). *Language, Education and Development: Urban and Rural Tok Pisin in Papua New Guinea*. Oxford: Oxford University Press.

—— (1994 *a*). 'Hau fo rait pijin', *English Today*, 38: 20–4.

—— (1994 *b*). 'Hawai'i Creole English as a Literary Language', *Language in Society*, 23: 527–54.

—— (1994 *c*). 'On the Creation and Expansion of Registers: Sports Reporting in Tok Pisin', in Finegan and Biber 1994: 59–81.

—— (1995). *Bilingualism*, 2nd edn. Oxford: Blackwell.

—— (1996). 'Pidgins and Creoles as Literary Languages: Ausbau and Abstand', in MARLIS HELLINGER and ULRICH AMMON (eds.), *Contrastive Sociolinguistics*. Berlin: Mouton de Gruyter: 271–89.

—— (1998). 'Introduction', in S. ROMAINE (ed.), *Cambridge History of the English Language*, iv: *1776 to the Present Day*. Cambridge: Cambridge University Press: 1–56.

—— (1999 *a*). *Communicating Gender*. Mahwah, NJ: Lawrence Erlbaum Associates.

—— (1999 *b*). 'Changing Attitudes to Hawai'i Creole: Fo' get one good job, you gotta know ho fo' talk like one haole', in Rickford and Romaine 1999: 287–301.

ROMMETVEIT, RAGNAR (1980). 'On "Meanings" of Acts and What is Meant and Made Known by What is Said in a Pluralistic Social World', in MICHAEL BRENNER (ed.), *The Structure of Action*. Oxford: Blackwell: 108–49.

ROSEWARNE, DAVID (1994). 'Estuary English: Tomorrow's RP?', *English Today*, 37: 3–8.

ROSS, A. S. C., and MOVERLEY, A. W. (1964). *The Pitcairnese Language*. New York: Oxford University Press.

ROSS, ALAN (1980). 'U and non-U', in NANCY MITFORD (ed.), *Noblesse Oblige*. London: Futura: 11–38.

RUSSELL, JOAN (1982). 'Networks and Sociolinguistic Variation in an African Urban Setting', in Romaine 1982: 125–40.

SANKOFF, DAVID, et al. (1989). 'Montreal French: Language, Class and Ideology', in WALT WOLFRAM and DEBORAH SCHIFFRIN (eds.), *Language Change and Variation*. Amsterdam: John Benjamins: 107–18.

SANKOFF, GILLIAN (1980). 'Language Use in Multilingual Societies: Some Alternate Approaches', in *The Social Life of Language*. Philadelphia: University of Pennsylvania Press: 29–46.

SATO, CHARLENE J. (1985). 'Linguistic Inequality in Hawai'i: The Post Creole Dilemma', in NESSA WOLFSON and JOAN MANES (eds.), *Language of Inequality*. Berlin: Mouton: 255–72.

—— (1991). 'Language Attitudes and Sociolinguistic Variation in Hawai'i', in JENNY CHESHIRE (ed.), *English around the World*. Cambridge: Cambridge University Press: 647–63.

SCHIEFFELIN, BAMBI, WOOLARD, KATHRYN, and KROSKRITY, PAUL (eds.) (1998). *Language Ideologies: Practice and Theory*. Oxford: Oxford University Press.

SCHMIDT, ANNETTE (1985). *Young People's Dyirbal*. Cambridge: Cambridge University Press.

SEBBA, MARK (1997). *Contact Languages: Pidgins and Creoles*. London: Macmillan.

SHAW, GEORGE BERNARD (1916). *Pygmalion*. New York: Brentano.

SIMPKINS, GARY A., and SIMPKINS, CHARLESETTA (1981). 'Cross Cultural Approach to Curriculum Development', in Smitherman 1981: 221–40.

SKUTNABB-KANGAS, TOVE (1984). *Bilingualism or Not: The Education of Minorities*. Clevedon: Multilingual Matters.

—— and BUCAK, SERTAÇ (1994). 'Killing a Mother Tongue: How the Kurds are Deprived of Linguistic Human Rights', in Skutnabb-Kangas and Phillipson with Rannut 1994: 347–71.

—— and PHILLIPSON, ROBERT, in collaboration with RANNUT, MART (eds.) (1994). *Linguistic Human Rights: Overcoming Linguistic Discrimination*. Berlin: Mouton de Gruyter.

SMITH, NEIL, and WILSON, DEIDRE (1979). *Modern Linguistics: The Results of Chomsky's Revolution*. Harmondsworth: Penguin.

SMITHERMAN, GENEVA (ed.) (1981). *Black English and the Education of Black Children and Youth: Proceedings of the National Invitational Symposium on the King Decision*. Detroit: Center for Black Studies, Wayne State University.

SPEARS, ARTHUR, and WINFORD, DONALD (eds.) (1997). *Pidgins and Creoles: Structure and Status*. Amsterdam: John Benjamins.

SPEDDING, ALISON (1994). 'Open Castilian, Closed Aymara? Bilingual Women in the Yungas of La Paz (Bolivia)', in Burton et al. 1994: 30–43.

SPENDER, DALE (1980). *Man Made Language*. London: Routledge & Kegan Paul.

SPOLSKY, BERNARD, and COOPER, ROBERT L. (1991). *The Languages of Jerusalem*. Oxford: Oxford University Press.

STANLEY, JULIA P. (1977). 'Paradigmatic Woman: The Prostitute', in DAVID L. SHORES and CAROLE P. HINES (eds.), *Papers in Language Variation*. Tuscaloosa: University of Alabama Press.

STUBBS, MICHAEL (1980). *Language and Literacy: The Sociolinguistics of Reading and Writing*. London: Routledge & Kegan Paul.

SWEET, HENRY (1890). *A Primer of Spoken English*. Oxford: Clarendon Press.

SWIGART, LEIGH (1992). 'Women and Language Choice in Dakar: A Case of Unconscious Innovation', *Women and Language*, 15/1: 11–20.

TABOURET-KELLER, ANDRÉE, LE PAGE, ROBERT B., GARDNER-CHLOROS, PENELOPE, and VARRO, GABRIELLE (eds.) (1997). *Vernacular Literacy: A Re-evaluation*. Oxford: Oxford University Press.

TANNEN, DEBORAH (1990). *You Just Don't Understand: Women and Men in Conversation*. New York: William Morrow & Co.

—— (1992). 'Reply to Senta Troemel-Ploetz', *Discourse and Society*, 3: 249–54.

TAYLOR, HANNI U. (1989). *Standard English, Black English, and Bidialectalism*. New York: Peter Lang.

THOMASON, SARAH G., and KAUFMAN, TERRENCE (1988). *Language Contact, Creolization, and Genetic Linguistics*. Berkeley and Los Angeles: University of California Press.

THURSTON, WILLIAM (1987). *Processes of Change in the Languages of North-Western New Britain*. Pacific Linguistics Series B, No. 99. Canberra: Australian National University.

TOLLEFSON, JAMES W. (1991). *Planning Language, Planning Inequality: Language Policy in the Community*. Harlow: Longman.

TRABELSI, CHEDIA (1991). 'De quelques aspects du language des femmes de Tunis', *International Journal of the Sociology of Language*, 87: 87–98.

TROEMEL-PLOETZ, SENTA (1991). 'Selling the Apolitical: Review of *You Just Don't Understand* by D. Tannen', *Discourse and Society*, 2: 489–502.

TRUDGILL, PETER (1972). 'Sex, Covert Prestige and Linguistic Change in the Urban British English of Norwich', *Language in Society*, 1: 179–95.

—— (1974 *a*). *Sociolinguistics*. Harmondsworth: Penguin.

—— (1974 *b*). *The Social Differentiation of English in Norwich*. Cambridge: Cambridge University Press.

—— (1978). 'Introduction: Sociolinguistics and Sociolinguistics', in *Sociolinguistic Patterns in British English*. London: Edward Arnold: 1–18.

—— (1986). *Dialects in Contact*. Oxford: Blackwell.

TWAIN, MARK (1935). 'The Awful German Language', in *A Tramp Abroad*. New York: Harper & Brothers: 1147–8.

UCHIDA, AKI (1992). 'When "Difference" is "Dominance": A Critique of the "Anti-Power-Based" Cultural Approach to Sex Differences'. *Language in Society*, 21–4: 547–68.

UNESCO (1953). *The Use of Vernacular Languages in Education*. Monograph on Fundamental Education VIII. Paris.

URELAND, P. STURE (ed.) (1980). *Sprachvariation and Sprachwandel: Problem der Inter und Intralinguistik*. Linguistische Arbeiten 92. Tübingen: Niemeyer.

VALDMAN, ALBERT (ed.) (1977). *Pidgin and Creole Languages*. Bloomington: University of Indiana Press.

—— and HIGHFIELD, ARTHUR (eds.) (1980). *Theoretical Orientations in Creole Studies*. New York: Academic Press.

VANDENHOFF, GEORGE (1862). *The Lady's Reader*. London.

VELTMAN, CALVIN J. (1983). *Language Shift in the United States*. Berlin: Mouton.

—— (1988). *The Future of the Spanish Language in the United States*. Washington: Hispanic Policy Development Project.

VRIES, J. de (1985). 'Some Methodological Aspects of Self-Report Questions on Language and Ethnicity', *Journal of Multilingual and Multicultural Development*, 6: 347–69.

WATSON-GEGEO, KAREN A. (1994). 'Language and Education in Hawai'i: Sociopolitical and Economic Implications of Hawai'i Creole English', in MARCYLIENA MORGAN (ed.), *Language and the Social Construction of Identity in Creole Language Situations*. Los Angeles: UCLA Center for African American Studies: 101–20.

WEBSTER, NOAH (1828). *An American Dictionary of the English Language*. New York: Converse.

WEINREICH, URIEL, LABOV, WILLIAM, and HERZOG, MARVIN (1968). 'Empirical Foundations for a Theory of Language Change', in WINIFRED P. LEHMANN and YAKOV MALKIEL (eds.), *Directions in Historical Linguistics*. Austin: University of Texas Press: 95–189.

WEST, CANDACE (1985). 'When the Doctor is a "Lady": Power, Status and Gender in Physician–Patient Encounters', in *Proceedings of the First Berkeley Women and Language Conference*. Berkeley: Women and Language Group: 62–83.

WILLIAMS, FREDERICK (1976). *Explorations of the Linguistic Attitudes of Teachers*. Rowley, MA: Newbury House.

WILLIAMS, GLYN (1992). *Sociolinguistics: A Sociological Critique*. London: Routledge.

WOLFRAM, WALT (1974). *A Sociolinguistic Description of Detroit Negro Speech*. Washington, DC: Center for Applied Linguistics.

WOOLFORD, ELLEN, and WASHABAUGH, WILLIAM (eds.) (1983). *The Social Context of Creolization*. Ann Arbor: Karoma.

WURM, STEPHEN (ed.) (1975, 1976, 1977). *New Guinea Area Languages and Language Study*, 3 vols. Pacific Linguistics C-38, 39, 40. Canberra: Australian National University.

—— (1982). *Papuan Languages of Oceania*. Tübingen: Gunter Narr Verlag.

—— and MÜHLHÄUSLER, PETER (eds.) (1985). *Handbook of Tok Pisin*. Pacific Linguistics C-70. Canberra: Australian National University.

WYLD, H. C. (1920). *A History of Modern Colloquial English*, 3rd edn. Oxford: Blackwell.

Index

Page numbers in *italics* refer to figures.